The Vanishing Point

W.O.
Mitchell

The Vanishing Point

⟦A DOUGLAS GIBSON BOOK⟧

M&S

McClelland & Stewart trade paperback edition published 2001 by arrangement with W.O. Mitchell Ltd.
First published in hardcover by Macmillan of Canada 1973

Canadian Cataloguing in Publication Data

Mitchell, W. O. (William Ormond), 1914-1998
     The vanishing point

ISBN 0-7710-6114-5

I. Title.

PS8526.I9765V3 2001   C813'.54   C00-932696-0
PR9199.3.M57V3 2001

Parts of this novel were first published in *Canadian Forum*, and in *Short Stories from Western Canada*, edited by Rudy Wiebe.

We acknowledge the financial support of the Government of Canada through the Book Publishing Industry Development Program for our publishing activities. We further acknowledge the support of the Canada Council for the Arts and the Ontario Arts Council for our publishing program.

ONTARIO ARTS COUNCIL
CONSEIL DES ARTS DE L'ONTARIO

Printed and bound in Canada.

A Douglas Gibson Book

McClelland & Stewart Ltd.
The Canadian Publishers
481 University Avenue
Toronto, Ontario
M5G 2E9
www.mcclelland.com

1   2   3   4   5   05   04   03   02   01

For Merna

PART ONE

ONE

FOR SEVERAL LONG MOMENTS HE LAY STILL. HE WAS ON HIS back. Dawn had just begun to dilute the bedroom's darkness. It wasn't his usual waking hour – must be well before true sunrise. There – the sound came again – like a rubber ball bouncing from step to step to step, a stubborn dribble beat that had finally worn through the edge of his sleep with placeless urgency. He could identify it now; a ruffed grouse drumming out again and again its invitation to join the living whole. Spring – actual spring by God!

No more brittle weeks below zero with hip drifts on the flats; no chill cling to every breath deeply drawn – mist exhaling from mouth and nostrils like those ectoplasmic clouds in seance photographs. All mediums seemed to have mislaid their hand-kerchieves. Media? Damn it – the floorboards were still cold to his bare soles, setting him into a defensive one-footed dance as he pulled on his pants. But the kitchen was kind; the stove still held a glow of coals. He poked in wood and once the coffee was on, the porridge pouting, he stepped outside.

Mountain spring exploded in his face. Fifteen years and he still wasn't emotionally ready for the chinook stirring over his cheek and breathing compassion through the inner self that had flinched and winced for months from the alienating stun of winter. Full reprieve! Smell, Sinclair – smell leaf mould and wet earth, singing with the menthol of spruce, bitter with the iodine edge of willow smoke from Esau's stove-pipe! The old man was still alive and it was Saturday morning – into-the-city day – Victoria day!

It had all the surprise of young love; spring truly was like first love. He was overdoing it, of course; this passionate delight simply because it was spring was just a little silly. Something must have happened to the fly-wheel of his emotions; look how moved he'd been the day before yesterday when Sarah Ear had brought the fistful of shooting stars up to his desk at recess. He'd recognized it immediately as a gift of contrition for chewing snoose in reading period that morning. Even so, the flowers had tipped him badly. There goes Sinclair – thirty-six-year-old adolescent, the Paradise Valley hermit, starved for the thrust from self to the centre of a loved one. But there was no loved one at all – just another spring. Latins didn't make the best lovers – cold-climate ascetics – puritans – the shy and lonely ones were the champions. Live your life in carefully low key and a few sad shooting stars apologetically proffered by a little Grade One could unhorse you – or a trip to the city – or lunch with Victoria! Sinclair's Law of Diminishing Emotional Returns; this spring was his cup of water on the desert.

Over dish-washing he reminded himself that the pendulum could swing back, the wider in one direction, the farther out on its compensating return. He cautioned himself again as he shaved; he could be in for a terrific depression hangover.

But he doubted that; one step outside the agency building and he doubted that like hell! This wasn't really Carlyle Sinclair at all – out of his dark winter nest and into total light, eyes squinted against sun dazzle, shouldering forth and lifting upright to swing his head from side to side, testing the crystal ring of spring now with this ear, now with that one. This was old Grizzly

Sinclair with his stomach shrunk fist-small from the long winter hibernation – no, sir – *young* Grizzly Sinclair possessed by a male grouse drumming life inside, membrane throat-bag flushed with blood, inflating, expanding incredibly more within him! But this was far beyond youth; he was being tolled all the way back to the toy room upstairs at Aunt Pearl's house. Until there were sparks, one of dead little Willis's balloons had resisted his mightiest efforts, then suddenly relented to blossom large under his nose. He blew and he blew and he cautiously blew till it was burst tight against the tip of his nose. The bubble grunted and squealed at the rub of his fingers; it threatened him till he released its stretched neck. He freed it to darting flight and the room was suddenly relieved by untidy crepitation. It died without warning in mid air, dropped to the floor – a stilled and shrunken scrotum. Blue.

Why – slightly dazed now by euphoria – why should he remember Aunt Pearl and Willis's balloon! To hell with you, Aunt Pearl! Eyes accustomed to the sunlight now, he looked out over the agency clearing, to the boys' and girls' toilets back to back, their doors facing decorously in opposite directions, the empty swings and then the tilted teeter-totters contradicting each other. To hell with you, Aunt Pearl! Oh to hell to hell to hell with you!

Thick and white the smoke rolled over Esau's roof, curled down and around the eave, was carried off low by the chinook. He'd better check out the old man.

Without knocking he pulled open Esau's door and the outrush of warmth against his face was instant. Passionate with heat, the dim interior was performing its usual smell concert, high, middle, low – active, passive – sweet, bitter, sour. The wild plangency of buckskin and willow smoke reached him first, then deep organic chords rolling out from black rags of elk meat hung to cure on a clothes-line length strung above the stove to his right. God – how Paradise had early taught him the use of his own nose! That lingering and contradictory sweetness must be the civet trace of a nocturnal pack-rat; the roquefort of feet was unmistakable. There was mould. There was mildew. There was the murmur of kerosene, and he was quite certain of urine's high soprano.

Smell didn't have its own art. Why not? Individual smells could be sorted out, then related in a register, used separately, blended, built to climax. Many were funny, some poignant. They accompanied birth, love, age, death. A performing art maybe. Have to be. Maestro Sinclair bringing down his baton – three peremptory whiffs of wood smoke or deer musk, then a fart chord full and long from the wind section. Good old Sinclair's Fifth!

That first year in Paradise – the coffee-can of water simmering on the schoolroom stove, its steam carrying the civilization of carbolic out to conquer twenty-nine active sets of sebaceous glands at their desks. But when Esau had visited him one evening in late winter, lifted his head and ostentatiously sniffed, Carlyle had been embarrassed.

"It's medicine, Esau," he'd lied defensively. "For the germs – it kills the germs – the ones in the air."

Esau sat silent, his eyes on the oilcloth of the kitchen table, and Carlyle cursed the disinfectant's authority, bringing bitterness right into the kitchen, even though the door to the schoolroom was closed. How much sharper in Esau's nostrils after the outside winter air.

"Hey-uh," Esau said, the Stony sound clipped off in the throat. It could mean almost anything: yes – no – maybe – you're right – you're wrong. "White people smell too."

"Do we?"

"Hey-uh." That was affirmative.

"How do you mean, Esau?"

"To us people, you know."

"We smell to you."

"Cow."

"I don't . . ."

"Quite strong."

"Oh – milky. You mean we smell milky to you?"

It was several deliberate seconds before Esau lifted his hooded eyes. "Hey-uh." This time he meant no.

Well, the disinfectant had been ungracious, if not insulting; he had not boiled another can of carbolic since. Now that his eyes had become accustomed to the dusk, the sight of Esau on the mattress at the far end of the cabin shocked.

"Esau – morning, Esau." Where had he found strength to sit up, let alone live for another day! Someone must have helped him; possibly when she came in to stoke her father's stove for him earlier, Susan had lifted him. Even so, what levitation magic still supported him in the welter of patchwork quilt, underwear top puddling around his waist?

"Sinclair, Esau."

Two grey ropes tied off into paint-brush tips hung down the bare chest, so articulate with its raised and ancient welts of Sun Dance scar; fever and hemorrhage had starved away almost all flesh. Only surpliced magpies could have done a better job on the incredibly upright skeleton with leg bones crossed before itself. One stir of wind and he would come free to bound away like a tumbleweed.

Carlyle stepped closer, looked down to the face that was simply skull and skin under the gothic arch of hair. He raised his voice. "It's Sinclair, Esau." Milky with cataract, the socketed eyes stared ahead without target. "Sinclair!"

Barely perceptibly the head nodded – or possibly – it had not nodded. Except for the dough smell of infection, a faint pickle of age, it was ironic that the old man smelled the least of anything in this hot cabin. But there was a faint signal from him; a

familiar and musty sweetness reminding Carlyle of rotten potatoes. God, yes! The funeral chapel's death breath! No! Lab
formaldehyde – a little green leopard frog offering its viscera,
skin pinned back against the cork, the acorn heart clenching
and unclenching like a tiny fist.

"What's that?" He'd heard the old man say something.

"Hey-uh."

"What is it, Esau?"

Again a syncopated mutter deep in the throat.

"In English, Esau."

Esau spoke in Stony once more.

"English, please, Esau."

"Hey-uh."

"Yes, Esau?"

"He went up."

"Did he?"

"That place."

"What place?"

"He come down out of there."

"Out of where, Esau?"

"Hey-uh."

Carlyle stared down at the beaded edge of the glass lamp-
chimney on the apple-box top; the wick curled round itself like
a pale, giant tapeworm preserved and floating within the lamp's
clear belly. "Raider," Esau said.

"What about Raider?"

"He come down out of there."

"Out of where, Esau?"

"That place."

They could go on all morning, circling nose to tail. "All
right, Esau."

"Stopped," Esau said.

"All right, Esau," he soothed.

"Gone now," Esau said sadly.

"Lost all happy days now, Esau?"

"Hey-uh."

The old man's torso must be lizard dry; not a sweat highlight glistened there. Carlyle felt a tickling trickle down his own fore-head, then the salt sting in his left eye. "I'm going into the city now, Esau."

"Raider said it."

Whatever Raider had said, there was little likelihood he was going to find out from Esau. "In town – anything you'd like me to get you there?" If you're still alive, Esau. If you are impossibly still alive!

Just as he opened the door to the blessedly cool outside, he heard Esau speak.

"Raisin bread." Esau said it quite clearly.

The chinook's breath was strong; for a moment he simply stood and savoured the fresh delight of it against his sweating forehead. Just like the witch and the children; today was one of the fair-weather days that had swung the children outside. For five months under the weight of snow those spruce branches had pointed down to frozen earth. Not any more! Released from pressure now they slanted upwards, dark finger-tips indicating blue spring sky, bud froth tinting river willows, the valley and surging hills around, committed to green. The earlier excitement was yeasting within him again as he took the path past Esau's backhouse, then cut across towards the river road. He was alive and well – well – well in every single Carlyle Sinclair cell; his own life was just as urgent as poor Esau's death!

Weathered grey, the ship-lap sides of the Powderface cabin were streaked regularly where nailheads had wept rust. One of the younger Powderfaces was by the step, a three-year-old wearing only his underwear top, stretched tight over the plump belly hatching out his nestling little privates. He held something in his hand; it might once have been red. Closer, Carlyle was able to recognize a battered and almost flattened toy truck without wheels. The boy kneeled; he growled motor sounds as he pushed the truck ahead of him, curving it wide-armed round one of the highways he'd engineered in the dirt. He pivoted on his knees, presenting Carlyle with his baby-fat buttocks.

Beyond the Powderface cabin and just before the path met the river road, he saw a magpie fly up; trailing its black tail it dipped and lifted in brief flight, then planed to rest on a near-by spruce. Hardly off the path ahead, a cloud of blow-flies had risen, dispersed, congregated, then settled out of sight again. He did not catch the smell of decay until he was almost on the pile of guts. This must be what was left of the elk Raider Lefthand had shot on Fir Creek. No horns; a stilting calf to starve somewhere, or, more likely, Raider had shot the orphan too! God damn it, he could have left his stinking guts somewhere else; one end of long intestine spilled out shredded faeces over the ground, the rest looped in a grey and glistening garland over the tip of a low-bowing cottonwood branch. Anywhere else! This was the bucking tree!

Old Esau had spoken of Raider; if the old man knew about this he would be upset too; there was a proper way to hunt and to kill and to dispose of carcass garbage – if only to avoid the Bony-Spectre. Was that what Esau had been trying to tell him? The elk strips drying over the stove would be from Raider's elk; maybe "that place" was Fir Creek.

Disgust rose in his throat as he looked down on the rotting pile populated and seething with fat, cream maggots that gave it illusory life. Now that spring was here the children would want to strap a folded blanket or pillow on the branch, to straddle and ride it while others bounced and jerked the make-believe bronc. She'd been ten – possibly eleven, because she'd always been small for her age – the day she'd slid around, lost her grip, and thumped earth – crying when he picked her up, brushed spruce needles and leaves from her back, picked twigs out of her hair. After he'd touched her elbow with iodine and decided that nothing had been broken, there had still come an occasional hiccup over ginger-snaps and milk. But not fifteen minutes later she'd been back on top of old Midnight, sunfishing out of Chute Number Two. Tonight when he got back from the city, he'd give Raider hell – tell him to have this mess cleaned up by noon tomorrow. Though he had given the old man a generous portion of the meat.

He stepped out onto the river road, and as he did he saw the men gathered in Archie Nicotine's yard. By the spreading cottonwood there, with his hands in his pockets, Prince Dixon leaned against the side of a truck. MacDougall Meadowlark and Rod Wildman looked down at two men cross-legged on the ground, facing each other. From the tree branch above them, the motor of the truck hung, still pendant two years after Archie Nicotine had hoisted it with block and tackle out of the half-ton. A sort of post-lynch sadness seemed to have settled over the group, Carlyle decided, as though they had no real purpose left for remaining together now.

The two seated were Watty Shot-close and Orville Ear; between them lay an opened checker-board, and from the number of whittled saskatoon and birch sections that had replaced the lost set of checkers, Carlyle estimated they must be half way through their game.

"Sinclair." Prince spoke from the truck side.

"Yes?"

"Archie was lookin' for you."

"Is he in the house?"

"He's gone."

He'd heard that Archie had finished cutting poles for Moon, had returned to Paradise from the Turkey Track. If he'd been paid, then he wanted a ride into the city, which in turn indicated why he had been looking for Carlyle.

"He thought he might go in with you if you went," Prince said.

"I was in seeing Esau," Carlyle said. "Did he find a ride?"

"He left," Prince said.

One more good thing about this spring morning; he would not have Archie Nicotine's abrasive company all the way into the city.

Watty leaned forward; he jumped one of Orville's pale birch checkers.

"Hey-up," Orville said with mild surprise.

"Crown him," MacDougall said.

"Moon paid him for the poles," Prince said.

Orville crowned the dark saskatoon piece.

"Sorry he missed me," Carlyle said.

"Rings and a rebuilt carburetor," Rod Wildman said.

"Any of you seen Raider this morning?"

"Hey-up," Orville said with regret. He had lost another checker.

"If you do – please tell him to gather up those elk guts and bury them."

"Your move, Orville," MacDougall said.

"It isn't healthy and it isn't nice for the children."

Orville moved.

"It's a mess I won't stand for again!"

The attention of all was on the checker-board.

"And also it was a God-damned cow elk!"

"Hey-up," Orville said with resignation. But it was only because Watty this time had taken two of his men.

He was relaxed by the time the road had reached the river, its banks shrill with green willow. Quite often Victoria used to come down here, to snare grayling, to cut kinick-kinick for old

Esau to peel and roast in his oven, to mix half and half with fine-cut tobacco. Ten from nineteen – nine. It seemed so much longer than nine years. He felt the peremptory thrust of the suspension bridge right up into his hip sockets; high over the Spray it gave and then it surprised with elastic response to each of his steps. That was what was needed really; some sort of suspension bridge that could carry hearts and minds across and into other hearts and minds. Indian Affairs ought to study the possibility of constructing and issuing them to every agent on every reserve.

Though it must be over a week since he'd used it, his car started with one turn of the key, needed only a couple of pumps on the accelerator to keep it going. He leaned back waiting for the motor to warm to full life. Had he ever made it across to any of these people? He had wanted to – from the first he had wanted to. With Victoria how he wanted to! Oh God how he wanted *her* to! He must not forget a couple of loaves of raisin bread for Esau.

As he pulled off the reserve and turned east onto the Valley road, he saw the coyote trot across ahead of the car. On the other side, before it would enter the clump of birch there, it stopped, head up high and turned sideways as though holding a pose for a fashion photographer. Not a coyote really, but Weesackashack. Yes, that was how she would see him – circling hungry on his own trail to discover scabs from his own rear end – eating them because he mistook them for food dropped by his grandmother. And when the chick-a-dees sang in the birches, they taunted, "Look at Weesackashack eating his own arse." Those welts had been whipped onto the white birch-bark by an angry Weesackashack. And that was how the birch tree really got its stripes, Aunt Pearl.

Cataract bridge damn near knocked his back teeth out; the municipality hadn't come by to fill in the approach. Yet! Going into the second year . . . almost as long as Archie Nicotine's truck motor had hung from the cottonwood branch. And it was just possible Archie might not drink up his pole money at the Empress this time, might actually buy the rings and carburetor he needed, could perhaps get everything back together in time to jolt over the twelve-inch shelf before the municipality did get out with gravel truck and grader to fill the trench in.

Did she still believe in Wendigo, the Wizard, the Witch, the Summer and Winter People? How did he know? How the hell could he ever know! How could he ever hope to understand what any of them sheltered secret inside themselves. Alien. After all these years he was still outlander to this valley. It was only theirs. He hadn't stained the dirt – grass – hills – mountains – with himself – with his own needs and his own fears. What bloody right had he to tell a little Stony girl this wasn't the land of people with removable hearts that could be hung on tree branches while they slept. For all he knew he was as strange to her as one of the backward persons. When she was younger. Maybe now – maybe for always! Goddam coyote! Come on, Wizard, change me over . . . contrary the backward. . . .

No Roman roads – no marble baths – coins – no *civilized* blood spilled to warm this dirt. Just Pile of Rocks there beyond Moon's road. How many centuries had it taken to grow so high? Pyramid magic of medicine men? Or had laymen created it, stone after stone tossed by grateful fists, in thanks for the blessed reprieve of life for another year till the next horse-stealing or buffalo foray out of the enclosing safety of high mountains, down the eastern slopes and onto the open plains country of the Blackfoot?

All the same – right or no right – he'd added eight rocks of his own; one for every year he'd spent in Paradise Valley. One for each fall, but this time – spring. He'd do it on his way back from the city. Hey-up!

A flutter of orange caught his eye and he felt his guts tighten against irritation. Gay and decorative they lifted out from the fence-post tips, snapping free in the chinook. They'd be spaced down the road all the way out of the valley – yellow – pink – blue – red. No right; they had no right to be here at all! These were not ribbons streaming from trees in a sacred burial grove; they did not signify noble doom at all! Oil-company markers tied on by last year's seismic crews during their season of subterranean hiccuping!

Interlopers! He could not see why they should be permitted to drive their drills into reserve property, insert and set off their explosive charges deep within the land. Fyfe had called his complaint unreasoned, but Carlyle had sent a letter to Ottawa anyway, though he knew it was like throwing a loved one into quicksand. There had been no answer, and Fyfe had advised him to wait and see what transpired. Wait until actual damage transpires – nothing can be done until we see what does transpire – Fyfe's favourite word – "transpire." And if damage transpired, then there would be legal action taken and there would be settlement: fifty cents per head per year to be added to the calf-crop money and the timber money and the grazing money and family allowance and old-age pension – one more package of fine-cut – one more bottle of beer would transpire!

Of course it had to be an open fall; exploration had gone on, and in early December he'd had to order one thick-booted and acned young bastard right out of the dance tent. Two weeks later they'd hauled their trailers, trucks, and drilling-rig with its yellow phallus out of the valley. Small satisfaction he'd had the afternoon he'd travelled down the road, taking the outrageous plastic ribbons off their proper fence posts and fastening them back again on different ones.

He swerved out to miss a gopher, bolt upright on the road edge, and as he did, he caught a glimpse of the car deep in the ditch, its front doors flung wide like the wings of a rusting butterfly. Mid January four years ago, pistons thirsting for cylinder oil, its engine had seized up with great finality; Mark Wounded-Person had abandoned it. In another mile there would be the chassis bones of Rod Wildman's truck, and after that the lock-jawed crocodile of MacDougall Meadowlark's Hudson with gaping hood held high. God, why did they have to leave this junk spoor strung along the ditches of the Valley road clear out to the highway! Why couldn't it mortify them!

And another ribbon waving from a fence post! But this one didn't annoy him at all. Red. How surprised he'd been when the Riders got to the school Christmas concert, and he saw that Susan hadn't braided Victoria's hair, that it flowed free as black smoke down her back. The scarlet, velvet ribbon had been his Christmas present to her. Gatine Nicotine had played "Silent Night" on the mouth-organ while the three wise councillors rode over the plains on their broomstick stud camels. Then Gatine had blown out "Going to Heaven on a Stream-lined Train" as Mary and Joseph, with the infant Jesus, fled from the Bethlehem Wendigo, helped by the angels, who'd laid out their wings over the deep snow for them. There'd been a bridge that Christmas night!

Now the tension and tautness were quite gone.

She'd be ready and waiting for him at the hospital, and it was spring, and they'd go shopping right away – have lunch later. A dress – possibly a suit – and purse and shoes to match. When she saw something she liked, there would grow the slow and infrequent half-smile, or perhaps no smile – the much deeper response of extra stillness in her face, the subtle semaphore he could sometimes read. But if she were truly delighted, she would lower her head, lift her hand half-closed to hide her smile. Gloves! By God, her hands were made for the extra grace of gloves!

He saw a figure up ahead with arm upraised, in time to slow down and stop beside it. Archie Nicotine climbed in, slammed the door.

"Thanks, Sinclair."

He shifted to second, to high. Damn it all!

"We got held up for the rings and for the carburetor. Moon underpaid me, but I still got enough for the rings and for the carburetor. Then we can get her rolling and I won't have to impose any more for a ride. On you."

Conversation with most of them was difficult, like trying to play catch with someone who wouldn't throw back the ball. Most of them. Not Archie, damn it!

". . . after he took out for the grup he said there was only forty-eight left . . ."

It was never a game of catch with Archie; it was a defensive and tiresome duel. He didn't want to fence this wonderful morning; he leaned over, pushed in the button on the radio.

". . . Moon always was a tight-ass and that's the whole situation."

". . . does not claim – has not ever claimed the healin' pahr. Heally Richards does not heal through the practice of medicine – chemo-therapy – the surgical knife – spinal adjustment – high colonic irrigation – deep analysis – hypnosis . . ."

He had instantly recognized the recorded voice, American, soft with the South, glib and truculent.

". . . deep heat – leechin' – cuppin' – transfusion – organic diet – Asiatic herb – sonic vibration – radioactive clay . . ."

Choice that wasn't really a choice at all; endless flow of primitive oversimplification from either the faith-healing evangelist or from Archie Nicotine.

". . . astrology – phrenology – or tea-cup readin'. Like I say, through none of these does Heally Richards – has Heally Richards – or will Heally Richards ever – lay claim to the healin' pahr."

The faith healer was a favourite with most of the Paradise Valley people, particularly Archie, for Archie was a religious joiner, had been in turn: original Methodist, Presbyterian, United, Baptist, Pentecost, Mormon. As nearly as Carlyle could tell, he was between dogmas now. When it came to a choice between Archie and Heally Richards, he preferred Archie. Which still didn't say a great deal for Archie. Carlyle reached over and shut off the radio.

"I generally listen to him," Archie said as Richards' voice paled to silence.

With fastidious tails held high, several white-faced and mahogany calves went rocking down the fence line.

"We have got a lot of sick people in our band – one way and another. I listen to him when I can," Archie said again.

The calves stopped. Springs unwound.

"I know, Archie."

"And he heals sick people."

"Not likely to do us much good."

"Why not?"

"Somewhere in the States, isn't he?"

"No."

"Yes, he is," Carlyle said. "That was just a recording – played all over."

"I know that. But if you listened to him regular you'd know."

"Know what?"

"That's alive."

"Is it?"

"Hey-up. He's here. Since all last week. Rally For Jesus."

"Oh."

"They announced it several times – for a month and he heals sick people. That's his business."

"It may be just a business."

"That's what I said. He heals them by faith. Through his hands."

"Does he."

"I never seen him do it, I just heard it over the radio. What I mean is, they wouldn't let him onto the radio if he couldn't do it."

"They might."

"Look at all this TB we got now. Whenever some kid gets his feet wet then he coughs and then he coughs some more and then he coughs some blood and then he coughs a lot of blood and then he dies out of it. All out of wet feet. That's the whole TB situation in Paradise Valley."

"Not quite."

"Esau coughed up a lot last night."

"He was sitting up this morning."

"Wasn't any TB in the olden days," Archie said.

"Maybe there wasn't but . . ."

"Before the white savage come," Archie said.

"That's right, Archie."

"Lots more wet feet then when we just had moccasins, before we had rubbers or boots – but all the same no TB then."

"There wasn't a single case of TB in Paradise Valley fifteen years ago!" Carlyle said angrily. "After Wallace Ear died and the unit came out – you're the one kept the others from getting X-rayed – you told them the machine was what *gave* people TB."

"Maybe I did."

"You *did* – no maybe about it."

"You think he could?"

"Could what?"

"Heal people."

"Who?"

"Heally Richards."

"Not so well as doctors and medicine."

"You figure they got a monopoly on it."

"All I figure is if I had trachoma like Susan Shot-close I'd take the doctor's advice. I wouldn't miss one single treatment if it went on through my whole life. If I had Mark Lefthand's hernia I'd go to the hospital and have it mended. All the faith healing there is won't cure Mary Roll-in-the-mud's diabetes."

"Like you said – he's sitting up this morning even though last night he let go half a slop-bucket of blood."

"Did somebody lay hands on him? Is that why . . ."

"No. Also there wasn't any doctor there or medicine, but all the same he did sit up this morning."

"He's a tough old man."

"Hey-up. But he wasn't tough enough to beat them TB germs. They won now."

"But he could have beat them five years ago if he'd gone to San. He refused to. You people have absolute sovereignty – nobody can make you do one single damn thing you don't want to do – even to save your life."

"Most the time that's piss poor . . ."

"I agree."

". . . and a lot of people die anyway in hospitals."

"More out of them."

"You're wrong there – more in."

"Oh – come on, Archie."

"Hospitals specialize in dyin'."

"What you mean is – they're full of patients who have contracted disease or – injury – they're in there for treatment – surgery – so naturally more people in hospitals die than the well people outside hospitals."

"More Indians die in hospitals."

"Just because white people go there sooner – when there's still some hope of recovery. They don't die like Gatine *after* his appendix burst. They don't wait for it to burst." Or pneumonia like Moses Rider – or eclampsia like Sarah MacLeod. All the deaths he'd died in nine years! Each one leaving him older – sadder – more helpless! Oh Jesus – the three smoke threads still wisping upwards like reluctant souls from three little charred bundles in the fire-scabbed tangle of bed-metal standing in the ruins of the Ernie Wildman cabin! Stop it, Sinclair! Stop it!

"Us people don't like to go in hospitals."

"Neither do us people."

"Us people get sick easier than you people do."

"Maybe."

"Germs can dig in quicker and easier and worse into us."

"Maybe."

"So I think a hospital crawlin' with all those goddam white germs from all those goddam sick white people herded up is one hell of a place for us people to go into." Archie lit the cigarette he'd made. He exhaled. "Especially when we are sick."

"They protect against that, Archie."

"Them germs is pretty small and there's millions of them and they can miss some easy. They just got to miss one germ – just let one of them get into us – or maybe two. Have to be two – wouldn't it?"

"What do you mean?"

"Take more than one I guess – bull and cow for increase."

"No. There don't have to be."

"Wouldn't want one of my kids in there – in the hospital."

"You telling me – if Maureen or Maxine or Marion got sick and the doctor said she had to go into hospital to save her life you wouldn't . . ."

"I guess I would," Archie admitted, "to save her life."

He might, but Carlyle was no longer interested in the possibility. Somehow their conversation had gone past a hidden significance. Earlier Archie must have implied something important, which Carlyle had missed. "Damn sight more likely to save her than some evangelist laying on hands." But even as he said it he was trying to remember what it might have been that eluded him now. "Just what were you driving at, Archie?"

"You said if one of my own kids got sick . . ."

"No – before. Nothing *is* wrong with your family – is there?"

"They all had a cold. I had one."

"I see."

"And our bowels loose – two weeks ago I moved my own bowels many times. We're all over that now."

As usual Archie had succeeded, manoeuvred him into the distasteful role of explaining – advising – preaching. It demeaned both of them. No – just himself.

"One good way to find out," Archie was saying.

"Find out what?"

"Heally Richards. If he can heal."

"He's not getting into Paradise, Archie."

The corners of Archie's mouth pulled in slightly. "He can't get in even if he might make our whole band healthy."

"That's right."

"You say that."

"And I suspect Mr. Fyfe – the department would say that too."

"You – Fyfe – the department say who can come into Paradise and who can't come into Paradise." Archie was actually grinning now. "Then I guess we just have to use some of that stuff, Sinclair."

"What stuff?"

"Absolute sovereign you said we got – even if it was to save our poor life."

He saw that the grin had widened full from ear to ear. "You just let me know, Archie – whenever you want to talk sensibly!"

Without relaxing his grin one stitch, Archie slid down on the seat. He laid his head back and he closed his eyes. "Hey-up."

Which could be Stony for "touché," Carlyle told himself sardonically.

He was just as annoyed with himself as he was with Archie now. Why could he not learn that impatience always delivered

him into Archie's hands. If only he could discipline his irritation, Archie wouldn't be able to score again and again; the best
defence was restraint of course, for counter-thrust only told
Archie he'd been successful. Archie made sure he never let you
know you'd pierced that smug certainty.

"Have you an objection if I listen to him anyway?"

"What?"

"Richards."

"Go ahead."

Archie turned on the radio.

"While he still has something left to . . ."

". . . everywhere – Jeeesuss Christ – EVERYWHERE!"

"Jesus, Archie – turn it down!"

". . . EVIDENCE – THESE SAME PEOPLE ARE the ones
will tell you Jeeesuss did not exist – that He did not live – that He
did – was not cruceeeefied – oh yes – they'll say – I have had them
say it to me – and you have had them say it to you – oh yes – it
is quite likely there may have been – ay – man – named Jeesuss –
ay – ordinary – everyday – mortal – man and His name may have
been Jeesussss – He may have hailed from Galilee – but He – was
– not – thee son of God! Oh no. He was not born of virgin birth!
Oh no. He was not risen from the dead and not ascended onto
Heaven. Oh no – oh no – oh no. I have been told this on the very
best authority – ministers of the gospel. Yes – I have! Presbyterian
– Methodist – Congregational – Episcopalian – all theossified
churches. No – not all – at least there hasn't been a Catholic
priest tell me that yet – no – not yet – nor Baptist. But – just you
give them time. They will – sooner or later they will – they'll all
tell you. Ay man – just – ay – man. That's all. Now – I want you
to do somethin' for me. I want you – please to do this for me; you
tell me – just – what – was – this ordinary mortal man's full name.
I know – I got his given name all right – but what was his last
name. Jeeesuss Brown? Jeesuss J. Jones? Jeesuss Kelly? Jeesuss

Kennedy? Oh – hallelujah! Jeeesuss Lenin or Jeesuss Stalin maybe – or was it just Jeesuss Marx of Galilee! Hallelujah! Not one of these mortals was born in ay stable in Bethlehem – was he! Not one of them was found there in any manger in swaddlin' clo'es – was he! By the three wise men who followed a star? You want evidence – existence of Jeeesuss Christ. Just you let me tell you where you can find it – everywhere – that's where. Why – in a little child's fairy tale – I can show you evidence – in 'Snow White and the Seven Dwarfs' I can . . . show you evid . . ."

But Carlyle had snicked off the radio.

"How could he do that?" Archie said.

"Walt Disney helped him."

"Generally he can explain all right," Archie said.

"I'm sure he has an explanation for everything."

"One time he explained the whole situation with us people."

"Did he."

"We are the lost tribes out of Israel."

"Hey-up," Carlyle said heartily. "A long way from home."

"One way to find out."

"If the Stonys are the lost tribes?"

"No – whether he can heal by laying on his hands."

"He's not coming out to Paradise, Archie." And, by God, he wasn't, though he possibly should not have said it again.

"I guess if he isn't a department civil servant then he can't get in even if he could make our whole band healthy."

The prick lay in the deliberate "civil servant," so he must at all costs be civil. "That's right, Archie. It might be difficult to convince them that Heally Richards could heal the entire Paradise band. Seventy-five families is a lot of heal . . ."

"What I mean was – one way to tell if he could heal or he couldn't heal – let him take a run at Esau."

"Oh – for God's sake, Archie – just leave Esau alone!"

"I'd like to find out if he could . . ."

"No healer's going to bother Esau!"

"If Esau requested him to heal him then . . ."

"Esau isn't likely to. It's the last thing Esau would want!"

"Maybe not."

"Look, Archie, let Esau alone – just let him die his own way – let him die Indian!"

"Us Indians didn't invent TB."

"Archie – no!"

"I just made a suggestion that might . . ."

"No!"

"Like a test – while there was time."

"There isn't time."

"Sure isn't. He hasn't time even to wait for his smart granddaughter."

"What?"

"For her to finish and come back and heal him."

So that was it! That had been the hidden jab! Victoria. He knew he'd missed something earlier; and how dearly important it was! "For once you are right. She is smart. She's the smartest child . . ."

"No child."

"Smart enough not to drop out the way Maxine did last winter – or the way Marion will before summer." Father of such moon-faced truculence, Archie had every right to be envious. "Don't ever give her a break, Archie!" Or me – spoil it! Spoil her whole life – make her fail!

"Sinclair," Archie said.

"Yes, Archie."

"I been thinking about a conclusion."

"That's nice."

"Whites make it their own way – everything. That's the whole situation with you people. Take cattle . . ."

"What about them?"

"Look at cattle."

"I am – I do – every day."

"Hereford out there."

"Yes?"

"All Hereford."

"Not all – there's Shorthorn and Galway. . . ."

"Few. Mostly the whole situation is Hereford. You people made it that way. Even cattle."

"What do you mean, Archie?"

"What I mean is white face – all white face – Hereford."

"That's right. That's one breed."

"Which you people made. You bred for that. It wasn't that way first at all. You know what I mean. You people want even your cattle to be white face too."

Carlyle felt a stir of his earlier annoyance. "I don't think that determined Hereford breeding at all."

"Sure."

"The breed came about . . ." Carlyle began to explain.

"It didn't come about," Archie corrected him. "You people made it."

"Possibly we did. Yes. I guess we did. Through careful selection, trying for the most beef for the least grass."

"Hey-up."

"Good foragers – tough – winter well."

". . . and that white face."

"All right – all right, Archie, but whether they have a white face – black face – spotted face – red face hasn't got anything to do . . ."

"But they haven't got it."

"Haven't what?"

"Got a red face or a black face."

"I know they haven't."

"Deliberate white face."

"I don't think so. Not deliberate."

"I do. Deliberate and that's the whole situation with white tits." Archie spit out the window. "Even if they snow-burn."

"Sort of silly if it were deliberate," Carlyle said.

"Hey-up."

Now he was truly annoyed with himself. "Nice we can agree on something, Archie."

"You don't. And they're lucky."

Always Archie started from the same conviction: white was lucky; red was not. He had a ready answer for his own envy of that luck; whites needed it.

Carlyle saw that one corner of Archie's mouth was caught up slightly with incipient amusement. In five more years and after fifty or seventy-five pounds more weight, the hairless cheeks would be glossed and plump; with the broad quirking mouth and the short neck Archie would no longer be subtly amused and cocky. Frog smug.

"Lucky they didn't make a white belly too," Archie was saying.

"Herefords generally are white underneath."

"Inside. You know what I mean. They got their stomach red inside."

"All stomachs are red inside."

"I didn't mean that. I meant a red stomach is superior to a white stomach. Herefords had a white stomach to go with their white face and their white belly outside then they'd be in trouble."

"Would they."

"Hey-up. Poor doers. You couldn't finish them off the grass then. Have to grain-finish all them delicate white stomachs."

"They already do – more cattle finished on grain than off range."

"I know. The whole situation is red stomachs are superior . . ."

". . . to white stomachs," Carlyle said, "inside."

"Deer – moose – antelope – they all got good red stomachs and Hereford still. I got a red stomach – but you got white. Your white stomach couldn't take what mine does – blue elk – bannock – them survival cookies for the kids with cocoa at the school or you take your bowels – you just try eating like us people eat – your white stomach – your white bowels you couldn't make enough bismuth hydrate to cork all the white ass-holes all over the white world."

Carlyle laughed. "All right, Archie. I do cork a lot of red ones, but I agree with you." He quenched the unkindness of a comment on liquor and Archie's superior red stomach. "I guess you don't have too much use for anything white, Archie."

For a moment Archie considered. "Anything they make, I do. That's the whole situation."

"What is?"

"Anything you people make is superior. Houses – cars – bridges – everything you make. For instance glass. White luck is the whole situation."

"What's so lucky about glass?"

"Somebody decides to make something hard you can see through clear. You know what I mean. He comes up with glass."

"Does he."

"And concrete is another good example."

"Of white luck."

"Hey-up. Very lucky. Not so lucky as glass maybe, because glass was so stupid to start with."

"Why?"

"To take something hard and fix it to see through it anyway – some fellow had nothing better to do to think of trying for that, he's worse off than the one pounded up rock so he could mix with water and sand to make rock out of it again. Both of them were lucky but glass was luckier than concrete."

"Maybe it wasn't simply luck."

"Oh yes. But goddam lucky at that. And guns and television
– soft ice cream . . ."

"And beer and rye and after-shave lotion and vanilla
extract . . ."

". . . clocks and X-ray and medicines and steel . . ."

"But, Archie, behind all these there were hundreds of thousands of men. There was research . . ."

"Hey-up. That's the whole situation. Whites herd better."

"I suppose they do," Carlyle agreed. "We do."

The smell must have been strengthening for some time, ever since
they'd come onto the flats. Usually it had achieved full rottenness
before now, but the strong chinook had been carrying it eastward
ahead of them. Now they were actually driving through the oil
field with its great metal birds tipping and sipping from deep in
the earth, releasing the stink of hydrogen sulphide from every
flaring vent. Thank God for prevailing west winds! They'd be out
of it in five more minutes. There'd been something he'd meant to
ask Archie about. What had it been? Something had reminded
him – oh – yes – the smell – and the smell – that was it.
Something about old Esau – what had upset Esau.

"You any idea what might have upset Esau this morning?"

"Coughing up blood last night."

"No – besides – when I talked to him he said something
about – that place – said Raider went up there. Would he mean
Fir Creek – where Raider got his elk?"

"Storm and Misty."

"Oh – and is that where Raider got his . . ."

"He got it up Fir Creek."

"But you said Storm and Misty."

"I said that to answer what you asked me," Archie said.
"With Esau – Storm and Misty is 'that place.'"

29

"What about it?"

"He went up Storm and Misty."

"Raider did?"

"Hey-uh," Archie said.

"Yes?"

"And then Raider come down out of it," Archie said.

"Great," Carlyle said.

"Maybe he told old Esau."

"What?"

"Didn't tell me," Archie said. "I guess he just told old Esau something – up there."

"Whatever it was, it upset Esau."

"Raider went up there to look for spruce poles."

"It has something to do with Esau sitting up this morning."

"Maybe."

"And by the way – Raider left his elk guts under the bucking tree," Carlyle said. "About time the Bony-Spectre got him, isn't it?"

"We don't buy that Bony-Spectre bullshit any more."

"I wish Raider did!"

"Superstition isn't civilized," Archie said.

"All right, Archie. Bony-Spectre may be superstition, but starvation isn't! Killing cow elk and leaving orphan calves and wasting meat – rotting piles of guts – are wrong!"

"I agree," Archie said. "Bony-Spectre bothers me."

"I thought you said it was supersitious."

"Old Bony-Spectre is. Not the one got Esau now. New one. TB Bony-Spectre's got him starved down good."

"Yes."

"He didn't find any."

"Hmh?"

"Spruce poles. Up Storm and Misty."

TWO

NOW THE HIGHWAY ARROWED NORTH SO THAT THE MOUNTAINS lifted to his left, with such superlative clarity it was hard to believe they were all of forty miles away. They comforted, yet they surprised at the same time. Was it because he'd been a prairie child? Today they seemed special – reassuring in their abiding presence – daubed with white almost thick against the blue. They looked just the way a child with a paint box would want his mountains to turn out.

Beside him he heard the low and prolonged growl of snoring; Archie's cheek was pushed up and resting against the back of the seat. Thanks, Archie.

When he was a boy, mountains had worried him slightly; at eight or nine he'd wondered how they ever got their railroad engines and passenger and freight coaches up the steep sides and over the tops and down the other sides of them. About Grade Four – before Mr. Macky – Miss Coldtart's room? The same time he'd wondered about the American border – decided that it must be a lot like the blue line they dyed into the ice at the Arena rink – the length of a whole continent – from Vancouver Island, across the prairies to the beak of Lake Superior, squiggling down around the Niagara Peninsula arrowhead, to the lower part of Quebec's throat, with New Brunswick and Maine reminding him of Aunt Pearl's goitre. Same time they'd taken up the vanishing point in art class. No – that was Mr. Macky's room. These highway edges and marching telephone poles disappeared before they could come together properly at a vanishing point; up ahead the blue was marred by long cloud – low – as though a deliberate thumb had rubbed and spoiled the whole length of an horizon carefully ruled with soft art pencil. Give them hell, Old Kacky!

Just five more minutes to the city's core. The gas gauge showed only a quarter; he ought to fill up on the way in if he was to have enough to drive to the hospital for Victoria – down town – back to the hospital – across the city and all the way back to Paradise Valley. But if he stopped it might waken Archie; avoiding that would be worth paying three to five cents a gallon more at a city filling-station.

Already he could sense the city's aura; in spite of rural mailboxes like little tin prairie schooners balanced on posts, the houses and outbuildings no longer belonged to farm and ranch. For the next two or three miles this was the territory inhabited by the periphery people. They raised rabbit fryers, chinchillas, budgie birds, Siamese cats. There – over a gate the cut-out silhouette of a poodle. Shetland ponies clustered in a fence corner. Though they had been drawn closer together in the city's constellating field, these half-way people resisted anonymity, clung still to first-name informality. They took their living not from their few acres but from cottage enterprises like: "Sid's Virgin Loam and Rotted Manure," "Charlie's Well Witching and Water Well Drilling," "Walter's Reliable Mushroom Farm."

"Under a quarter," Archie said.

So he was awake! "What?"

"The gas."

"Yes – I know." It had been too much to expect him to sleep considerately all the way into the city.

Archie was looking ahead now. "On our side – half a mile up – you could pull into the station there."

"I intend to."

"Forty-seven cents a gallon . . ."

"I know it is, Archie. I generally fill up there." And now that Archie was awake, there was, of course, no point in waiting till they were any nearer the city limits.

"That's for extra, you know. Only forty-three for the cheap grade. Once you're in the city, then it's over fifty cents there."

"I said I was going to fill up now." He pulled over into the right lane.

"I guess it doesn't make any difference anyway," Archie said.

"What do you mean?"

"To you."

"To me?"

"Hey-up."

"I don't understand what you're . . ."

"It's Indian gas, isn't it?"

"No – it isn't!"

"I thought it was."

"It is government – department gas!"

"Hey-up. Indian gas – Indian car."

"No – God damn it! The Indian Affairs department owns the car. It pays the operating expenses – and it gets the money from taxes – tax-payers of whom I suspect damn few are Indian! Whatever you think, I'm careful of expenses – my own or the department's."

"You missed the turn-off," Archie said.

And he had! He glanced in the rear-view mirror, jammed on the brakes. He did a U-turn on the broad and empty highway, then crossed it and drove in under the filling-station canopy.

In so doing he almost ran down a congregation of dwarfs. Dwarves? He did manage to miss them barely, then corrected in time to shave the island edge of the gas pumps. Actually he had driven in the wrong way. Archie's fault! As he looked back through his window, he saw that all the dwarfs were dressed identically in green, and smoked matching clay pipes. Arrest that man – I saw him do it – leprechaun hit-and-run! Oh God, what satisfaction it would have been to maim – no – pulverize half a dozen of the pot-bellied, bearded, little bastards, wearing similarly pointed and equally limp caps folded down over the same ear, each accompanied by his own toadstool!

"You're on the wrong side of the pumps."

"Oh, shut up, Archie!"

And now he saw the bear cubs. There were an incredible number of them between the car and the building. Every one had been frightened precisely half way up a grove of cast trees truncated at exactly the same height. Each cub embraced his own stump. The fearful desperation with which every single one looked back down over the same shoulder did not suggest climbing nearly so much as ursine masturbation. In perfect concert!

Nobody yet had come out of the office to serve him. He pressed the car horn.

He looked back to the dwarfs. Dwarves? Leprechauns? Smug contentment echoing from face to face to face to face. Fat, green little breeches all buttoned up. But just the same . . .

He honked again.

Even as he did, a man in a turned-up baseball cap was bunged past the left corner of the building. He was little, yet still considerably larger than the cast dwarfs he trotted through. There was deft monkey grace in the way he made a quick cranking correction of the last sale, snatched the gas-line's curved nozzle up out of its cradle, unscrewed the tank cap, poked in the nozzle. Luton – Luton – your goddam tootin', this was Luton. Five years of stopping here and the man's first name was all that

Carlyle knew him by; it was stitched in free hand over the green twill of his uniform jacket.

Except for the unknown surname, Carlyle suspected he knew everything it was possible to know about Luton. He was married to a truculently wordless and cigar-shaped woman, who sometimes manned the gas pump. He could not remember when this conversationally costive female impersonator had ever answered a question. Luton never shut up. Into a family of eight: seven boys – one girl – in southern Manitoba in 1912, April 3rd – father a railroader – Luton had been born and early infected with verbal diarrhoea. Quite possibly congenital. His father had permitted him – at the age of seven – to carry a lighted lantern into the barn – even though the loft was full of tinder-dry hay and Norny D. was three years older – Norny D. married his childhood sweetheart, Sadie – lived in Saskatchewan now – wasn't a blockman for Cockshutt any more since he and Sadie fell into artificial flowers – late in life – after Sadie's operation – breast cancer. Just walk through any Five and Ten or look in any city florist window or supermarket or Econo-Mart or funeral parlour and you'd see Norny D. artificial flowers there. You couldn't miss them. This was the time of year – spring – when Sadie and Norny D. would be rolling out in their little trailer with sample arrangements, writing orders all over the three prairie provinces and clear into B. C. – pull in right here any day now – then west again as far as the Crow's Nest Pass anyway and maybe right to the coast – way they'd done every single year since they'd fallen into artificial flowers. Luton had a left-hand rupture and also something else down there that the doctors hadn't been able to do anything about. Carlyle could believe that. Luton's breath stank consistently.

It stank now; the soft spring air must be tainted right to the highway; the inside of the car was superlatively polluted.

"Couldn't get to you any faster. Round back waxin' flamingo moulds." Face at the open window, he leaned on his elbows, forehead wrinkled under the tilted peak of the baseball cap, just a bunt of a nose, a fine, ginger line delineating his lower lip and putting a snoose period to each corner of his mouth. ". . . them thin, skinny legs you got to get it into every single crack and nook because if you don't then you have an aitch of a time to pop them out your goddam tootin' an' if you force them out then bang goes your mould." Mustard and beer and garlic and the sweet edge of snoose! How could people complain of the smell of Indians! ". . . most people's taste runs to flamingoes on their lawn and they're the worst but they still kick when you tell them the price – just can't figure why flamingoes should go higher'n goose an' goslin's or prowlin' panther or wild-stallion wall placks. Well, there's the labour and to begin with there's the original cost of your flamingo mould alone . . ." Light – sour – not mustard – mould – God – Luton's ancient rupture had finally gone mouldy in him! ". . . your moulds can't last for ever, you know – limited life your goddam tootin' – whether it's cartoppers or dune-buggy bodies or bed-pans – shower basins – septic tanks . . ."

He couldn't help it; he flinched from the man's breath, then considerately exaggerated the movement so it would seem he had deliberately leaned across Archie to reach the glove compartment. By fumble and recognizing touch he found the credit card in its little leather folder, then, taking down and holding a deep breath, he straightened up to hand the card over to Luton.

". . . don't write in an' say, 'I want to get hold of your moulds,' because it won't work all that easy because they protect their mould people – have to – got to protect the ones payin' 'em royalities from any Tom Dick an' Henry gets the notion to scab off his own moulds." He'd been the champion breathholder out at Tourigny's swimming hole; not even Mate had

been able to beat him. Two decades later he was going to have
to set a new record; Luton had taken the card, simply by lifting
one hand at the wrist and accepting it, both forearms still inside
the car. ". . . orders from the Okanagan – Oregon – clear to
California – God, we're back-ordered on everything and before
summer you'll see licence plates from every province the
Dominion – every state the Union your goddam tootin'. . . ."
Luton's head still in the window – his own faintly ringing. Not
a motorist in sight on the highway, to pull in and draw Luton to
either pump. Archie simply sat there so that escape by the other
door was cut off!

". . . when Else pitches in you can tell we're real desperate
because she ain't fussy about . . ." Windshield hopelessly clean!
Carlyle was actually dizzy now and his face must be red with
pent breath!

"Aren't you going to make out the goddam card!" It was
released from him like steam from under a locomotive.

"Not till she's filled, I can't." His head indicated the glass
window on the gas pump, cents and fractions of gallons flickering and tumbling there.

And now, of course, to compensate he was dragging down
magnificent gulps of splendidly foul air. Closet panic knifed
him and knifed him again! They had him strait-jacketed! He
burst from the car, sending Luton staggering back on the
swinging door.

"Sorry – sorry!" He almost ran in the direction of the wash-
rooms, felt his right foot turn slightly under him, heard the bell
ring inside the filling-station, cleared all the climbing, wicked
little bear cubs to enter a couchant flock of does, each with the
same double corner to one foreleg, the other thrusting a licorice,
cloven hoof straight out before herself. Little dappled Bambis
were beyond their mothers, then the spiking stag horns, then the
geese and their goslings, ducks and ducklings, donkeys with

twinned side panniers, and finally a fluorescent flock of flamingoes, stick legs thick as first-growth lodge pole pine, great beaks like inverted scimitars much too heavy for the pink, serpentine necks.

Thank God, the Men's door was unlocked! For once the washroom deodorant was completely successful in its illusion of piny freshness. He was not going to be ill, he thought, as he stepped up to the urinal.

He had just proffered himself when Archie entered and stood to his right. The smother feeling rose in him again, then as quickly subsided.

"You people are careful what you do with this."

Without too much difficulty he kept himself from asking Archie what "this" was.

"And that." A backward jerk of Archie's head indicated the toilet bowl, pristine in its square shrine.

"If we weren't it could pile up pretty high."

"Hey-uh." Archie rump-shrugged, was busy with his fly. "They look nice too."

"Anything wrong with that?"

"Expensive," Archie said.

Carlyle turned away from the urinal, stepped over to the wash-basin.

"Just to take care of shit," Archie said.

"Oh, Archie!"

"Excuse me – I guess they can make a lot of shiny white dishes to catch it in, but they didn't make a nice word to put it into yet."

"I'm not objecting to the word." The soap dispenser was empty!

"I thought so."

"I'm simply not interested in discussing it." He shook water off his hands as he turned away from the basin.

"Not interested in what I have to . . ."

"That's right." He pushed past Archie.

"I have come to a conclusion that . . ."

The towel dispenser was empty! "I'm not interested in any philosophic conclusions you may have come to on – it! Or – on the manner in which we handle – it! Or – what cultural importance you may attach to – it! Or that we do – or don't! Shit, Archie, is shit and that is the whole shit situation!"

"Hey-uh," Archie said with satisfaction. "Exactly what I wanted to tell you my conclusion I come to."

"That's nice," Carlyle said. With his wet hands slippery, he had a brief problem with the stiff door-knob.

As they pulled out onto the highway again, Archie said, "So that's the whole situation with civilization – a lot of people – a lot of germs – a lot of shit."

"Just part of the whole situation."

"Your wars."

"Wars didn't have to wait for civilization."

"The big ones did."

"Look, Archie, let's just forget it between here and the city."

"Sure," Archie said, then only a moment later, "You didn't . . ."

"No more, Archie . . ."

"I was just going to tell you . . ."

"I mean it! Shut up!"

". . . that you forgot to do up your fly yet."

He managed to zip it up without diminishing speed or veering from course. And Archie said nothing more. Decent of him after all those cast ornaments. Unusual restraint. Just give him time though – later – when you least expected it.

The car interior was almost free of Luton's breath now. What a moat! And how lonely it must have made him – all his life. It would take a lifetime to accomplish that breath. Poor little ten-year-old – six-year-old Luton all alone in the schoolyard. And at home. "No – I said no, Luton – you can't climb on

my lap – Mother's busy – run out and play with Norny D." But
of course Norny D. didn't want him – or any of Norny D.'s
friends. They couldn't stand Luton's breath either – made their
eyes water – spoiled their marble aim – telegraphed their presence in hiding games – once they'd scrambled to safety down
their holes the gophers never put their heads back out to be
snared. It was quite likely the father had handed little Luton the
lighted lantern because he was unable to stand the child's breath
one moment longer – simply to get him out of the house.

He heard the snoring beside him – dropped deep into sleep
again – easy as cut-the-dead-man's-throat. God, they had a
relaxed style of life! How did Else defend herself? Very early in
marriage she'd been forced to turn away from Luton; possibly
that was why he had populated the yard with garden ornaments.
Little bearded dwarfs didn't show revulsion; cast does and fawns
couldn't run from him, or flamingoes take instant flight.

Had bad breath ever served as grounds for divorce? It must
be the reason Else never said anything when she came out to the
gas pumps. The less she said, the less he said, and therefore
the more his mouth would be closed. No – incredibly she had
come to terms with Luton's breath – before marriage. The garden
ornaments had driven her to taciturnity; year after year in this
gay zoo had driven her into herself, and there had been no
escape there – just trapped hopelessness. "Please, Luton – please
– let's get out of them – away from them – sell – get rid of the
moulds – destroy them before they destroy me!" And he just
looked at her – with his mouth open – at first – and then he
accepted that it was important to her. "All right, Else – all right
– that's it – not another one – bear cub – wild-stallion wall plack
or goslin' or flamingo." And he stuck to his word. One by one they
left, and as their numbers diminished, so did Else's apprehension
and despondency. She sang as she tidied up the house – herself.

She talked to him, took up painting by numbers again. They planned for the time when the last little dwarf and bear cub had gone – a new life raising frogs or mushrooms. Possibly they might get into a Kentucky Fried franchise. They might even build a Kiddyland near the park gates – east of Banff on the Trans-Canada – Shetland pony trail rides – plywood teepees – a dear little turreted castle Luton would design himself and build entirely out of mortar and bottles. Listerine bottles. But they stayed dreams; there never rose a bottle-cobbled Kiddy Kastle to twinkle in the sun. Flamingoes: 29 – dwarfs: 13 – climbing bear cubs: 17 – Bambis: 22 . . . And then with dreadful inevitability despondency darkened her. Flamingoes: 49 – Bambis: 31 . . . They'd increased! Almost doubled in one night since her count! Dwarfs and toadstools were the same but – Luton was moulding again! Hysterically she accused him. He denied it, but she knew – nights – while she slept! Honest, Else – honest to God! He'd smashed the moulds two weeks ago. It wasn't Luton who'd been busy nights. Only then did they realize the full, fornicating horror of it – out of their control now – simply a helpless matter of time until the entire defenceless world would be up to its arse in fluorescent flamingoes!

"Hey-up, Archie!"

"Huh!"

"Wake up – nearly there." Now that they were well into the city he wanted to talk with Archie. "Need your company – just had some frightening thoughts." Surprisingly all irritation had evaporated, was replaced by something else: incredibly warm affection for Archie Nicotine. "I just come to a conclusion, Archie. Luton's menagerie back there – something missing."

"What?"

"Whooping crane."

"Hey-up," Archie said.

"Late afternoon I'm heading back. I'll be stopping in at the Super-Arcade for groceries. Five-thirty – six. If you want a lift back to Paradise, meet me."

"Flyin' Saucer?"

"Sure. Might stake you to hamburger and soft ice cream."

"I'll have that left over after the rings and carburetor."

"All right."

He made the right turn onto Johnston Trail, and they began the shallow descent into the city's heart. Far ahead, the Devonian Tower thrust with stiff arrogance fully a third higher than the tallest of the office buildings around; from the broad cylindrical base the concave slope sides soared six hundred feet, so that its glass revolving restaurant, boutiques, gift shop, broadcasting station, CSFA, floated above traffic smog. Pretty nearly the only six-hundred-foot concrete erection in the British Commonwealth. With a May basket balanced on its tip – that twinkled with coloured lights at night. North America. And had a red oil derrick to spear the last fifty feet. The world. Who forgot the bear cubs!

"Heally Richards."

"What?"

Archie was pointing out and down through his car window.

"What do you mean?"

"Big tent."

He saw it then, beyond the railroad below, in an open area between the Stampede Grounds and the south edge of the industrial section following the river.

"Now – look, Archie – I meant what I said about Esau and . . ."

"Hey-uh."

"Where do you want me to let you out – Empress Hotel?"

"It'll do."

He wished he hadn't said it, but Archie had asked for it, stubbornly hanging onto the evangelist. And he most certainly would end up in the Empress beer parlour, drink up all the pole money. Hundred to one odds. No – a thousand to one. There'd be no Archie Nicotine to meet him in the Flying Saucer, and tomorrow morning when the phone rang, it would be Archie, and the charge would be drunk and disorderly. It wasn't the bail he minded so much as having to make another trip into the city.

"Snakes," Archie said.

And he wouldn't mind it so much at that. Victoria would be free for the afternoon. Sunday. Possibly they could visit the island.

"Maybe it was snakes at first so they cut it off short like that."

Given the certainty of Archie's failure to stay sober, to buy his rings and carburetor, to stay out of jail, to keep the rendezvous at the Flying Saucer, he'd have to make another trip in tomorrow morning.

"For the kids crawlin'."

So – he must keep a picnic in mind when he bought his groceries at the Super-Arcade, where Archie would fail to meet him this evening. Just thinking about it gave him a lift.

Their route was taking them through the residential area of Meadow Lark Park; still Johnston Trail, but now it was as though development surveyors had kicked a tame jack rabbit in the rear, followed it faithfully. They had been followed by others with a weakness for euphemism – unable to call a street a street: Pekisko Crescent, Palliser Trail, Willow Road, Diefenbaker Lane.

"No chance of snakes now, but they keep right on cuttin' it down."

The binder-whip trees were in swelling bud; here and there tulips and daffodils held their stiff, bright ranks. Sprinklers whirled and sparkled or lifted up and over, combing the spring air with slow regularity. Fyfe lived here. The lawns were lush.

"What did you say about snakes, Archie?"

"Grass all cut down short. I guess they did that first time so the little kids could play on it and not get bit. Snakes."

"That's very generous of you, Archie."

"There's a couple."

"Couple what?"

"Them pink whoopin' cranes."

"I knew you wouldn't disappoint me, Archie." Picnic tomorrow with her would be just lovely! "Try to make it to the Flying Saucer."

THREE

ARCHIE NICOTINE STOOD BEFORE THE LADIES AND ESCORTS entrance of the Empress beer parlour. Forty-eight dollars – rings sixteen – carburetor from Hercules' Salvage – maybe eighteen – thirty – thirty-two – maybe fifteen over – ten anyway. Forty-eight. He could feel it almost warm against his left thigh – in his pocket there. Also he could use a beer. Way a man's tongue stuck to the roof of his mouth and his throat got stiff for the tickle of beer and the earth taste of beer.

A Hutterite passed him, turned into the Men's door; funny for them to be so religious, but you still saw a lot of black pail hats in any beer parlour all the same. His eyes idled over the passers-by – not one of them had to think twice about whether to go in and have a beer or not. Another man pushed past him and into the beer parlour. Denim smock – flat boots – farmer. Forty-eight – rings sixteen – carburetor eighteen. Twenty – fifteen dollars of beer was one hell of a lot of beer. Beer never hurt him – never hurt anybody. Let everyone suck it down and not a drop for him!

Red luck right from the start. There was the difference – how you were born was the whole situation. You either got born a horse or a fool-hen or a link. Or red or white. His luck he got dropped red in the corner of a reservation bull-field, laced into moss in a *yo-kay-bo*, weaned on an elk bone. Tag around the tent or cabin – beans and bannock and tea when it was there – roll in or out when you felt like it – colt roping or grabbing hold of girls from thirteen on and "Onward Christian Soldiers" washed in the blood and all the white religions said no beer at all. With their flower-pot hats and their long noses and their twang, Latter Day Saints said it loudest. Mormon missionaries could ride and they could rope all right, but they got the coal oil onto their fire over beer – or even coffee – tea – coke. So that washed up the L.D.S. How sweet the name of Jesus and the taste of beer – beer – beer – and the salt taste of beer cooling down your hot throat!

Sinclair was so smart; on his face you could tell he figured all the pole money would end up in the waiter's apron, then drunk and disorderly, and into the bucket before dark.

A Black and White taxi had stopped. A woman got out. High heels behind. And Sinclair said no laying hands on Esau too, so maybe he ought to just visit Heally Richards at that tent. Not with beer on his breath though. Tent. Church tent. Maybe it was some kind of a red religion from across the line with those little mushrooms you ate and they gave you a vision. Not very damn likely.

He caught a smell sweet as wolf willow, from the woman who pushed past him and into the Ladies and Escorts door of the Empress, her perfume winning over beer bloom through the opened door. Buh-beer – buh-beer – buhbeer – it beat in him like a Chicken Dance drum. The taxi was still at the curb, its driver, head down, making a notation on the seat beside himself. Sinclair was so smart pushing people around, so first thing was to go see Heally Richards to lay hands on old Esau – then Hercules Salvage for rings and the carburetor for the truck – then the Flying Saucer and Sinclair with surprise all over his face because he hadn't figured it out right at all.

He stepped across the street to the taxi. The driver looked out and up to him.

"You busy?"

"Get in." The driver leaned across and pushed open the front door.

Archie opened the back door and got in. The driver pulled shut the front door. He straightened up, tucked his note pad under the sun visor. He stared into the rear-view mirror. "Where to, Chief?"

The mirror framed the driver's eyes, his bridgeless nose – two punches of cheek bone; on the left one there was a faint linger of bruise. "I said where to, Chief?"

"The big tent."

"In the sky, that is."

"No. Other side the Stampede Grounds – just off Johnston Trail."

"Oh – that big tent." He thrust the car into gear and pulled away from the curb.

Sinclair could get one hell of a surprise. Come to think of it, he was a little surprised himself. "Turn south," he advised the driver as the car stopped at the Johnston Trail red light.

"I know, Chief. I know the way."

Maybe he ought to tell him how at fifteen he'd been top rider in the bareback and the calf roping – in the money for steer decorating – second highest – would have been all-round Little Britches Rodeo champion if it hadn't been for the saddle event.

"You Blood?"

"No."

"Sarcee?"

"No."

"Blackfoot."

"No."

"Sure as hell ain't Hooterite."

"You're correct," Archie said.

They had turned off Johnston Trail. The car did a double hiccup over the railroad tracks.

The tent was a lot bigger than it had looked from up above when he and Sinclair had driven into the city. Its khaki canvas scalloped above the slack guy ropes, swagging deep from the high poke of four poles. On the street side where the taxi had stopped, a framed banner said: GOD IS NOT DEAD!, the message centred in a curlicued margin of circus doodle decoration. It was as though the original portraits of freaks and wild animals had been painted out of the centre and the reassuring announcement substituted.

The meter read a dollar fifteen. Archie handed over a dollar and a quarter, waited till the driver leaned again to the opened window. "Thanks." The taxi driver dropped a dime into the hand Archie held out. "Chief."

"I'm not."

"Friendly form of address."

"It isn't."

"All right. Honest mistake then. Under the impression only chiefs could afford to ride taxis."

"I'm a duly elected band councillor."

"So you're travelling on an expense account. Red is beautiful."

"No, it isn't." Archie looked up to the baroque banner. "Guys like you it's the shits – and that is the whole situation."

He turned towards the revival tent so that he didn't hear what it was that the taxi driver growled, but a moment later he felt the angry pelt of gravel against the back of his leg.

Two men had just emerged from the tent opening. One was little; one, large. The Reverend Heally Richards was large, and he was also pure. His shoes, socks, pants, suit coat, vest, shirt, tie, made a white total in the spring sunlight. He could have been carved from lard except for his face; the white hair and white eyebrows, even the white eyelashes, jumped out from the darkly tanned face. The slight jowling of his cheeks, a fullness at the mouth, suggested beaver to Archie. The other man's totem had to be old mosquito. The Reverend Healy Richards was frowning, the old man talking, as they reached Archie.

". . . isn't I'm complaining, Reverend Richards. That isn't it at all. When I came to the front last night for you to touch me . . ."

"I recall I did, Brother Hillaker."

"I know you did, but I still had to get up seven times last night."

Richards' voice sounded just like it did on the radio. They had stopped, seemed quite unaware of Archie. And now the evangelist's big white back was to him; that was what made him think of the backward people. Anyone could heal people from being sick, a backward person might do it. Healy Richards should have walked backwards out of that tent.

"Isn't automatic, you know," Richards was saying.

"I know it isn't, Reverend."

"Nobody commands the Lord. You've got to understand that right now. You can't push Him around."

"No – no – I wouldn't – I don't want – but I figured if tonight you could touch me again . . ."

"Of course I will, Brother Hillaker – but first you have just got to understand this one thing – it is not for you to demand blessin' – or – is it for me – to guarantee – what the Lord does with His blessin'. After all . . ."

"Oh yes – yes – but I figured if you were to touch me right – then maybe He might . . ."

"Praise the Lord! Praise Him!"

"Hallelujah," Mr. Hillaker said obediently.

"You want your sufferin' lifted. . . ."

"Yes, I . . ."

"I can understand that and praise God it may be. But – the way I touch you isn't all that important. You should see that. Lord's the One does the healin' itself. Not me, Brother Hillaker. His Heavenly Pahr . . ."

"What I had in mind for tonight," Mr. Hillaker explained, "was if you took me . . ."

"Praise of the Lord."

"Hallelujah," Mr. Hillaker said automatically.

"Praise *of* the Lord," corrected the Reverend Richards. "What I'm tryin' to explain to you is that praise of Him is the prime mover that is what primes Him. You say you want His blessin' to pour down on you – then you have just got to prime Him with your praise."

"Sixty years," Mr. Hillaker's voice thinned earnestly. "I been praising Him over sixty years – forty-two Baptist – nineteen Pentecost! But that isn't the point I wanted to bring up with you."

"There you are, Brother Hillaker. That is *just* the point. Praise is the point – first point – first there must be praise and then there is blessin' in the form of pain an' sufferin' lifted. Why was not yours?"

"Huh?"

"Your sufferin'? Why wasn't it lifted?"

"Oh – well now – way I see it – it was the way you touched me last night and also the time before – and also it was where you touched me. . . ."

"Where I touched you? No doubt about that, Brother."

"No, there isn't and I thought maybe tonight you might . . ."

"In the presence of the Lord – I touched you. There is where I touched you. There was loud praise – there was harmony – Gregorian – Pentatonic – just the five notes – there was myriad tongues and there was very great glory in that tent last night."

"Well, if there was so much glory then why wasn't my . . ."

"I touched you . . ."

". . . on the back of my neck and the front of my forehead!" Mr. Hillaker said with tight exasperation. "And that just ain't where my prosperous gland is at! Now can you see what I'm getting at? I been trying to get at? Where you touched me was all wrong – wasn't it? Now – if you were to grab me more where – the trouble where – the right location of my . . ." His voice trickled out.

"Brother Hillaker – in front of a thousand people in that tent tonight – instead of your forehead you askin' me to touch your – are you askin' me – do you really expect me – to grab you by your Baptist balls!"

"Reverend!"

"Haven't you got faith that the Lord knows where your crotch is?"

"I got . . ."

". . . that even if I touch you somewhere else on your body – which He made – in His own image – He has got a pretty clear notion of where your prostate gland is?"

"Sure I . . ."

"Then bring it with you tonight – lift up your praise to Him – praise the Lord – praise Him!"

"Hallelujah," Mr. Hillaker said. "I guess maybe . . ."

Heally Richards turned abruptly, saw Archie, shifted his course. "I'm already late for a tapin'."

"All I wanted," Mr. Hillaker called after him, "was for you . . ."

". . . any more time wasted I won't even make it to 'Your Line Is Open.'" He turned his head to Archie, who had fallen into step beside him. "That is a live show – I am now late for."

"I would like to talk to you for a minute, Reverend Mr. Richards."

"You heard me – of course not."

"It was about healin' somebody – one of our people that's pretty sick now."

"All right – all right. Bring him tonight – or her – right now. . . ."

"We got quite a few people sick and that's the whole situation at Paradise."

"Paradise!" Reverend Heally Richards stopped.

"Eighty miles south-west. I come in . . ."

"Oh – Indian reservation."

"Hey-up – and I come all the way in from there to see you about this matter."

"Possibly tonight – bring your sick with you tonight."

"How can I do that? Him back there in Paradise Valley – both ways is nearly two hundred miles."

"We worship every night. Three times on Sunday."

"The reason I wanted to talk with you is to see if you could."

"Yes – yes." The evangelist had stopped again. "Could what?"

"Heal those who are sick with pain and sufferin'."

"I don't. The Lord does."

"Hey-up."

Richards began to walk away, stopped, turned back to Archie. "Tell me something, Brother – ah . . ."

"Archie Nicotine."

"Brother Nicotine – there is an Indian – some taller than you – not young – middle – early thirties. He has a scar on the one side of his face – corner of his mouth to his ear. You familiar with a man that description?"

"There's quite a few Indians around, Mr. Reverend Richards."

"I suppose there is."

"They come in to this city from five different reserves – and there's a lot aren't treaty any more and it's a big city. We're just a small band and there isn't anybody like that in our Stony band."

"Just an off chance."

"One way or another we got a lot of sick people and we have one person who's very sick right now. That was the purpose of my visit with you. To tell you the whole situation with this person and see if you can do it."

"Not me. The Lord."

"To see if He makes very much use of you for this purpose."

"Mmmh?"

"It would be pretty hard on this person to bring them all the way in here when they're so sick and the Lord's blessings didn't come down on him and lift up off him his pain an' sufferin'. . . ."

"Depends on the Lord, doesn't it?"

"And you."

"I serve as His instrument."

"That's what I was interested in."

"What?"

"If you are."

"Are what?"

"One of these instruments."

"Considerable sick and sufferin' has been healed durin' my ministry."

"You could have a good opportunity for it on our people. There's sickness on them most of the time. You could get in a lot of good work there amongst them."

"Perhaps – now – wait – you don't mean for me to come there – to your – to Paradise?"

"Hey-up."

"Oh – now. I don't think you understand. I couldn't get away from here and go to your reservation, Brother – Nicotine."

They had reached the street corner, turned, Heally walking quite quickly now. "You specialize in city people," Archie said.

"No – they come to me – people – from the city and from the country. They come to me."

Archie increased his pace. "Maybe I could catch a lift with you."

"If your destination is down town – anywhere near the Devonian Tower."

"Not far," Archie said, and then he saw the Reverend Heally Richards' car.

"You're welcome, Brother – ah –"

"Nicotine," Archie said absently.

"Brother Nicotine." Heally Richards opened the car door. "Praise the Lord. Praise Him."

Cadillac! White! "Hallelujah!" Archie said fervently.

As the magnificent car floated over the railroad tracks, Archie said, "I'm sorry to impose on you for this ride."

"That's all right, Brother."

"My own truck isn't running because I'm rebuilding her motor. I'm getting the rings and a carburetor today for her."

They had turned south on Johnston Trail.

"But that place isn't near the Devonian Tower."

"What place?"

"Rings and carburetor. The second light is the Bow Valley Road. If you turn west there. Five blocks then south again. Two blocks you could let me off there. Then it isn't much out of your way."

"All right, Brother Nicotine," Heally Richards said.

Five minutes later when the car stopped to let him out, Archie sat for a moment. "I'm Stony. He isn't."

"Hmh?"

"So I didn't see him in our band. But I did see him."

"Who?"

"The one you asked me about. He isn't treaty any more."

"I don't think I understand you, Brother."

"I seen him around a few times."

"Who?"

"The one you asked me about."

"Oh – oh – do you know him by name?"

"He isn't on any reserve now. The department don't want him there."

"And what's his name?"

"Norman. When they take out their life treaty they can't go back on the deal."

"Norman who?"

"His sister too. They would both be trespassers."

"Norman who?"

"Catface."

"Thank you . . ."

"His sister is Gloria."

"Indeed . . . thank you, Brother Nicotine."

"That's all right," Archie said. "Norman Catface is a wicked man." He got out of the pure Cadillac, held the door open. "Gloria won a contest."

"Contest?"

"Hey-up. For beauty. Miss North-west Fish and Game of 1954."

"Well – that's interesting, Brother . . ."

"Now Norman made her wicked too," Archie explained. "Mr. Reverend Richards, it wouldn't be very smart for you to have anything to do with them."

"As a matter of fact . . ."

"The Lord's blessings isn't likely to pour down if you lay hands on Norman. . . ."

"It isn't that, Brother . . ."

". . . or Gloria Catface either. About old Esau . . ."

"Esau?"

"The person I told you was so sick in our band."

"Look, Brother . . ."

"With TB. If you have laid hands on any TB . . . lately . . ."

"I am one half-hour overdue at CSFA now!"

"Hey-up. If you have been very successful with TB . . ."

"Some other time, Brother!"

"If we could . . ."

"The tent – any time – any day before or after worship."

"You sleep in that tent?"

"I sleep in Room 517 at the Foothills Carleton."

"Hey-up." Carefully Archie closed the door of the white master car. He turned to the Men's door of the Empress Hotel beer parlour.

FOUR

THE LIGHT HAD JUST TURNED RED AS HE REACHED THE intersection; he remembered it as a long and complicated one, green and red alternating with lighted arrows. Now it was the turn for cars on the outside lanes to his left and to his right to move out to the centre, meet opposite partners, swing and pass each other in opposite directions. The green arrows blinked off, but his own light persisted red while the cross-traffic was released. The double flow of pedestrians past his windshield was almost uninterrupted – four – five deep. Purse, shopping-bag, brief-case, parcel, ice cream cone, top-coat over an arm – almost all of them carried something. Those who did not seemed to; the white-egg burden of their own life perhaps. They made such work out of walking, as though the pavement were tipped against them, and all were engaged in a communal pantomimist illusion of walking up an invisible slope. Some of the women did seem to be descending stairs, swinging their free arm back right through the wrist, as though they were persistently but unsuccessfully trying to brush off a webbing that had caught at their skirts and was trailing behind them. How gracelessly whites walked!

Ever since he'd dropped Archie off, driven round the base of the Devonian Tower and across Main, the carnival feeling had been deepening within him. Theatres, restaurants, hotels, offices, shops were on display for him, and when he left this evening they would all be taken down till it was time for their next stand. His next visit.

He must be getting bushed! But it always did seem a show to him – put on by curious people who did not lead innocent lives. They performed for the benefit of those who had paid to come onto their carnival grounds. They weren't freaks – exactly – but they were somehow exotic and unrelated to him. Nine years in Paradise Valley had set him apart with this perspective. He supposed it was a dehumanizing one. Not just for them – for himself as well. Very dangerous for himself.

A concerted arrest of the pedestrian flow had caught a couple by surprise, so that they teetered at the sidewalk edge. They regained their balance, one of them pulling back a foot that had stepped down and found the pavement hot. All stood now with heads up and eyes front, not as though they were looking, but as though they were listening. Behind Carlyle a car honked impatiently, and he saw that his light was green now.

How did he justify – explain anyway – his long self-indulgence in fantasy? It had gone back much beyond his Paradise Valley days. The year he'd moved into Old Kacky's room in Sir Walter Raleigh School? Before that. At Aunt Pearl's when he'd spoiled the order of her things on the top of her bird's-eye maple dresser – during the lonely hours up in dead little Willis's toy room with its balloons and steam-engine and magic lantern! The habit had grown and strengthened through later years when he had shared manic moments of silliness with Mate.

Fifteen minutes till half past one when he was to meet Victoria in the General. With another ten to get across town, he had a margin of five minutes. Not that she would mind if he were late, or, if she did, that she would show it. What inexhaustible patience she had. That was her true strength – her real talent. She was capable of such stillness, the ability simply to *be* for so long a time. Dear little lamb, Victoria! Sometimes it could disturb; he was always on the look-out for apathy, the one thing that could truly frighten and defeat him. Every waking moment in Paradise Valley it greeted him from a hundred faces; the despair that grew out of the will-lessness of others – that was the one that beat you. Your own was bad enough, but that of others dependent on you was the turn of the screw. At least you could try to do something about your own. And she would make it – by God, she would!

Perhaps that was why he fantasized – at first it had been some sort of day-dreaming escape for him whenever pressure or abrasion had become too much for him. Escape from outer lunacy. But he always played fair when he took these inner trips. They were not comforting ones really. The journeys always began in actuality, with the itinerary already set out for him, the destination determined ahead of time. He must be some sort of artist, a very private one performing only for another part of himself, that stepped back and away to share the illusion and to applaud. And laugh – oh yes, that was it! Always to laugh! Why not? Life made so many comic promises that the destination simply had to be funny.

More and more fool mines hidden under the life field and silly triggers to set them off – Luton's goddam tootin', cast garden ornaments – the magic lantern of television and film – thronged supermarkets and department stores where so many ludicrous threads were braided together. In his own smug way Archie Nicotine knew what he was talking about! Just a year ago – after he'd bailed Archie out on the drunk and disorderly charge – they'd walked through the Super-Arcade's Green Magic Garden Centre on their way to the grocery section. Archie had stopped by a counter covered with sprays and fertilizers, fungicides and insecticides, peat pots and rooting hormones. He had picked up what looked like a dark, miniature pillow of plastic. "The Real McCoy," he read from the label. "What's that?"

"Fertilizer."

"Twenty-nine cents. Must be strong stuff."

"It is. Organite."

"What's that?"

"Manure."

"Horse?"

"No."

"Cow."

"No."

"Sheep? Chicken."

"Human," Carlyle said.

"Hey-uh! Who fills them?"

"By-product of disposal plants."

Archie stared at the plump plastic bag in his hand. "You people charge for that."

"I guess so – now."

Still Archie stared at the earth-dark fertilizer. He lifted and smelled it carefully.

"It's been processed, Archie."

"Can't say it now."

"Say what?"

Archie tossed the bag back onto the counter. "Something isn't worth a shit."

"I guess not. Any more. Just have to say something isn't worth twenty-nine cents."

"Hey-up."

When the escalator bore them down to the basement floor, Carlyle had stood sideways, one hand on the moving black rubber banister, across from him the rising line of people caught in the undertow of the upward escalator. There should have been the flat, cracking whap of .22 target rifles, the spice-sting of gun powder acrid on the air. The fat, worried woman with the nearly albino child, the narrow-shouldered man with the tragic mask face and his fists punched down into his sweater pockets, the two clown-faced and giggling teen-agers – one after another they should ring and stiffly flip over backwards and out of sight like rabbits and ducks and four-leaf clovers and clay pipes and squirrels.

He stepped off at the bottom, rounded the end of the escalator, to bump into Archie, transfixed, staring at the plastic nether-parts of a woman in panty-hose, drum tight. It was as though she had trustingly lain back to do her bicycle exercises on the counter, and someone had taken a completely successful swipe at her with a scimitar. Truncated, she rested on her waist stump, knees gracefully bent, toes pointed, one leg almost outstretched. Through the tipped and proffered crotch, looping down and around the buttock cheeks, hung garlands of pearl necklace. They'd moved on to the grocery section. Archie said nothing. He'd got bingo that day!

Why was it – in a city with over a quarter of a million population – he saw always the same people in the Super-Arcade. He did again and again, their faces calling out to him for remembrance. That day a year ago with Archie and the severed woman, he'd figured it out; there were people who lived in department stores and supermarkets. They were born in Infants' Wear; they grew up through the difficult and insecure years of adolescence in Teen Town; were married in Bridal Belles. They bought their contraceptives and douches and sanitary napkins in Drugs; ate and slept in Furniture and Bedding; their dishes came from Glass and China; their clothes from Men's and Ladies' Wear; they did their laundry in Electrical Appliances, where they also watched colour television, unless they wandered over to Sporting Goods for a game of snooker or billiards. They weren't trespassers; management knew all about them: the hidden people. What the hell happened to them when they died though? Ah – that explained city parks – hidden people cemeteries actually, and the geometrically exact flower beds with mounding earth fortresses were graves. KEEP OFF THE GRASS signs were put up to prevent desecration of ground hallowed by a white web of hidden-people bones spread six feet under.

It was before visiting hours so he had no difficulty finding a parking space. He didn't bother to lock the car – nothing to worry about – just in and get Victoria and out again. After lunch and shopping maybe she'd like to go out to the island – flowers would be lovely now in the Herbarium – they could walk along the river – must mean a lot to her to get away from the hospital. What a pang when he'd left her here last fall! Days already short – grass no longer green – and no birds sang. But they had. After he had left her and her bags before the desk – as he had walked down the steps and stopped and looked back and up to the lucent windows – contemporary vertical honeycomb – suddenly he'd heard the untidy twittering of birds settling down for the night – thousands of them. It was a mechanically persistent skreeking – a taped minor complaint turned on according to schedule and broadcast by hidden speakers. The bird-lime streaks on all the sills were real though.

He ran up the long bank of shallow concrete steps to meet Victoria.

She was not down yet. The receptionist behind the desk, with head lowered, was intent on something before herself there. A commissionaire was travelling from ash-tray to ash-tray with a trash bag. Carlyle took a seat on the chrome-and-black plastic bench that ran along the side windows, and the smell enclosed him, an old familiar he had known in the house of his childhood, for it had stolen in from his father's surgery; it breathed through the pre-med lab of his university days, and until old Esau had straightened him out, it had lived in the agency schoolroom. Such bitter authority!

Light glinting from the glass of a large picture on the opposite wall caught his eye: girls' heads in ovals. He felt a shock of recognition that was at first hard to identify, and then he was remembering a much, much older graduating class – 1902 – the nurses' caps more Florence Nightingale-ish – bonnet type. One of them on his mother's dark head. What incredible chance that had brought her from New York to Saskatchewan prairie to a typhoid epidemic to a meeting with his father to the creation of Carlyle Sinclair. . . .

"They put this pacer in you know – my heart – that was three weeks ago – will be Monday."

Hands in the pockets of his faded hospital bathrobe, the man stood before Carlyle.

"Eatin' solid food inside two days off the table – plumbin' goin' in twenty-four hours – both of 'em. No gas pains at all."

One of the lonely accosters; it always surprised him how often – in restaurants – waiting rooms – on elevators – at bus stops – people initiated conversations with him – spilled precious intimacy.

". . . back in again – you know why?"

In beer parlours – on park benches – trying to play darts in the dark. He must disappoint them, because listening was an active act, and he wasn't any good at it. He was no priest or psycho-analyst – even amateur! Their direct and unflinching gaze made him uncomfortable. They always tried for the eyes. It wasn't fair to them – just to listen, and they weren't all that entertaining – except for the fellow one time – the informative one. ". . . this guy invented stuff to keep sheep from belchin' – sheep always belch and they have it figured down so fine now it paid them to come up with something to stop sheep from belchin' – yeah – they got it down that fine – they proved – they're worried about loss of meat an' wool from belchin' – proved a sheep that doesn't belch does better than a sheep that does belch." This man did look rather sheep-like – puffy look about the mouth – badly fitting dentures?

"... reversed – they got to get her beating right you know – I guess I got the only reversed heartbeat in Canada – beating upside down you know – can't have that."

He'd taken the space on the bench beside Carlyle. What in hell was holding her up!

"... you listening to me?"

Carlyle nodded.

"Upside down."

"Your heart," Carlyle said.

"No – not the heart. They got the pacer hooked up backwards – reversed her. I got the only living heart – maybe in the whole world – that's working backwards – that's what I meant when I said upside down, you know."

"I see."

"Mind you it's their look-out not mine – you'd think they'd know enough to do a simple thing like that."

"What simple thing?"

"Hooking her up right."

"You'd think they would."

"I'm not making any fuss about it, you know. I don't want to lose anybody their job over it, but at the same time I don't want some other poor guy to walk – to come in here and walk out with his heart backwards – wouldn't be fair to the unsuspecting public. Would it?"

"No."

"Well all right. Strange thing about it is I feel fine – alla that blood racing around backwards and I feel good – appetite's ay-one – bowels regular – sleep fine. You know what just struck me now?"

"No."

"Maybe it isn't backwards – oh sure it is – what I mean is – they changed her all right – but – consider this – the reason it is working so good now is – originally my heart was reversed – I was born with a reverse heart – and they didn't know it and went ahead and hooked her up backwards so now my heart's beating right for the very first time in my whole life. Think that's what might have happened?"

"The doctors will know."

"Well – that's what I'm back in for – get her changed back so she isn't reversed any more."

"Or if it's already beating right," Carlyle suggested, "just reassure you."

"Huh?"

"In case you were born with a backward heart – as you said."

"Oh – yeah – it isn't simple at all, is it? No. Confusing. I do get confused easy." He had turned sideways towards Carlyle; now he leaned to him, put his hand on his knee. "You been listening to me – you been paying attention. Yeah. You have. So I better tell you – they didn't put in any pacer at all. And maybe my heart don't beat backwards either. But I'll tell you something – there is something reversed – I'm not saying it's my blood – at least I did say it was, but maybe it isn't – not my blood – maybe there's some kind of a electric current – now – don't laugh – through them electrodes in your head – my head – wouldn't that explain why a person could get confused? Huh? Sure, it would. That's right."

"Just a minute." Carlyle got up. "Miss Ogden."

The girl who had stepped out of the elevator was not in uniform, so it had taken him a moment to recognize her. Holly Ogden, Victoria's room-mate, a pale blonde girl with skin so unflawed and fragile as to suggest the translucence of Belleek.

"Mr. Sinclair."

". . . they just bumped one of them electrodes when they –
you can understand why a person wouldn't want to tell a total
stranger they reversed your electric . . ."

"Please!" He went over to Holly. As so often happened
with such fairness, the slightest fatigue showed dramatically,
and now it was as though her eyes were faintly bruised. "I've
been waiting . . ."

". . . so maybe they could fix it by putting in a brain pacer."

"Any idea what's holding Victoria up?"

But the sheep-faced patient had rounded him and come
between them, his fists jammed down into his bathrobe pockets.
". . . and by Jesus, if they get that one backwards I won't go easy
on them – when they monkey with people's brains . . ."

"Holly." He shoved the patient aside. "I've been waiting over
half an hour for Victoria – what's keeping her?"

". . . sure it would – everybody walking around with their
eyes looking in instead of out . . ."

"I want to talk with this young lady right now."

". . . hearing their insides instead of their outsides."

"Please, shut up and let me talk with her!"

"You'd better get back up, Mr. Dabbs. Go on now." She
watched Mr. Dabbs turn obediently, walk to the elevator, then
she faced Carlyle again. "Mr. Sinclair, Victoria isn't – she isn't
up in our room."

"She isn't! She – but she was to meet – twice a month I get
into . . ."

"Breathing out when they should be breathing in . . ." Mr.
Dabbs called over to them from the elevator door.

"She isn't here, Mr. Sinclair – at the hospital – she . . ."

"What do you mean – she isn't here! She's – she's your
room-mate."

"I went home for two days and when I came back she didn't
– she didn't stay here that night."

". . . everybody left-handed instead of right-handed."

"Where is she?"

"I don't know – when I came back – Thursday – I didn't say anything to anybody – like – she was gone – not the night I left to go home – the night before and I didn't say anything because I thought she'd be back when I got back but she wasn't."

"Monday! She's been gone six days!"

"A week ago Tuesday, Mr. Sinclair – I went home."

"Good God – you mean – almost two weeks."

She nodded.

"How in hell could she be gone for two weeks without anyone notifying – without anyone telling – what's wrong with this outfit!"

"I told Matron when I got back."

"What's wrong with her! Doesn't she take any responsibility for the girls! Where do I find her?"

"She'll be in her office now – it's 4A – you take the elevator up to 4, then turn left and down the hall."

"How's your electric current?" Mr. Dabbs said to him at the elevator door.

Oh, Jesus, dear Jesus, little girl lost!

"If it's backwards a person could go off and get himself knocked up."

Dear little lamb, Victoria!

FIVE

THEIR TABLE WAS IN THE MIDDLE OF THE SLOP AND CLINK and bung and banter of the Empress Hotel Ladies and Escorts room. Archie Nicotine had bought the first round for Norman and Gloria Catface and himself. Then the young man with the brush-cut and the acne all over his face like purple yarn bits had joined their table, bought two rounds. His entire interest was for Gloria.

Five years ago she had rightfully won the zircon diadem of Miss North-west Fish and Game of 1954. Her blackberry eyes were large and lovely; she was dark-madonna beautiful still. Just as she poured the rest of her bottle into her glass, there was a signal look from Norman, a suggesting movement of his head; it seemed to include the young man. Norman's hair was a black aster centred in the middle of his very round head, falling in thin petals above the tilted seeds of his eyes. His face had the oval grace of his sister's, but also fixed derision because of the old knife scar slicing up from one corner of his mouth to a vanishing point just below and in front of his right ear. He did not know, had never known, just who had given his face extra mouth value. In the middle of Stampede Week, the same year that his sister had won her contest, he had lost a drunken one. He'd passed out in the lantern dusk of the chuck-wagon barn; before all life could bleed from the severed facial artery, Gloria had found him lying in the sweet alfalfa. Twenty-nine stitches. One half Cheshire cat. It was not a completely frightening face. He and Gloria were almost inseparable, not only because they were brother and sister, but because he pimped her as well. From time to time whenever need was great.

Gloria set down her empty glass. She stood up. "I got to go."

"Sit down," the young man said. "Buy you another."

Gloria shook her head and turned away.

"Hey, Taffy, over here!" Norman called. The young man stood up. "Hold on for us, Taffy," Norman said. "You said you was buyin'."

"I changed my mind."

"I already called him."

"You can pay him too. I bought twice." The door was closing behind Gloria.

"Archie and me could use another . . ."

But the young man had left the table.

Norman stared at the empty glasses and bottles. "You gonna buy a couple?"

"No," Archie said.

"I can't. We didn't even eat too good this week."

"Haven't you sold her much?"

"They stopped her four times. How you fixed?"

"I can't help you."

"Next time he takes her in – and me." He looked up to the waiter, who stood now with a tray holding beer bottles. "Never mind."

"If you're all through, don't hold up the table."

"I'm just talkin' with my friend. We may change our mind later." To Archie he said, "Next time they'll lay a charge against her – me. It's spring."

Archie stood up, put his chair back. "I can't help you any."

"I just thought you might have something."

"It's for rings and a rebuilt carburetor." Surprise, very near consternation, showed on Norman's face. "Jeses! You got enough for rings and a carburetor!"

"Hey-up."

"Hey, Taffy – a couple here! Hold on." Norman hooked Archie's belt with his hand, the other raised high with four fingers extended.

"I'm not buyin', Norman – let go."

Norman jumped up. "You can't leave when you still got . . ."

"Let go my arm, Norman. Sit down. I'm goin' to Hercules Salvage now."

"Sure – sure." Norman put his arm over Archie's shoulder. "Let's . . ."

Archie shoved Norman away, but Norman turned and grabbed at him again. Archie pushed Norman's chest, so that the chair caught the backs of Norman's knees. Norman sat down.

"All right – none of that!" It was Taffy – but without a tray this time.

"Alone," Archie said. He left Norman.

In the Men's all the china stalls were full. He went out to walk down the narrow back hallway, then opened a door to the bright alleyway. He walked along the brick back of the hotel building till he came to the parking lot. There he paused in the shelter of a truck to relieve himself. It was half-ton too. But red.

He felt the hand on his shoulder almost as soon as he heard, "What the hell you doin'!" He turned his head – carefully, for there had been three bottles. Behind the policeman was a black and white car with the red gum-drop light on top.

"I just had three, and that is the whole situation," Archie said. A policeman partner sat behind the steering wheel, the motor still running.

"Better come with us."

"Just a minute," Archie said.

In front of the Pioneer War Surplus, one block down from the Empress Hotel, one block the other way from the Devonian Tower, Gloria Catface faced the young man with the pitted face, who had caught up with her, then asked her the question. She answered him. "Ten."

"Ten!"

"That's right."

"Hell . . ."

"If you got it."

"I got it."

"All right."

"Yeah – but most the time smoked gash is free."

"Crabs free too?"

"Now look – no sense gettin' unfriendly about it."

"You started it."

"I just said ten seems kind of high."

"It's been higher – lots."

"It couldn't!"

"Sure as hell could – when I was Miss Fish and Game . . ."

"You aren't now, and ten's steep!"

"Uh-huh."

"Five."

"Ten."

"For all night?"

"Middle the afternoon – two o'clock," Gloria explained to him.

"Then ten is too goddam . . ."

"Ten is for once. You want more? Buy supper – beer – then all night?" He considered. She said, "Twenty-seven fifty."

"Hell, no!"

"You don't want all night. Maybe you don't want once either."

"It's just that ten . . ."

"Go on over to Ninth east where they got the head in the window."

"Huh?"

"Two bucks."

"Nobody gets screwed for two bucks in this town."

"The gipsy girl there . . ."

"I don't want some money blessed."

"They charge five for that – but for two she'll let you take a look at it."

"Hell, I need more'n a peek at . . ."

"All right. Ten bucks. Make up your mind."

"I did."

"Then let's have it."

"Don't be funny. Where's your place?"

"Couple blocks."

"Hotel? Which one?"

"Just a room – like a room. Let's have the ten."

"Look, you may of been Miss Fish and Game an' I'm game but I'm no fish. Ten's the deal – when we get there – after."

She shrugged and turned and walked away from him. He caught up with her in front of the Brenda Kaye Savoir Faire Model School and Agency. "Complete Courses in Modelling and Self Improvement . . . Fashion Shows . . . Hostessing . . . Television Promotion . . . Advertising." Through the spring sunshine they walked together past the Devonian Tower.

In Studio B of CSFA-TV, "high atop the Devonian Tower," the Reverend Healy Richards unbuckled his belt and pulled down his fly zipper enough to drop the mike cord inside his trousers. He wiggled it down and along his leg, retrieved it from his pant cuff. This extra care was necessary because when he worked he liked to pace back and forth; a black cord showing would flaw his white totality. The Burning Bush Hour pulpit was white as well.

On discreet rubber casters the camera glided sideways, then wheeled and aimed on the evangelist. The camera man, with shoulders hunched and eye at the lens, said "Three minutes, Reverend," and then softly, "Carl, come here." He stepped aside when the other man came over. "Take a look."

Carl leaned down to look at a miniature white Heally Richards before a white pulpit, with white Bible in his dark hand, white crest of hair above his dark face.

"Hit you too, Carl?"

"Yeah – yeah." Eye still at the lens, Carl emitted a light, incredulous laugh. He whispered, "Looks just like a goddam photograph negative!"

Gloria Catface and her young customer passed the Liberty Café, then the high-fenced space to the corner. They turned and walked along the great sign: BLACKFOOT BUILDING SUPPLIES, with its huge black foot, the giant and bony toe pivoting on the rest of the foot, activated by a small motor behind the sign, moving slowly up and down with its rabbit-eared bandage bow: SPECIALIZING IN RUMPUS AND GAME ROOMS . . . POLYNESIAN IS IN EVERYONE'S BUDGET.

She led the young man round the end of the sign, then down the narrow space between it and the south wall of the Liberty Café.

"Room! Call this a room!" He looked at the space canopied by two orange war-surplus parachutes; sheltered under them, a nest of Arctic-down sleeping bags, two Coleman gas camp-stoves, a rank of olive-coloured canisters.

"We're campin' here," Gloria said.

"Shee-yit!"

"We are all sinners – we're humans – we're mortals an' therefore we are sinners. Congratulations. Now – I did not say hopeless sinners. No – I did not. For Jeeesuss Christ was cruceeeefied for us – poor – mortal – sinners! Those spikes were hammered through His dear palms for us sinners. Sin. Ay word – 'sin.' Ay old-fashioned word, isn't it? It is not ay in-word – today – not with ay-dultery – not when our young are rottin' their bodies an' minds with booze. Sin is not in. I should say – the *word* – 'sin' – is not in. But sin itself is in! Sin is very, very popular! Don't you tell me it isn't! My friends, sin is today – more popular than it ever was – more popular than it was when Jeesuss of Galilee healed the sick – more popular than when the Caesars held sway! Oh – I know – the word 'sin' can bring gales of laughter from our leaders and from our legislators and from our modern clergy and from our teachers and from our professors in their tickley tossel-swingin' mortar-boards! Sin is taught today: kindergarten sin – grammar-school sin – college sin – graduate sin – sweet sin-uh – rotten delicious sin-uh – deeelightful sin-uh!"

"Easy – easy!" Gloria said. "Take your time! You wanta tear my pants! Goddammit – it isn't gonna go away!"

"Now then – 'Hell' is another unpopular word today! You don't like it – so just forget it – then it'll go away! Hell will go away!

There just simply isn't any Hell any more! You don't want there to be a Hell, so just you close your eyes and it will vanish! You don't want Hell – nobody wants Hell – so – there – is – no Hell. Isn't that dandy? No Hell – no sin – well then, I guess I can just go right out and loot and riot and rape my neighbour's wife and teach sin and preach sin and legislate sin and encourage sodomy and butcher unborn children – because there is no Hell and there is no sin! But oh, my friends there is a Hell – and the price of sin comes very very high!"

"That'll be thirteen ninety-five," Gloria Catface said to the young man with the acne-ravaged face.

"Our deal was ten."

"I said it before."

"What's different now?"

"You tore my pants – that's what's different now!"

He turned away from her. "So just clip another pair next time you're in Ladies' Underwear."

"I paid! Three ninety-five just last week!"

"Don't bother showin' me the receipt." He had begun to walk away. "Our deal was ten."

He was half way to the alley when she called after him, "All right – you're right! Maybe ten was too much! No charge at all for rabbits!"

He kept on walking.

"Your face may heal up," she called after him, "when you're older!"

That stopped him. He wheeled, took several quick steps towards her before he saw the knife in her hand. Then he stopped again. He stared uncertainly at her, at the knife.

"Tight ass!"

He grinned with sudden relief. "You sure as hell wasn't, Miss Fish an' Game." He was still grinning as he turned to leave.

". . . tell that to Jacob gruntin' and sweatin' and strivin' to lock a full nelson round the neck the angel of the Lord! Don't tell Lot's wife because she can't hear you, but you tell Abraham about the God that spoke to him and said to him, 'Abraham hold back on that knife there!' Tell that to Jacob and his brother Esau eatin' his bread an' pottage of lentils! Tell it to all the children of Israel fleein' over the wet sand floppin' an' gaspin' with needle-fish an' mullet – with prison-fish an' sting-rays an' whip-a-rays all wonderin' what happened to their Red Sea the Lord dried up under them! Tell it to Daniel an' all those prowlin' lions! Pull open that fiery furnace door and tell the news to Meschach, Shadrach, and Abednego. Tell Jeesussss – tell Him!"

The Reverend Heally Richards stopped, turned full to the camera, which slowly dollied, then zoomed to close-up on his face.

"Jeesuss," Heally Richards said, "I got a bereavin' message for you – they say your Daddy is dead."

The red light on Camera One blinked off. The evangelist unclipped the mike from the V of his white vest, unbuckled his belt and pulled down the zipper on his fly part way, then wiggled the mike down his white pant leg, extricated it from his white pant cuff.

"Stony," the constable at the receiving desk wrote down. "Paradise Valley Reserve." He looked up to Archie. "Empty your pockets, please."

"Look," Archie said. "I am a duly elected band councillor and this time is wrong. I just had three in the Empress, and that is the whole situation."

"Isn't the charge though. In this case it's indecent exposure."

"How much does that one generally cost?"

"With a kind-hearted magistrate, maybe ten and costs. Empty your pockets, please."

"That's easy," Archie said as he began to comply. "I got forty-five – still got enough left over for . . ."

"Keep goin'," the constable said. Then, "What's the matter?"

"I been robbed out of my rings and rebuilt carburetor!"

"You can lay your own charge later. You want to make a phone call?"

"I don't know where to phone him now. Maybe tonight when he gets back to Paradise. . . ."

"You just let us know."

SIX

Just inside the living-room, off the entrance hallway of his Meadow Lark Park home, Ian Fyfe, Regional Director Western Region, Indian Affairs and Northern Development Department of Indian Affairs Branch, MS Group 4, faced Carlyle. "Just a moment, Carlyle."

"Damn it – she – that girl has been missing for over two weeks!"

"So she has – I'm not saying she . . ."

"And the department has known it! Two weeks! The matron said she got in touch with you. . . ."

"She did – actually Hugh took the call – he made a note of it. . . ."

"Look, I am not interested in how your damned machinery . . ."

"I was in Ottawa – I did not see Hugh's memo till I got back – after the week-end."

". . . then failed to let me know! You did not bother to . . ."

"Carlyle – Carlyle – you were coming in – the next day – Tuesday you were to come in. I intended mentioning it to you. . . ."

"Intended was not good enough!"

"You did not come in."

"And you did not phone!"

"I tried. Five times. Your telephone was out. I don't know if it's up – even now."

"It's up."

"All right. But I did try."

"You could have got word down to me! Sent someone down."

"My God!" Fyfe was startled. "Sent someone down! Hundred-and-fifty-mile trip – let's be reasonable about it – it isn't a matter of life and . . ."

"It sure as hell is!"

"I don't think it is."

"I do!"

"Carlyle . . ."

"She has no money!"

"Of course she hasn't. . . ."

"Where's she sleeping! How's she eating! She's defenceless!"

"She certainly would be if she were . . ."

"She can't take care of . . ."

"Carlyle – will you listen to me! You know as well as I do – what's happened."

"She's lost!"

"No – she is not lost! She had her day off – it's spring. She passed the bus depot – homesick for her family – Paradise Valley – she had enough for her ticket – she weakened. It's happened before – it's happened now – it will happen again – why should this time be special?"

"Two bloody weeks!"

"Yes. It is. That's unfortunate. I'm surprised Susan and Jonas have been so successful."

"Successful!"

"Hiding her."

"What!"

"You haven't thought of that? It's what has happened. They're sorry for her unhappy in here – so they've helped her – by keeping her out of sight."

"They couldn't. Not for two weeks."

"They could. You know they could. She may not even be on the reserve – back up Storm and Misty. Not so hard to hide her from you when you don't even know she's left the hospital – is it? Isn't as though you'd been looking for her two weeks."

"I would have known – two weeks."

"I'm a little surprised at the – ah – response – the strength of your response to . . ."

"You know what can happen to her!"

"I know."

"Then how can you say . . ."

"Quite likely I'd be as upset as you are – if she were in the city. She isn't. She is somewhere in the bush. I can understand your concern – easily; what I can't understand is why – if you are so concerned – you haven't started to use your head – tried to see it in proper proportion. If you had, you'd know she is with her father and mother in Paradise. That's what's likely. Isn't it?"

"I don't know."

"I do."

"She's special, Ian! You know that."

"Yes. Because she is, you'll do everything you can to – ah – cope. Emotion doesn't accomplish anything. You've got to turn that reserve upside down – systematically. Another thing – how does the hospital feel about it?"

"I don't know."

"You don't. Well – what did the matron say?"

"I didn't ask her."

"You didn't. What was her response to – Victoria's – disappearance?"

"Hard to say."

"It was. Did she – was there any indication at all that the damage was irreparable?"

"I don't think so."

"Beyond the usual matronly disapproval – was she displeased – angry – disappointed? Impersonal about the whole . . ."

"Some disappointment."

"That's good. When you find Victoria and bring her back – have you any idea what her attitude might be – then?"

"She's a just woman."

"Would the decision be hers?"

"Maybe."

"More likely a higher one?"

"I think so."

"Which she could influence."

"Yes."

"When you flew at her . . ."

"I didn't fly at her."

"That's good. Think she'd recommend reinstatement for Victoria?"

"She might."

"Have supper with me?"

"I guess I did come on a little strong with her."

"I thought you hadn't saved it all for me. Stay for supper?"

"She should have got in touch with me! She didn't! Victoria gone the whole goddam week-end before she got around to . . ."

"Matter of point of view, isn't it? She's looking at a lot of girls in her charge; you're looking at just one."

"All the same . . ."

"All the same she's probably on our side."

"I think so."

"That's good. We'll just have to see what transpires. Now – for the third time – will you stay for supper?"

"I'm supposed to meet Archie Nicotine."

"When?"

"Around seven – Super-Arcade."

"He still hasn't got his truck running?"

"He hopes to buy his rings and carburetor today. This time."

"He's got the money?"

"Yes – Moon paid him for some poles he cut."

"Where'd you drop him off?"

"The Empress Hotel."

"So – he hasn't managed to get past the Empress for two years – stay for supper."

"He might this time," Carlyle said.

"Early supper then. You could still meet him by seven." Fyfe put his hand on Carlyle's elbow. "Let's have our drinks in the conservatory." The pressure on his arm persuaded Carlyle gently.

"She is in Paradise."

"Of course she is."

"Jonas and Susan – I should have seen it that way – but why didn't I?"

"Because you're too personally involved."

"You really think they're hiding her – she isn't loose in the city?"

"I do. You do too – actually – do you think Nicotine will manage his rings and carburetor this time?"

"No."

"Is that an emotional judgment?"

"No."

Fyfe released Carlyle's elbow, reached for the knob of the glass conservatory door. "Dead certain he won't."

"Almost."

"So am I." Fyfe stepped aside. "About both of them. You go on in. I have a bottle of Scotch I've been saving for just a time like this. Old country – liqueur."

"Don't open it for . . ."

"Death-bed whisky."

"Thanks – but rye and water."

"All right. Go in and sit down – there are some nice brasso hybrids opened. On the lower bench – to the left there's a rather lovely bi-foliate for the first time. The new star type – superior to the Harrisoniae alba stud. I think I can get it larger."

Fyfe's hand left his shoulder. Carlyle stepped through the door and down the three conservatory steps. Entering the glass bubble surprised him. It always did – first with benign humidity, then the vanilla and lily scent of orchid blossoms, usually faint, but much stronger this time. As he sat down in one of the wrought-iron chairs, he recognized the fleshy white of gardenia flowers against their dark leaves, so it was a sort of perfume harmony really – Debussy smell-poem, edgeless and lovely except for one persistent discord. Bark rot – a long decay note that was not unpleasant – rather comforting – like the soft smell of leather in a saddle and harness shop. Raisin bread for Esau!

Oh, dear God, little girl lost – dear little lamb, Victoria!

Fyfe was right! Jonas and Susan were hiding her! And all the others in on it too. Probably Archie had known about it, kept his knowledge hidden all the way into the city; he'd made a jab about her being in the hospital – knowing that she wasn't there at all would delight him with secret irony. Then he'd come back to it again. Yes, Archie had known that Susan and Jonas were hiding her. Everyone had known but him. And now he knew – not because Fyfe had persuaded him of it. Fyfe had simply called his attention to what he should have realized right away. Right after first shock. There was no other sensible explanation. She had headed for the reserve unerringly! That was that! Have a drink – supper with Fyfe – don't listen to the apprehensive traitor inside himself! Just don't listen to him!

No more invitations to him! Emotion never solved anything, Fyfe said. Have to see what transpires, Fyfe always said. My escape to beauty – how many times had Fyfe said that.

He'd said it as he'd ushered him in here for the first time early in March – seven, eight years ago. There'd been a mountain blizzard, dizzying with wind-driven flakes, as Carlyle had bucked drifts all the way out to the highway. He had come free of the bewildering storm and into full sunlight finally at the city outskirts, then visited with Fyfe and his outrageously beautiful orchids. Thirty below outside, and the inside face of the glass bell rimed white with its own hoar jungle of fern and plume and palm frond. Down the long curves of the conservatory's metal ribs, condensed moisture had run and hung and frozen in clear tears.

He had drifted down the benches with Fyfe, pausing now and again before a breath-taking flower – luminous somehow – and on close examination, almost crystalline. Candled from within themselves. Fyfe would lift a tag with a finger-tip, pull out a plastic pedigree strip; he reminded Carlyle a great deal of Moon showing off how well his yearlings were doing. Except that Moon didn't lecture. Fyfe had an inexhaustible supply of orchid information. They were not parasites, but epiphytes.

"In a sense they're immortal. One – sometimes two new growths a year. That means a new pseudo-bulb – but then there's always a back one dying out – the leaf drops off – bulb shrivels – roots go – so it's a new growth on the front and losing an old one on the back so they travel across the bark, you might say. That's why they have to be repotted every third year – every two sometimes if they're growing well or if the bark breaks down – it decays and gets mushy. You always have to be careful about watering because the roots – those white things over the edge of that pot – that one needs repotting – they're actually aerial roots in their natural state – meant to clutch tree bark or rock and feed on organic matter the rains wash down to them – but here they're in pots – roots enclosed in the bark chips in the pot so there's danger of root rot always. . . ."

They had stopped finally before a plant holding high a pastel cloud of small lavender flowers.

"That's lovely," Carlyle said.

"A miss," Fyfe said.

"But it's beautiful. . . ."

"Hoping for a red – or a dark at the very least. It's a complete miss."

"I still say it's . . ."

"It has substance – that's all. The sepals curl back – petals on the narrow, skinny side – look at the gaps there – very poor form – the idea is to get – with the petals – sepals – labellum – as nearly a perfect circle as you can. And that colour – just species colour – it's slightly larger than species, but that's about all you can say for it. Complete miss."

"Who says?"

"Eh?"

"Who says it's a complete miss?"

"I do – any breeder would – or show judge."

"What's the orchid say, Ian?"

"What!"

"Just – well – has the orchid been disappointed? Does it consider itself a complete miss?"

"You crazy?"

"I don't think so – it just strikes me funny."

"Funny!"

"All the hybridizing – breeding – how long is it from the flask – eight years. . . ."

"With timed light I manage in four – but you're not serious. . . ."

"I think I am. You're trying to – for something that hasn't got anything to do with what the orchid wants."

"Orchid wants . . ."

"Impertinent."

"To what?"

"The orchid's concept – destiny – it takes a little longer than the few years you – what it has wanted for millions . . ."

"There haven't been orchids for millions . . ."

"No – but there are millions of years in them . . . all the same. Not just decades – it's not all this simple – no chances – no surprises." He looked down at the tag. "BLC PANDORRA 4N X SELF – BLC – that's . . ."

"Brasso-laelia-cattleya."

"And 4N?"

"Tetraploid."

"Oh sure – double the chromosomes – great – stacking the gene deck – next thing you know you'll be . . ." But he hadn't said it. He'd stopped before he said it. God Almighty, a man was getting into bad trouble when he couldn't keep his fantasies inside himself. Listen to the orchid, Fyfe – let her tell her own delight and need! He could just see Fyfe, with his rigid concept of beauty erect, taking – with careful passion – a purple, velvet blossom big as a bread and butter plate, and the result noted on plastic tags: BLCH Fyfe 4N – orchid-like Fyfe or Fyfe-like orchid offspring, in rows and rows of nursery flasks. Would he then be so dispassionate about his misses?

He hadn't actually seen it enter – whether it had wandered through the open door or bumbled in under the raised bank of side windows; he had just heard a tiny insect sawing, abruptly amplified by the glass bell of the conservatory. Now it took a wide swinging loop over the mahogany pouch of a cypripedium, lifted above the grass leaves of a pink cymbidium, then, in slow and heavy flight, idled down the front bench.

The buzzing stopped as it landed on the top sepal of an orchid to his left. There were three in the spray, snow pure except for a mint tint in the labellum. He watched the bee crawl down to the trumpet lip, then work its black-and-gold body up inside. Almost out of sight.

Fyfe came back with their drinks. He would get in touch with the matron right away, ask her to start things rolling towards Victoria's re-admission to the hospital and her training. He would keep in touch with Carlyle, and Carlyle must let him know what transpired at the Paradise Valley end. He was quite sure that Jonas and Susan wouldn't be co-operative; indeed he would be very surprised if Victoria were with her family at all, and Carlyle must look for a camp that might not even be on the reserve. Somewhere in the rough Storm and Misty country, was his guess. Sooner she was found, the better. Get Archie's help. Look how he'd found the frozen hunter two years ago.

When they left the conservatory to put on the steaks, the bee was still in the flower.

Dinner over, Fyfe had suggested they take their liqueurs out to the conservatory again, since it was early and still full light. Thank God for Fyfe! He wasn't magnificent but he was meticulously adequate. He was a responsible and honourable man – above all, practical. Fyfe's assurance and advice were just what he'd needed. He owed Fyfe a lot really – all the gratitude accretion of eight years. Too bad Fyfe was finishing this year. He'd miss him.

"I'm not looking forward to retirement," Fyfe had said several times over the past three years, and now he said it again. "I'm not looking forward to retirement. I have looked forward to the Island – ultimately moving out there for good – not just holidays – but now the time's come . . ." He shook his head, took a sip of his Drambuie. "You know, Carlyle, when you first came with us, I warned you – told you the same thing I tell them all – don't let yourself get personally involved, and it's true, you know. It really is true and I wouldn't be taking this retirement quite so hard if I'd followed my own advice. Forty-five years."

"Long time," Carlyle agreed.

"All over. You think you've prepared yourself for it – but when it happens you aren't prepared at all. Still a shock."

That bee was still in the white orchid blossom; quite possibly it had never backed out all the while they'd been eating their dinner.

". . . can't help wondering what you've actually accomplished in forty-five years."

He couldn't think of anything to say that would comfort Fyfe.

"Held the fort," Fyfe said.

"I suppose so," Carlyle said.

"Hasn't been easy."

"I guess it hasn't," Carlyle said. Usually a bee shopped from blossom to blossom – and in time, with pollen sacs loaded, took off for home.

". . . the biscuit. Even if that were all – I think the biscuits by themselves were important enough. Certainly there's satisfaction in seeing them in general use now – if only in our own country."

Yes, the cookies. Fyfe did have those. Every morning at the end of recess, in every agency school, for each child at each desk – one Fyfe Minimal Subsistence cooky – one perfectly round, quarterly creased cooky, dimpled like Victorian upholstery, containing all the carbohydrate-protein-vitamin richness necessary for twenty-four hours of life. Very early in his years with Indian Affairs, Fyfe had confided in him the birth of the Fyfe Minimal Subsistence cooky.

The idea had happened in his very first year on his first reserve with the Assiniboines of the Moose Mountain country.

". . . resort area as well – cottages along the lake shore – and with the Indian cabins and teepees removed some distance from the resort itself – they leased the shore area to the cottagers – very poor band – great deal of scrofula so the men pretty nearly all wore bandanas down from under their hats – for flies and mosquitoes of course but also the – it curtained the sun off lesions on their neck skin. Incredibly disorganized – primitive – you won't believe it – over half of the families were under canvas – year round – those incredibly bitter Saskatchewan winters – in teepees!

"Mrs. Fyfe and I were very young – we were there five years – the day we were all packed to leave, she sat on the trunk and cried – said she'd never leave – but we did leave – oh, we did leave. Lovely tennis courts – beach – it was after tennis and a bathe – going up to the cottage for lemonade – no spirituous beverages allowed on the reserve, and the cottagers were quite decent about it. Not even at the dances – there was a screened octagonal dance hall run by Mr. Diamond – ten cents a dance – set in the trees – and under every tree an Indian – just standing there watching the young couples dancing – 'Marquita' – 'Roses of Picardy' – 'Barney Google' – Maggie loved to dance. Every Dominion Day the Indians put on a powwow – did the Chief Dance – Grass-Snake-Hoop Dance. Twenty-five-cents admission. They watched us dance – we watched them dance. Fair enough. They'd stand and watch the bathers too during the day. In all five years I never saw one of them go in bathing.

"But – I remember this one afternoon on our way up from the beach – on the point we passed Sheep Skin and all his clan sitting on the ground under a birch tree. They were having their dinner out of a fire-blackened old wash-tub filled with some stew – no – not stew – stew would have to be cooked and it couldn't have been cooked because it was quite red and what the meat was I don't know – dog – coyote – some sort of rodent bouillabaisse of jack rabbit – ground squirrel – gopher. And they all just reached in and down and grabbed out a handful – children with the red mess in their fists – all over their mouths. Except for the grandmother – Sheep Skin's mother, I think – toothless – she had a tin can of some sort with the jagged lid bent back for a handle so she could dip up the raw muck and then dig it out with her finger. She had the baby on her lap and every once in a while she'd lift it and hold its face up to hers and transfer some of the stew from her mouth into its. The baby wore a black velvet bonnet all hung with dimes.

"Right then it came to me. Oatmeal! Nearly everything a human needs to sustain life. If they could be seduced – not too strong a word . . ."

"Not strong enough."

"Eh? If they could come to accept oatmeal – not your rolled oats – body – meal! Has to be cooked for hours before it breaks down and releases its nutriment – that thick, glossy, glue quality that can build young bodies – bone – muscle. I was young – optimistic; looking back I'm amused at how I oversimplified things. The Assiniboines simply were not receptive. . . ."

"Oatmeal is pretty well Scottish," Carlyle said, "culturally."

"Oh yes – that's right – they hadn't the patience to keep a fire going evenly – cooking it that long – taking care about lumps forming – stirring – watching and not scorching it. They simply could not handle oatmeal preparation. And they refused it anyway."

"But not the other."

"Hmh? Oh, yes." Fyfe snorted. "Too bad – if it could only have been reversed."

"Accepted the oatmeal – refused the whisky."

"Aye-he." The very, very few times that Fyfe had ever used the sound, it had reminded Carlyle of the Stony "hey-uh." Less clipped, more drawn out, and with reversed emphasis – but still in the throat.

"I didn't give up though," Fyfe said. "You must never do that. There'd have been no Fyfe biscuit if I'd given up."

Carlyle could see Sadie Wildman stirring the great cauldron of cocoa on the kitchen stove, hear the shrill excitement of the schoolyard at recess, then after the children came inside, Toots going down the aisles and setting out one cooky to each desk, Raymond Ear behind him with the cocoa to be ladled into their cups. The schoolroom was staccato as child after child cupped his cooky in his hand and rapped it against his desk corner or clapped it flat on the maple top. One after another they were successful, put manageable shards into their mouths, then took mouthfuls of cocoa and waited with bulging cheeks for the hot liquid to conquer the cooky fragment.

". . . for the little ones – it grew out of their own terrible need. Still the oatmeal base – and I had several who would co-operate – you know how there are always a few to encourage you – that you can depend on – the large Standing There family – I knew they'd see the children were consistent – were eating them regularly – under some sort of controlled system.

"They were not instantly and completely successful. I noticed in spring – a number of the oatmeal biscuit children twitching – little Violet Standing There took fits – tetany. But it was in spring and that was an indication – with growing children – ultra-violet rays of the spring sun Vitamin D had become effective in depositing calcium in the bone – by robbing the blood of its calcium – and rickets – stunted little things with their pot bellies – then Vitamin A and we had scurvy whipped. No denying the biscuits constipated the children. But the constipation was a relative matter."

"Relative?"

"Yes. Starvation deteriorates the gut wall – that means diarrhoea – so does rotten meat. Enough biscuits rich in calories – carbohydrate – protein – vitamins – and the gut wall improves – the constipation cause was no mystery."

He had never been able to tell Fyfe how he spent noons and after-fours sweeping up cooky fragments – whole cookies more often – from around the desk legs and all down the aisles. The children hated them.

And now he had a new insight into Fyfe. Paramount equalled immediate. Fyfe saw the Indians – all of them – as terminal cases to be made comfortable as possible within the terms of the reserve system – the budget and the Indian Act – and the civil-service machinery. All you could do for terminal cases – wait and see if they expired. Well, God damn it, Victoria's disappearance had transpired, and it was easy to predict what else would transpire. Oh, God, why had it stabbed him like that! She was not in the city. Jonas and Susan were hiding her in Paradise! He'd find her – he'd find her!

"When is your retirement date, Ian?"

"November," Fyfe said. "Christmas on the Island. Brentwood Bay."

"That's nice," Carlyle said. He could still see a black-and-yellow fur bit deep in the white orchid blossom. Thing must have gone to sleep in there. "You'll probably be very fond of it."

"I hope so." Fyfe sighed. "So much to do – so little time. I've listed the house. All the plants . . ."

"You have to sell them."

"Oh no! They go with me!"

"Can they?"

"It'll be awkward – but I'll wrap them myself – one by one – and into barrels at the very last – with peat and sphagnum well watered. Then when they get out there – unpack – repot. If necessary they'll hold for two, three weeks – but if I get my timing right it'll be just a matter of days."

How simple Fyfe was able to keep his concerns – always. Possibly that was why he'd been so effective in his forty-five years with the Indians. Focus. Choose very small priorities, and focus.

". . . *epidendrum radicans* – *odontoglossom grande* – all the species plants – the Herbarium is delighted to get them – and the Bird of Paradise and the *achmea bractiata*. All the years I've had it, I haven't been able to get the achmea to bloom and I doubt they will either. I think it has to have the cold nights. Sun through glass isn't the same – some vandas are like that – won't do well under glass no matter how careful you are. Do you like the new white?"

"Hmh?"

"To the left there."

"It's nice."

"Star type – shape and colour and substance perfect; I'm going to cross it with General Eisenhower – I have the pollen in the fridge."

"General Eisenhower's?"

"Yes."

"It looks very nice now."

"It could be larger."

"There's a bee in it."

"What!"

"There's a bumble-bee in it."

SEVEN

Now why hadn't he told fyfe about that bee sooner?
He'd watched it enter the flower, he'd sat and chatted before and
after their supper. My God, Fyfe's response had been violent,
snatching up a spray can from one corner of the bench, nailing
the bee in a bitter cloud, so that it had tumbled out of the
blossom and dropped to the tiles.

"Did you see him enter?"

"Through the door or under the side windows . . ."

"No – no – the flower – did he get into any other ones before
that one?"

"I just saw him go in that one – on that spray."

"Just this one."

"I think so. That was the first and only one."

"Well." Fyfe relaxed. "Not so bad." He was already putting a
twist of red plant-tie round the stem of the violated flower.

"Spoiled it for General Eisenhower?" Carlyle said.

"Yes. Mucking around in there – pretty sure to be selfed."

Then he had gone out, returned. Carlyle had watched him
open two small, plastic sacks, draw them carefully down over the
two unmarked white blossoms.

"Should have taken the precaution sooner."

He'd recovered, and the incident had got him off the sad subject of his retirement this fall – and the Fyfe Minimal Subsistence cooky.

"Eskimo is a new problem for us now, you know – at least it's quite evident now – industrial development of the North – it's probably a very short matter of time. Pipelines and all that sort of thing." Fyfe snorted. "The other night – oh, last week – on television – possibly you saw it . . ."

"We can't get reception out there."

"Oh, yes – of course. This was a panel – sometimes they do very good public-affairs things – they had an environmental scientist – an industrialist – oil – gas. They talked about the fragility of the tundra skin and all the cat-train tracks criss-crossing and breaking through it and leaving it black so the sun's melting action was magnified – made a very good case out of it – particularly if the pipelines are built and they block the caribou migration." Fyfe snorted again.

"Not very funny . . ."

"No – no – not at all – it means the caribou's number is up – I was just remembering what the industrialist said – defen-sively – he said they were just as concerned as any ecologist – that they'd have to do something for the caribou – like the gates for spawning salmon – you won't believe it – he was quite serious – he said they would certainly construct some sort of steps for the caribou herds – over their pipelines – he really did."

Fyfe had reassured him again before he left that Victoria was in Paradise. See Susan and Jonas first thing in the morning. Fyfe was right. Susan and Jonas were hiding her. Confront them with it – make them admit it – tell where she was. Jonas might not, but Susan would understand; she was ambitious for Victoria – always had been. Susan was the best thing he had working for him – and for Victoria.

He pulled off and into a parking space at the Super-Arcade quite a bit later than he'd promised to meet Archie at the Flying Saucer, but as he and Fyfe knew very well, Archie would not rendezvous with him. Just inside the entrance, by the magazine section, he saw the long tobacco counter and remembered that he was nearly out. There were three ahead of him, so he had to wait with his cartons. Almost all along the magazine rack stood a line of hipshot men and boys, their heads down as they turned their magazine pages.

Nearly forgot. He went through the counter gate of the grocery section, was blocked for a moment by a cart with a child sitting high in the front, the mother indecisive before the detergent shelves. He picked out two loaves of raisin bread, and then, where cubes of winter were created and trapped, dipped his hand down into the chill of the frozen-food bin for a cellophane-wrapped tray of pork chops. Steaks – ribs – roasts – cutlets – not really meat or bone or blood, any more than the florid illustrations in his father's medical books had been. Another thing – check up on Raider Lefthand tomorrow – see if he'd cleaned up and hauled away his elk guts from under the children's bucking tree.

Archie's smug face was nowhere around the Flying Saucer – give him fifteen more minutes just in case.

"You like it on me?"

The man's nose was a reversed parsnip, the pale eyes anxious and magnified behind his glasses.

"Just bought it."

He meant the hat obviously, a straw confection with canary cockatoo crest. He turned his head so that Carlyle could see a miniature set of golf clubs under a palm tree in the rainbow band.

"Too young?" He waited for Carlyle's judgment. "For me?"

Carlyle shook his head.

"Just caught my eye on the counter when I cut kitty-corner from the east entrance – by Men's Wear. Caught my eye – on special – so I bought it." He waited again.

Carlyle nodded.

"Huh?"

"Yes."

"You aren't just sayin' that?"

"No."

But the piscine eyes still searched his face, looking for something there. Carlyle willed the man to turn away. "Springy. You think it looks springy?"

"It's all right."

Still the eyes under the boob hat questioned. The pike mouth tightened, then saddened. "Yeah." The man nodded as though he had just confirmed something again for himself. He turned away.

Archie did not show up.

He felt his tension releasing even more as the south flow of traffic thinned. Banners and neon lights signalled hamburger and root beer stands – used-car dealers' car herds – fried chicken – fish and chips – pizza and pancake palaces. The city was briefly industrial and superlative: ZENITH – ACME – UNIVERSAL. The speed zone changed – the Bluebird Motel – Shirley-Dan – Round-up – Arrow – Pioneer – Stetson – Mecca – Oasis. He accelerated at the city limits – PEERLESS EXTERMINATORS FOR SPARROW, PIGEON, STARLING, SILVERFISH, MICE, RAT, BAT AND SKUNK CONTROL. He flashed by your goddamn tootin' Luton, lifting a fluorescent flamingo into an estate wagon by the pumps. SID'S VIRGIN LOAM, PEAT MOSS AND ROTTED MANURE – CHARLIE'S GOLD STAR DRAIN CLEARING AND SEPTIC TANK INSTAL-LATION – WES'S TRENCHING, BACK FILLING, BRUSH

CUTTING, EXCAVATING, LEVELLING AND CRUSHING.
Arnold's, Pieter's, Vein's, Les's, Oscar's, Walter's . . .

Actually he felt quite optimistic now. He would find her; he would talk to her; he would encourage her; he would get her all straightened out and back into the hospital. Have to be tomorrow, because it was going to be too late to do anything by the time he reached home. Why did the trip back to Paradise always seem shorter – like reversed and speeded-up film in which horses and riders leaped backwards over hurdles, water fountains sucked themselves down into themselves, the diver arced out and up to land tip-toe on the spring-board end?

Orange flares had turned the oil field into a flame-fitful purgatory. The metronome birds still sipped. Too late to stop at Pile of Rocks. He was not so sure he would have anyway.

Just before Paradise his lights picked out the sign on the right-hand side of the road: antlered silhouette of a jumping deer. DEER CROSSING. But the illiteracy rate for deer was so high – possibly not so great as for moose, but still quite high. Elk – much lower. That ecologically responsible, industrialist son-of-a-bitch whom Fyfe had watched on the C.B.C. television panel! Caribou steps over an Arctic pipeline! How far apart? What a dreadfully difficult decision! Every thousand – five hundred miles? Hundred-mile intervals perhaps? And at half-way points there would have to be large signs: CARIBOU CROSSING FIFTY MILES NORTH – CARIBOU CROSSING FIFTY MILES SOUTH. With pointing arrows. Printed in Caribou. The migration steps could be made even more effective still by constructing guiding fences, fanning out for ten or fifteen miles over the tundra. Just as plains Indians had done with buffalo driven to their destruction over jumping pounds, migrating caribou could be funnelled – but now to salvation.

If the steps proved prohibitively expensive and the caribou perished, the Eskimo could still be saved. The Fyfe Minimal

Subsistence cooky alternative. Thousands and thousands of tons of them could be mixed and cut and then fired in great Northern Affairs kilns, to be borne aloft in the metal bellies of Air Force jets. Flight after flight after flight winging north, vapour trails threading high over Ontario, Manitoba, Saskatchewan, Alberta, whose provincial legislatures would protest the Damoclean threat of inadvertent destruction – through cooky abortion – of every major Western town and city. But the mercy cooky flights would go through to seed the Canadian Arctic with Fyfe cookies. OPERATION SCAFC, the only way left to pull the Eskimo back from the vanishing point. Just spray the entire tundra with Fyfe cookies; no need for the planes to lower altitude one inch. Dropped from any height, Fyfe cookies were guaranteed not to shatter, crack, or chip on impact. Harpoons at the ready, Eskimo hunters crouching by their walrus and seal breathing holes would simply have to dodge the brittle manna – those who had ignored the Ottawa short-wave alerts and cooky-dropping schedules prepared by the Department of Meteorology. Consumers' Affairs would issue bulletins designed to discourage them from hunting and fishing any more, now that there were less primitive sources of vitamin and protein.

Mostly through braining, there might be some further unavoidable loss of polar bears, but the Eskimo would be saved; he would not join the caribou and the buffalo and the passenger pigeon and the whooping crane. Just send the children out cooky gathering – anywhere. Even art would be served and insured; indeed it would be enriched through an entirely new form of Eskimo art: Eskimo cooky carving. Though there would be a much higher carving-tool replacement than when the work had been sculpted in soapstone, whale bone, and walrus ivory.

Oh, Jesus, dear Jesus, little girl lost! Dear little lamb, Victoria!

EIGHT

Anxious as he was to talk with susan and jonas, it was much too early for them to be up yet. He took time over his breakfast, did his dishes, made his bed, returned to the kitchen-living-room to have another smoke on one of the three ascetic chairs there. They knew damn well they couldn't keep him from knowing they were hiding her. He must handle it carefully, listen and look for inadvertent clues; the first thing – convince them he knew beyond doubt that they were hiding her from him. He already was sure of that. Way to do it – find out casually if they'd made a trip into the city the week-end of Victoria's disappearance. Then – a few leading questions – how Victoria was – how she was doing. The key would be their denial that they had seen her – after their earlier admission that they had been into the city.

He ought to straighten out the dispensary before he went over – wash the floor. Chaste – most anchorites would approve of that linoleum, the book-case of boards and brick, the fumed oak table monastic in its square ugliness. Chesterfield and chair under the windows were wine-coloured though. But if they did say they'd seen her that week-end, then he'd ask them when they'd returned her to the hospital – precise time. If it didn't

coincide with her hospital hours – too soon – too late – well
then – be another indication. He could tell – he could tell – he
could read all the signs of her presence in Paradise!

The two waxed loaves of raisin bread, the fibre tray of pork
chops, reminded him. He stubbed out his cigarette.

Smoke was rising blue from Old Esau's stove-pipe. There was
the probable explanation; her grandfather's illness could have
been the turn of the screw for her. Inside, cacophony of smell
saluted him. The old decay clock was still ticking, for Esau was
sitting up in his blankets at the end of the cabin. Carlyle put
down the raisin bread and pork chops on the table corner.

"Morning, Esau."

No blood in the bucket.

"Morning, Esau!"

"Hey-uh."

"Susan been in already?"

"Hey-up." It was quite strong with crankiness and it meant
no.

"I got your raisin bread for you."

"Hey-uh." Even stronger.

"Pork chops too – if you can manage them." And this
morning he just might. "I won't put them on the stove now – I'll
tell Susan."

Esau muttered something.

"What?"

"Beulah."

"What about it?"

"Raider."

"What about Raider?"

"He went up."

"Yes?"

Esau said something in Stony.

"Yes – you told me. You told me, Esau."

Esau said quite clearly, "Victoria."

Oh, God!

Esau spoke in Stony again.

"English, Esau."

A roupy edge had roughened Esau's breathing. He coughed.

"What about Victoria?"

It had turned into a long chain of coughing. He leaned over the pail, then sat back, his breathing harsh.

"Raider."

"What about Victoria?"

"Hey-uh."

"She's not here now, is she, Esau? She's – she's in the city – the hospital – training." Had he seen her – recently – had Susan brought her over to see him? She must be in Paradise!

"He come down out of there."

"All right – all right, Esau."

"He told me."

"Told you what?"

"Raider did."

"Just what did Raider tell you?"

"Hey-uh."

Something to do with Victoria – had Raider come back down from Storm and Misty and told the old man his grand-daughter was camped up there? No use trying any more with him.

Blood in the bucket now.

Bare-bottomed in his underwear shirt, Peter Powderface's littlest sat in his own dirt nuisance ground, littered with the crushed red truck, bent-handled tablespoon, a yellow plastic sand pail cracked and missing its bail. His broken-toed riding boots were adult discards. He was engrossed in a severed chicken foot. His fingers, pinching the end of a white tendon, pulled so that the glossy toes scaled yellow, straightened out. He released and the foot clutched again. He gave the tendon end a series of quick jerks and the foot obediently performed, twitching open and shut and open again.

"All the red kids got to play with."

Carlyle turned. Orville Ear.

"My kids too."

"Raymond had his hockey."

"Not now."

"No – season's over, Orville."

"He quit Christmas."

"Did he."

"Hey-uh."

He could not be passionate about Raymond Ear's hockey career with the Shelby Cougars in the foothills juvenile league.

"He's good hockey player."

"Sorry he quit last Christmas."

"He broke his stick – coach give him old stick."

"Did he." How could he bring up Victoria Rider without seeming to?

"Made him play with that old stick instead of a new one. Before – he gave that white boy good stick."

He supposed Raymond had finally missed too many practices, but he'd better not mention that. "How old is Raymond now?"

"Right away after he gives Raymond old stick."

"Nineteen?"

"Hey-uh. Right away after he gives Raymond old stick would break soon like the other one."

"That's too bad."

"Worse – other one was good stick."

"Well – hockey season's over now – maybe next year."

"Hey-up. Raymond's discouraged."

"Raymond – he and Victoria are the same age."

"Hey-uh."

"I just looked in on Old Esau."

"Still livin'?"

"Better this morning. I left him some raisin bread and pork chops. Think you could drop in on him – stick a couple on the stove for him – cut some bread?"

"Hey-uh."

"He – uh – also – I think he'd like to see Victoria."

"She's in that hospital now – in the city."

"Yes, Orville, I know that, but I thought – isn't she – from what Esau said I thought she might be back for a visit – been in to see him."

"I didn't see her."

"I'm just going over to Susan and Jonas – they'll know."

"Like with Raymond – maybe they discourage her too."

"I don't think they will."

"Storm and Misty."

"What?"

"Riders left yesterday."

"For Storm and Misty?"

"Hey-uh."

"I see."

"Raider Lefthand family too."

"Oh."

"Raider needed them."

"What for?"

"Poles – Moon."

"Uh-huh."

"Department should do somethin' about that."

"About what?"

"Them white coaches – givin' the red kid old stick. Raymond's good hockey player."

"Yes. Yes, he is, Orville."

He'd have to go into Storm and Misty himself! He did up some bannocks, put them with bacon and tea and sugar into a flour sack, wrapped it into his bed-roll, then his slicker.

He walked up to Sam Bear's, found him home and willing to lend him a horse. He led her back down, tied her outside the agency building. He got his own saddle and bridle out of the bedroom closet.

She had a beautifully smooth gait that covered ground fast; Sam had given him his half Tennessee Walker, which was pretty decent of him. He watered the sorrel at Beulah. He had never seen the stream this low – even in fall – just brook-width in the exposed pebble bed. He pulled up the horse's head, sunlight glinting off the water stringing from her nose.

He was pretty certain he could find his way into Storm and Misty all right, though it had been three years since Archie had taken him in there. He had to ride west for about three miles beyond the reserve limit, then cut south up Daisy Creek for about five, where he must turn out east again, then up over a high ridge to reach the forestry trail. It was almost impossible to get up Beulah, Archie had explained, though there was another way in from the east – but longer.

He rode along the cut bank on the west side of Daisy Creek till it sloped down to the point where he and Archie had crossed it and left it. Daisy was high. Before he climbed the ridge he ate his lunch of bacon and bannock.

It must be near here that Archie had found the hunter two years ago. The first severe spasm of winter – mid December – with a wind-chill factor of sixty below – the man had wounded a cow moose from his Volkswagen on the road, then followed her, wearing his war-surplus golf jacket, his red-margined rubber boots and ankle socks. Archie too had followed the scarlet stains in the snow, then simply the hunter's tracks after he had left the moose carcass. He had finally come upon the hunter, a frozen windmill, to be kicked loose from the snow, lifted and propped against a fir trunk. Then Archie had turned to the feat of getting himself out of Storm and Misty alive – wading through hip drifts and trying for the delicate balance between too much effort, which would make him sweat, and the not enough that would lead to capitulation and death.

In the agency kitchen he had thawed out his feet in a steaming wash-tub, his toes suet white. He had limped around Paradise for almost a week. The hunter, Carlyle discovered later when the young Mountie came out to do his investigation, had been a baker in the city, and somehow that made it worse, when he thought of flour powdering the fine hair on the backs of his hands, his forearms, yielding dough being punched and kneaded, the protecting smell of bread baking.

Great thinking – just the sort of thing he needed now!

He was not so sure any more that this was a forestry trail at all; if it was, it had been neglected for years, kept open only by elk and cattle turned out for summer graze. At no time as he had climbed had there come to him even the faint vanilla smell of cows, nor had he seen fresh manure, but of course it was a month too early for cattle to have been turned into Storm and Misty. This should be the forestry trail. It had been three – no – four years ago that Archie Nicotine had taken him in and they'd picked it up, just under the ridge – on the south side, coming from Daisy Creek. From the top, the draw had looked right and the trail had seemed definite. So – now – get up, then down the other slope and he should come to Storm and Misty canyon. He should – didn't mean he would, if this wasn't the forestry trail.

Damn it – any one of his children would have known – ironic if he got himself lost trying to find Victoria, who knew exactly where she was. He had congratulated himself when he'd come to the trail back there, when it had taken him mostly down, switching back upon itself lower and lower – but not at the bottom when it entered burnt-over land. He was forced to lead his horse through a jack-strawed maze of grey trunks tilting, tangled, lying flat, spotted with the charred obscenities of spruce stumps, even their burn-bared roots checked and gleaming carbon. Appalling – he picked his way through sable wasteland where no order of growth remained. Without a backward glance, when high flame rolled and roared through tree tops, the forming soul had fled for ever.

When he had finally given up hope that there would ever be an end to it, he was free of it, found the trail again and was climbing once more. So he'd made a small error – not one but two draws – another ridge and then Storm and Misty, where she was camped. If it was the right forestry trail, he'd know when he reached the top.

It was. On the clear ridge he rested himself and the horse. Later in the afternoon than he'd thought, the sun lingering only over the upper rock to the west, flushing the higher flanks with late light. Mountain spines and glacial teat peaks blazed steadily with snow purity, as the radiance melted upwards, the following darkness erasing valley veins and fluting rock. He mounted again and began the descent; the trail was as open as he'd remembered it. And then when he came out of the jack-pine, he recognized the broad meadow he and Archie had angled across to the south. Actually he hadn't done so badly: five – maybe six saddle hours according to his aching thighs and bruised buttocks – since he'd left the agency.

As soon as he came to the cut bank, he'd have to hobble the horse, climb down. She would be deep in Storm and Misty canyon itself – probably by the spring. She'd had help – her mother and father – the Raider Lefthands – initially when she'd set up camp – and now lifelining her with any supplies she needed. It didn't bother him that he hadn't come across Jonas or Susan or the Raider Lefthands; they could have come by the east trail. They could have.

He had hoped that there might be smoke trace showing when he looked down into Storm and Misty, a semaphore of white canvas – up or down. Just meant that she'd made sure of not being found. That was all.

As he went over the edge, he remembered the cold breath that had rushed up to meet him when he and Archie had climbed down the first twenty steep feet, then, sitting with their heels digging in ahead of them, dislodging stones and shale crumbs, slid all the way to the shallow pan of roots tipped up by the fallen fir. It still bridged the lower part of the Storm and Misty cleft. It would be farther up the canyon, near the springs, that Victoria would be camped.

He ducked under the fir trunk and began to walk through the canyon's own early twilight, for the sun had dropped below its high west edge. And there was the canyon sound now, a deep chord, persistent, much more than wind sigh through leaf and needle branches. This hum was a master thrumming, as though Storm and Misty canyon's lofting sides formed a giant rock viola to give the wind a resin edge. When he had come in with Archie, he had thought this was a shaman place set aside from ordinary places. Here a hero could seek vision and solution so that he could lead his people out of want and danger. Here he could purify and prepare, and be absolved from self, and that was the great trick – the true magic – not to turn into an osprey or a falcon or an eagle or a magpie – but to fly free of self. This was the seed place where Esau had dreamed of leading his band, to find the happy days that they had lost.

Archie had told him that this was where Beulah began, flowing north, now above, now underground. Right here it was hidden, and they'd had to walk up the canyon a hundred yards to drink from it. It had made Carlyle's teeth ache. When he and Archie stood again, they could see up to the springs, a white water web down the rock face where the end of the canyon narrowed – was almost blind. The high sides there were bare of trees, the rock carved by millennia of wind and frost and water, suggesting the clump bodies of grazing buffalo, a bear, a goat, and unmistakably – a third of the way up the eastern wall – a demon face – witty – derisive.

The rock cup where he and Archie had drunk was dry. No water wept down past the demon face. This was what Raider had found! This was what Old Esau had been so disturbed about! "Stopped now." Like the old man, Beulah was almost dead; all that had been feeding her since the seismic crew had mortally bumped an earth fault last fall had been surface melt and run-off.

Above where he stood, there was no tent. And he knew that down below he would not find Victoria either.

Just at dark he made it up and over the edge. He unsaddled the sorrel, stood uncertain for a moment with the moist warmth of the saddle blanket over his arm. What now! What could he possibly do now! He'd have to spend the night here, ride back early in the morning, but that did nothing for her – when he was back at the agency, then what was he going to do!

He threw his slicker over the saddle against night dew already lowering, spread out his bed-roll. He lay with his eyes up to the sky and told himself over and over again that he must do something. He listened to the tearing crop of the horse, the idle swish and crush of hooves as it moved on – stopped – moved on again. A coyote howled. There'd been no great danger waiting here for her – but in the city – oh God, in there! Why had she done it! And what could he do for her! Why had she failed! He must do something; nothing was accomplished – ever – by this sort of spiralling thought that left hopelessness to return only to hopelessness again. The coyote howled once more. Oh, God, why had she failed!

Hours later, cold and damp nagged him awake to a muted world – tree shapes blurred by mist almost absorbing dawn light. He got up, his knees trembling with hunger weakness and the day in the saddle. Before he went after the horse, he ate the rest of the bannock and the two strips of bacon left. His mouth was still bitter, his tongue sticky with thirst.

He began a wide, stumbling search, standing still now and then in the swathing fog to catch any hoof click or halter shank clink. After an aching time he knew he'd have to wait till the mist had lifted. He lay down under the blanket and slicker. He dozed a while. He sat up. A cigarette pushed back the thirst slightly.

He could take another try at it, because it was brighter now. When he stood up this time, his knees almost gave out under him. He began to slap his arms to revive circulation, walking slowly and carefully. The warmth had just begun to rise in him when he saw something move – to his left. It was the sorrel – fifty feet away under a group of spruce.

When he lifted the bridle over her head, his hands shook so badly he could hardly hold the bit; the buckle was almost too much for his knuckles, from which cramping stiffness had sucked all strength. He had to turn his back to the horse, then straightening his knees from a crouch, with the strap over one shoulder, use his leg and back muscles to tighten the cinch. He rested before he climbed into the saddle.

He looped the lines around the horn, slid his hands between his crotch and the saddle for warmth. As he rode, he was filled with strange lightness, his mind walking just along the edge of consciousness.

Without any idea of how long he had left the horse to her own sense of direction, he straightened in the saddle with a start to discover that he was warm once more and the last shreds of mist were dissolving ahead of him. They were still following the well-cleared forestry trail. Another hour and they had made it through the burnt-over land. He dismounted at Beulah Creek; he and the horse drank from the narrow trickle of water there. Late in the afternoon he rode into the schoolyard.

After his supper he sat for a long time in the kitchen. No use seeing if Susan and Jonas were back or not. Victoria was in the city, and they knew or they did not know that she had left the hospital. If they didn't know, they couldn't help him; if they did know – they wouldn't. No one could now. There was nothing he could do to help her. Nothing!

He did not know how long the phone had been ringing. It had sounded first – possibly – without his even hearing it, and then again as he paid no attention to the ring pattern – short-long-short. He lifted the receiver. Long distance. Yes – he'd pay the charges. Dim and distant, Archie Nicotine's voice came to him through wire hum and crackle.

"Sinclair."

"Yes, Archie."

"They only let you have one call, you know."

"What is it, Archie?"

"I can't hear you very good."

He raised his voice. "Same old thing, Archie!"

"I lost one call because you didn't answer it. You weren't there."

"I know."

"And then I lost another one he let me, and he said it was the last one I could have."

"You've got through now. What is it . . ."

"But I explained it to him . . ."

"What's the trouble?"

". . . if I didn't talk to you then it didn't count – so he gave me another chance to get through to you."

"I've been out."

"I know, and if you didn't get back I could be stuck in here."

"Jail."

"Hey-uh."

"Oh hell – Archie!"

"Hey-uh."

The insect whine of the line went on and on. "I only had three," Archie said.

"Archie – I am sick and tired . . ."

"I got robbed my rings and carburetor or I paid it myself. You come in and you get me out of here."

"No."

"Get me out of here."

"I am not driving all the way in there just to . . ."

"Get me out . . ."

"Just don't get in there!"

"I'm in it now, aren't I? This time is not justice. Different."

"No – it isn't – it's never different – and there's nothing accomplished if you won't learn . . ."

"I guess I learned something new this time. . . ."

"No – you didn't – and I'm not going on and on – even though you do – there has to come an end to it – I am not coming in just because you got drunk again."

"No – I didn't – not this time."

"If you didn't get drunk, you wouldn't be in there."

"Hey-uh."

"But you are."

"Hey-uh."

"All right then!"

"I just had three – then Norman Catface robbed me my rings and carburetor – then I went out back the Empress and they picked me up."

"They would not arrest you if you weren't drunk and disorderly."

"I wasn't and they did it anyway."

"Then – why . . ."

"I didn't know about it before. I was just taking a piss I needed."

"Archie! What the hell are you in for – this time?"

"Indecent explosion," Archie said. "You got to come in get me out of here because I got no money for the fine – I would have it if Norman didn't . . ."

Carlyle hung up the receiver.

The kitchen was as cold as the bedroom. The fire was out; the wood-box was empty. Some time during the night the snow had started falling, was still coming down, a last contradiction of the mountain spring. On his way to the wood-shed he had to kick his way through the stuff; it had pillowed the swing seats, the teeter-totters; it piled itself high on the spruce branches now pointing down. In a sense it was merciful, for it swathed the roofs of cabins and backhouses, tilting posts and broken fence lines; by now, with feathering stealth, it would have covered all the derelict cars in ditches, hidden Raider's elk guts. Probably hadn't reached out east as far as the abandoned cars. Most of it would be gone by noon.

Kitchen range first. He glanced up at the clock: 7:15 – better get to the school stove instead; it would need from now till nine to warm up the schoolroom for the children. His breath steamed ahead of him; all the black-boards were cloudy. Janey hadn't come near the place since he'd gone into the city Saturday. He looked down at the floor – unswept – Fyfe cooky bits – crumpled paper – dried mud. It had never been that way when Victoria . . . He pushed his thoughts away from her. When he had the stove roaring he slid the side draughts shut, pulled the damper half out. Oh, God, she was loose in the city! No doubt about it! And what was he going to do! What could he do! No use phoning Fyfe, who'd just tell him to wait and see what transpired! Let's just get through this day, Sinclair – just take it easy – you got through yesterday and last night – and you will make it through today and then tonight – but will she! Oh – will she!

Just before the noon break, he looked up from Toots Powderface's scribbler, saw that it was snowing again. Toots, waiting for his arithmetic correction, fidgeted – just a nervous rustle; with his ears protruding famously, his fist of a forehead, he reminded Carlyle of a house mouse. The tiny hands gripped the desk edge as he waited to see what the judging pencil would give him, the long tailed "C" or the plough-share check mark that meant a mistake. Carlyle could see the veins through the short hair above his ears, blue crayon marks scrawled beneath scaling dirt and dandruff. An anxious smile flattened out the sharp twin peaks of his upper lip, showed large front teeth like shrivelled corn.

"Very good, Toots." He wrote "OK" on the bottom of the page. That was it. That was it for the day.

As soon as he told them, there came the silent, pushing rush to the jacket and hat corner, then the hissing, wound-up excitement of getting outside. They poured through the door with thin hoots bouncing back from the hills, running in short spurts all over the schoolyard, and then up over the first rise. He watched them through the doorway, saw one boy with his hands in his pockets chicken dance along – then stop to stand spraddle-legged, sunlight catching a glinting arc. Even the girls were unrehearsed in modesty; he'd often seen one left behind by the others in a homeward group, squat and relieve herself, then run with skirts and braids and kerchief flying to catch up again.

It really meant to snow. He didn't bother with lunch – lay out on the couch and, with no sense of time passage whatever, stared up to the long windows above. The flakes falling, eluded; at glass touch they melted and ran. A flight of blackbirds scarved the length of the windows – disappeared – returned out of white nothing – only to vanish again. Individual flakes had become indistinguishable, just loosed from above without identity, myriads bewildering with vertigo.

He slept on the couch. Very early the next morning, his mind awoke and found itself caged in a body still sleeping. From the sea-caves of self, he tried to call out his will; it was far too deep and far too weak, and the labour of freeing himself from the paralysed flesh was far beyond the power it possessed. But he must wake up the imprisoning body, release himself from strait-jacket terror. Only by perfect concentration on the big toe of his left foot could he end the leaden drowse. He willed one first twitch and then another and then another and then the leg shake that broke the body chains.

He had not found her in Storm and Misty; he must find her in the city before she perished there. He'd call on Ezra Powderface, ask him to notify the parents that school would be closed for the rest of the week.

Jesus, dear Jesus, I'll find you, little lost lamb, Victoria!

PART TWO

NINE

HE HAD OFTEN WONDERED IF IT WERE REALLY POSSIBLE TO make a decision, then act on it so that a person truly changed the flow of his life? He had resigned from Shelby School; he had applied to the Indian Department – that seemed decisive enough – until he looked at the reason for the decision: that everywhere he turned, the town – the people – reminded him of Grace. He could no longer pass the hospital to or from school without remembering the baby daughter there wouldn't be. The window seat in the living-room, where Grace had sat so still for hour after hour, saddened him; it was there that Bruce had given her the hypo so that they could take her into the city. He hadn't made any decision; a calcified placenta, post partum psychosis, finally death, had made the decision for him.

When he'd signed his contract in Ian Fyfe's office in the city, the district head had told him Indian Affairs were delighted he would be teaching in Paradise reserve. For three years the Reverend Dingle had done his best until a proper teacher would be available, and now the minister could return to Hanley reserve, north of Paradise, to take care of his Stony congregation without the extra load of teaching. The Paradise band of twenty-five families was actually satellite to Hanley, which was the responsibility of Mr. Sheridan. Paradise was too, though

119

Carlyle's duties – since Mr. Sheridan must live on the main reserve – would necessarily be much broader than those of simply a teacher. But Sheridan would get down twice a month, the doctor from Hanley perhaps once, Reverend Dingle even less frequently, since Ezra Powderface was a lay minister experienced in conducting church, burial, funeral services.

Because they'd been talented hunters and trappers almost a century ago, the Stonys in the eighteen-seventies had voluntarily chosen Paradise Valley, generous with game – 25,000 acres of long-grass grazing that lifted behind the agency building in three wide benches, each one a meadowing expanse edged with spruce and dotted with their cabins and tents. It was isolated – thirty-four miles from the foothills town of Shelby, eighty from the city – but then Carlyle would not have applied for and accepted the teaching post if he hadn't considered this isolation with some care. The telephone line shared with ranchers along the Valley road was often out; indeed, even when it was unbroken it did not give too satisfactory communication, for there were a number of stretches dependent on barbed-wire fence line. Carlyle must keep after the Paradise people to make sure they repaired their part of it whenever it was down.

The suspension bridge from the Valley road over the Spray was awkward; it meant Carlyle must leave his car on the north side of the river. The department had promised a bridge, but it was an expense of great magnitude; government machinery did not move as quickly as one would wish it to, and they would have to wait and see what transpired. Quite likely in time there would be a bridge; Carlyle must keep after them to check the cables, or rather, do that himself – especially in June at high water.

The Paradise Stonys trapped little now, Fyfe explained, shot deer and elk and moose only when the lash of hunger drove them to it. That could be the fault of department paternalism, federal government bounty in the form of band rations, the ten-dollars-a-head treaty money, family allowance, old-age pension – the usual welfare apathy relieved by spasmodic periods of seasonal work for neighbouring ranchers in haying, harvesting, fencing, rail- and post-cutting, once or twice a year, the per-capita distribution of money from the sale of the communal herd calf crop.

Next week – the beginning of it – Fyfe promised – he and Sheridan and Dr. Sanders would visit Paradise – when Carlyle was settled in. "Yours is possibly the most rewarding work there is with these people. If there's hope for them, it lies in their children and – eh – one bit of advice I always give to young men beginning with us – do not let yourself become too personally involved."

Before Carlyle had left Fyfe's office, Sheridan had showed up on an unscheduled visit. He was a slight, nervous man in his late sixties, a chain-smoker with mahogany fingers. Over coffee he did not speak with very great warmth of the Hanley or the Paradise people. Most of his advice was cautionary: don't give them any begging letters; don't let them get into the habit of coming into the agency house; don't lend them any money; don't take any back talk from any of the younger ones – especially Harold Lefthand – Archie Nicotine; don't rely on their word; be sure that the school was locked after four and the house, of course, if he left it. Nicotine had enough natural shrewdness and enough education that he would bear watching.

Three months' vacancy meant a whole morning of scraping out pack-rat droppings that had crusted in cupboards and corners; there were piles of blue-and-gilt fly bodies to sweep up after he'd sprayed. Not until he had aired some of the mildew mustiness out of his own living quarters did he go into the schoolroom through the doorway to the left of the stove. He paused just inside by the stone water jug. Half way up the centre aisle, in a square space of its own, a pot-bellied stove; at the dead front of the room hung a picture each of the King and Queen, staring out over empty desks, with the impersonality of coins. He walked slowly along the back of the room looking at the magazine pictures and cut-outs on the wall; a plump-cheeked girl in the middy and skirt of Canadian Girls in Training held up her hands in horror – LET'S FACE IT – NOBODY WANTS A COLD. Then by the side door, where the children would see it at noon and recess and after four: BE SURE YOU WASH YOUR HANDS. He paused for a moment before a calendar advertising cattle vaccines and serums – a Russell painting: TIGHT DALLY AND LOOSE LATIGO. It showed a bearded cowboy standing with all weight on one stirrup of a saddle, about to slide under his horse's belly, his lariat fast to a plunging Texas longhorn.

He came to the beginning of the side blackboard, examined curling sheets of onion paper on a nail, a list of the band's councillors and members. Then he saw the framed verses with illuminated letters, done in Sunday School Gothic:

God has not promised
Skies ever blue,
Flower-strown pathways,
Blessings for you.

God has not promised
Sun without rain,
Joy without sorrow,
Peace without pain.

But He has promised:
Strength from above,

Unfailing sympathy,
Undying love.

Staring at the framed verses, he knew that he had just met Mr. Dingle, his predecessor in the schoolroom.

There came a tapping at the school door. He opened it to an Indian in a long, black coat, a squat man in his late sixties perhaps, thick of lip, nostrils flaring to give his nose a squashed look.

"Mr. Sinclair." The deep voice vibrated against Carlyle's chest.

"Yes."

"I am Reverend Ezra Powderface. I came over to shake your hand."

The pulpit was in that voice, Carlyle decided, still unable to believe the anciently cut coat with six cloth-covered buttons down its front. He looked into the face with its tenting eyelids, the broad nose. The man was missing a lei!

"I also come to tell you there was a meetin'. Today. This meetin' is gonna be held at the dance tent. This afternoon at two o'clock. The meetin' is for you, Mr. Sinclair. Archie Nicotine will call for you and he will take you thence." He waited – not at all awkwardly, but with relaxed patience.

Carlyle said. "That's fine, Mr. Powderface."

"If there's anything you want – if you could use some boys they will carry anything. . . ."

"I might – later – this afternoon – some of my stuff is still on the other side."

"I'll send them. God – be praised!" The "be praised" came almost as an afterthought.

Nicotine showed up just as he was doing his late lunch dishes. Carlyle judged him to be in his late twenties, a blocky man with a curious eye that darted about the room.

"With you in a minute." He hung up the damp dishtowel.
"Hey-uh."
He took his jacket off the back of the chair.
"Mrs. Sinclair – she's not comm'?"
Oh, God! He still wasn't ready for it when it came!
"There – isn't any Mrs. Sinclair."
"You're single then."
"I guess so."
"But you been."
"Yes – I've been."
"Hey-uh."
Sheridan hadn't been too far off the mark.

Archie Nicotine guided him up and onto the first bench, where the dance tent was pitched. Ezra Powderface met them just before they went inside, introduced Carlyle to half a dozen men – the band councillors. Carlyle did his best, as he shook hands with each in turn, to fix them in his memory.

He met Jonas One-Spot with his age-skimped braids, standing with bowed legs wide apart, knees bent and shaking with palsy. His was a caved and toothless face without sex clue; the small eyes were almost lost in wrinkles; at the lower rim of each trembled a clear tear that could have been distilled from the pearl clouds covering the pupils. The mouth corners were drawn back and up in a smile of fixed and bereft anticipation, as though his ears awaited the hearing of some delightful thing his blind eyes could not see.

He shook the small hand of Esau Rider; under snow hair, Esau's narrow temples and prominent cheek-bones gave him a death's-head appearance, though he was obviously younger than Jonas. Deep furrows ran down past the corners of his sickle mouth. Finally he met Prince Dixon with his raisin eyes and a brush-cut; he looked about the same age as Archie Nicotine.

They entered the great tent, the inside phosphorescent with afternoon sunshine. He saw that many of the women had babies on their laps; the brilliant kerchiefs and the pink, green, yellow, red, blue, orange and white rimmed smoked glasses, soothing eyes fogged with trachoma, cataract, snow glare, were vivid as a mixed poppy bed. Empty baking-powder tins were spaced around the dirt floor; then he saw the flat, round boxes travelling from hand to hand; many were chewing snoose; the tins were for spitting.

Ezra Powderface led him to the far end of the tent, invited him to sit on a cracked leather car seat there. The minister left for the centre.

"This meetin' gonna be opened up now – sing by the hymn book."

Thin, black books appeared in brown hands; the Indian to Carlyle's left touched him on the elbow and handed one to him.

All around the tent walls legs uncrossed themselves; everyone stood. The tent was filled with staccato Stony for several bars before Carlyle recognized the revival bounce of "Rescue the Perishing." Beyond Ezra Powderface he saw a man earlier introduced to him as Wayne Lefthand. His head was back; his eyes were screwed shut; his voice rode high and pure above the others.

The hymn came to a ragged end; Ezra Powderface raised both hands above his head, brought them slowly down.

"I'm gonna pray."

All heads lowered together; eyes closed and faces took on an intensity almost of pain.

"Heavenly Father, we're gathered here in this tent because we got a teacher now for our kids – Thy children. We thank Thee, Heavenly Father, for sendin' us this teacher. We're grateful to Ottawa for sendin' us this teacher for teachin' our kids for us. While I'm at it, I want to thank Thee for these people too, for the no frost this spring so's there gonna be berries for puttin' up in the fall. And for the fencin' there is now for some of these people on Moon's place and the Turkey Track and so on, and for the hayin' and green-feed stackin', the stookin', for the thrashin' that may come later for these people that just want to work a little without a starvation. But the main thing now is this teacher, Mr. Sinclair, that come to live amongst us. We needed him and Thou sent him to us. Well – thanks. Now we got cabins and canvas and the wind blows through, Heavenly Father, and the children get sick out of it. Hold on, Heavenly Father, I'm comin' back to Mr. Sinclair Thou sent us in a minute. As I said it – we lost all that now – and still there isn't anything yet in its place, is there? No, Heavenly Father, there is not yet. The old Indian good-livin' and the new white way – these people are between that now. So here is where this teacher Thou sent us comes in. I will explain. We want to make homes like the white people make – we want to grow vegetables like the white people grow. We want to live the white way now and put the suffering out of our souls. I know the old people cannot do this, Heavenly Father; I guess this isn't possible for some of the young ones too. I guess there will always be the ones from about fourteen years old and on up that will go right on havin' blanket marriages and not gettin' these sanctified in Thy sight the way I keep harping at them to do it. I know there will always be some not bring their infants around to be baptized in Thy name – but Thou take the young ones, Heavenly Father – the kids and the like of that. These are the ones! Especially where their father and mother make them speak English – these are the ones Mr. Sinclair will teach to read and write. These are the ones will live the white way and there is why we thank Thee for sendin' us Mr. Sinclair to teach them and educate them and make this possible. We are thankful to Thou. And while I am still here – maybe Thou would work it Harold Lefthand give back the 30-30 Joe Dance says he took from him his place when he was into Shelby last Tuesday no questions asked – in the name of Jesus Christ Who died for us all – Amen."

Ezra's arms came down; there came a sudden and terrific burst of clapping that cut off as suddenly as it had started. Began. Stopped. Took up again and was finished.

"That's all," said Ezra. "If you will please step up one at a time, I will let you meet Mr. Sinclair."

Sheridan and Fyfe, carrying a brief-case stamped gold and scarlet with the royal coat of arms, came down the next day. They stayed till after lunch, and just before they left, Fyfe said, "Eh – Dr. Sanders was to come too, you know – eh . . ." He cleared his throat, seemed to be searching for what to say next. "He – he'll be down in a week or so."

But Sanders came two days later, a lean, sandy-haired man in his early forties. His cheek-bones were as high as any of his patients'. He had what Carlyle considered a "cold eye" – which actually meant a mature or reliable one! He'd already made his calls when he came to the agency building, introduced himself. "I'd been down sooner with Fyfe and Sheridan – but – drunk – been out with the X-ray unit – so – I tied one on."

He'd begun work at the kitchen table, after excusing himself, his pencil marking in numbers under the form headings: "common cold," "infant diarrhoea," "VDG, VDS" – then finally under "tuberculosis pulmonary – new-found" – "three" – then under "refusing treatment" – "three." In spite of its tan, Carlyle noticed that Sanders' skin had a glossy softness, almost as though no beard had grown there to be shaved and shaved again. He looked up to Carlyle, the colourless brows lifted. "Green liniment – white liniment – epsom salts – castor oil – no point in my coming down really – your dispensary takes care of them – when they want me they're moribund."

He added to Carlyle's store of information about the Paradise community. Harold Lefthand was a truculent rascal, Peter Dance, the biggest scrounger, John Roll-in-the-mud or Allan Tail-feather, the laziest, Orville Ear, the stupidest, Matthew Bear, the vainest, the Wounded-Person family, the most tuberculous. But this time there was praise too: Susan Rider watched the family's credit at the Shelby store; Mary Shot-close kept a spotless cabin; Wayne Lefthand sang like a meadowlark; Matthew Bear could dance; Peter Powderface loved all children.

"Look at his father, Ezra – result of the valiant Methodist missionary work – started almost a century ago – you can – must have already noticed the influence."

"Yes."

"Ezra's their shining-success example – Methodist right through the peritoneum – camp meeting – washed-in-the-blood Methodist. The old boys saw great possibilities in him when he was a child – sent him to residential school – even before that I think he lived in the missionary's home – today he'd make Wesley turn over in his grave – and the old missionaries – over the years he's thrown in a pinch of Weesackashack here – Wendigo there – it's hard to tell where Methodism leaves off and Ezra begins. The amalgam's damn effective too. What about you?"

"Hmh?"

"How come?"

"How come what?"

"How come you're here – taking on this job?"

"Why – I – reasons."

"I won't say it's none of my business – it is."

"I have – come."

"Oh. Were you gold medallist at St. Johns or St. Andrews –
Acadia – McMaster – Newton?"

"No."

"B. D. Used to pack them into the cathedral church till you
began to hit the sherry too hard – couldn't get along with your
deacons – elders."

"That how I strike you?"

"No."

"I've always been a teacher – never been – I'm not a minister."

"Thank God – let us pray."

"Tissue bank came up with too many bad checks on you –
too soon from the party to the operating theatre – they couldn't
ignore that twenty-two-year-old mother who might have had a
baby girl if you'd been lucid enough to see pre-eclampsia?"

"Nope."

"Illegal operation on a little black-eyed hooker in nightgown
– daisy white – that was the friendly one but she . . ."

"Nope."

"All right then!"

"Two sisters and my mother died in Qu'Appelle Sanatorium.
I've had to watch it ever since I interned. No sputum cup yet."
He grinned suddenly. "I guess they might call me a disease
brother. You fish?"

"Yes."

"Fly?"

"Yes."

"That's nice – you are now up to your ass in the finest
rainbow and cut-throat water in North America – the Spray –
Daisy and Beulah Creek. Want me to show you some good runs?"

"All right."

They walked down to the suspension bridge, but did not
cross it, walking instead to the west up the Spray bank. Sanders
led the way, turned off from the river course, through thick

willow. The slap and scratch of a branch across the face came less frequently, and then Carlyle caught water glint through pin cherry and saskatoon.

"Beaver dam," Sanders said.

They stopped at a broad pond reflecting perfectly the silver of wolf willow, the spearing green of bulrushes. Carlyle stared down at cloven-hoof pocks deep in the edge mud. Reversed hearts. The punctuate plop of a frog, startled. He saw the water surface crease with the lilliputian wake of a water bug in minute epilepsy. Stopped. Held quite still – twitched itself again over the surface.

"Swim first?"

Carlyle knelt and began to unlace his shoes.

With mild chill the pond embraced him; he pulled himself down through the cool murk of underwater, then, arching, broke the surface to expel pent breath and spray. Hooooough! He turned over and lay floating face upwards with the sting of water at the back of his nose, the earth taste of it in his mouth. As though they were not part of him, his hands fluttered gently at his sides; his knees moved lazily as he stared up to sky and still cloud. The fluid intimacy of water against his nakedness won him.

Slapping mosquitoes and deer flies, they sat on a rock to dry off in the sun.

"Smoke?"

"Nope," Sanders said. "About these people – one thing to remember . . ."

"Never let yourself become personally involved."

"Hah!" Sanders laughed. "No – you've taught, so I assume you know children. You'll hear everyone refer to them as children. Horse shit! They are children, but with adult drives – grown-up hungers – mature weaknesses – envy – love of power – of their own children; they have vanity and – what's very – the key – a terrible feeling of inferiority. If you know that – and that they are child-like – then you won't give them too much of a load to carry; you won't rant at them because they failed to carry what you piled up on them. Don't expect too much of them – don't let them get you angry. They will – don't let them know it. You know what you are – to them?"

"What?"

"Ever wonder what a shock it must be to someone – seeing himself in a mirror for the first time in his whole goddam life? That's what you are – to them. There's a phrase you'll hear them use a lot."

"What?"

"I'm ashamed. One way that's worked for me – give them praise – just if they've earned it. Be a good guardian."

"Was Dingle?"

"Poor Dingle. Hey, I'm dry."

Later, as they stood side by side at a long and beautiful and utterly unproductive run on Beulah Creek, Carlyle asked again about Dingle.

"I can't help you much with him. He is the most well-meaning man in the world. I am not fitted to give you Dingle – not really. He loves his fellow man with a great, big, happy, boob heart; for twenty years since he left white charges, he's indulged himself in a sort of absent-minded masturbatory loving-kindness that has borne no fruit. Oh, maybe some – the Indians all know he's good – they can't understand him but he's good. Until you hear him preaching to them – talking to them – until – was that a rise?"

"I think so."

"You know – you can tell a lot from the way a man fishes." There came a thunking splash; a ring was spreading under the tree leaning out from the opposite bank up stream. "God – be praised! Here – use a grey hackle!"

"I have some."

"I saw them – bloody shaving-brushes. They'll do for fast water in the Spray, but you . . ."

"For Christ's sakes I've fished trout before."

"Sorry – I get nerved up – like my first woman every time. I was really pleased to see you fished a fly at all. Dingle uses a three-dollar telescope rod to lob out a hardware counter of lead and hooks of worms and grasshoppers – then wears a blazing white shirt to put them down a half mile up and down stream. Don't get me wrong about him – he is a sweet bastard, but your taking over the school is the best thing since penicillin."

"And Fyfe?"

"Fyfe – oh, he has a Stradivarius of a rod – Hardy reel – exquisite flies – uprights – spiders – bi-visibles – nymphs – he has nymphs with wing pads – literal with setae – egg sacks – do you know he was responsible for one of the Hardy patterns – Paradise Valley Spent-wing – year ago – late August hatch; he scooped some off the water, sent them to London in a match box and they made up the artificial. Got one! Aaaaaah – he's off! Me – I guess I'm in between."

"What?"

"Fyfe and Dingle."

Before they headed back Sanders had his limit, for the hatch that was happening had stung the trout into a voracious and unselective rise. Carlyle took four on his shaving-brush bucktail.

While they cleaned them on the bank, Sanders said, "Archie Nicotine distresses Dingle."

"Why?"

"Religion; Archie tries them all on. A good sign, I think – shows he's got some elastic left. Archie has a liquor problem – like most of them – and me. He'll get under your hide too."

Carlyle stripped off willow leaves for his creel.

"Examine why he does," Sanders said.

"Why?"

"You'll see – he doesn't herd well."

"Sheridan warned me about him."

"He would. In his own context, Archie's still effective."

"You like him."

"I can't stand him most of the time, and that's the whole Archie Nicotine situation. I think he's Mormon now – if they haven't excommunicated him – maybe I should say – if he hasn't excommunicated them. Now Fyfe . . ."

Carlyle laughed.

"What's funny?"

"Not really – yes, I guess it is. Mr. Fyfe – my Aunt Pearl."

"Oh."

"Year I was six – most of it – I stayed with her. Year my mother died. Aunt Pearl had a boy of her own – Willis – once; he died in the flu epidemic of 1918."

"That's funny as hell."

"No – Aunt Pearl burned string."

"Huh!"

"Kitchen – toilet – her stool was white. She'd always burn a length of string after. Guess I would have grown up with her in dead little Willis's toy room – I hadn't stuck my prick in the magic lantern."

"What!"

"Tell you about it some time."

"I can hardly wait."

"When I know you better – trust you."

That night he lay in the strange bed; the high sign of spruce came through the open window, and with it a penetrating fresh-ness of needle and blade far beyond the fragrance of the hot day. How come Aunt Pearl had floated up – or what was it about Sanders that had moved him to confidence? Doesn't come easily to you, Sinclair, and you just met him today. Sibilant at the screen, the night wind was musty with sage, singing with wild mint – enough to make saliva flow. God, smell must be civilization's first casualty! Scents strengthened and fainted upon the chill air, vivid as he had remembered them ever to be in his prairie childhood: the quinine of willow smoke, burnt sweetness from a frightened skunk far off, or perhaps it breathed from a goddam pack rat up in the rafters!

Several times an owl laid deliberate melancholy upon the stillness. Somewhere up on the benches, a coyote howled long. Another answered him – or else there was one ventriloquial coyote. He'd sleep tonight.

He heard Sanders cough in the bedroom on the other side of the partition. For the first time in the two years since Grace had died, he was pretty certain he wouldn't have the wading dream with the steady tug of the current at his legs, so real that panic would wake him.

He dreamed of Mate and Tourigny's swimming hole.

TEN

ALMOST EVERY DAY OF THE TWO WEEKS LEFT IN AUGUST, A west wind urged the spruce, their tips swaying in shallow arcs against the mountain sky; on the high brass bed he fell asleep and he woke up to their persistent sighing, mind-filling as waterfall hoarseness. As much as it ever would, the aching loss of Grace had withdrawn, or at least, it came to him less frequently. He supposed their two years together would contract more and more, for time – like distance – must have its own perspectives. Sad.

Late one afternoon, as he came down the river, he saw Esau Rider sitting on the rock slope at the foot of the suspension bridge. Third time he'd seen him there; the old man must spend many hours on that rock where the afternoon sun fell warmest. Carlyle stopped a hundred feet up stream to watch him, elbows on his knees, hands hanging loose. Possibly hours that way – stirring only to fill and light his pipe – staring down at the rock, where orange fungus scaled its minute foliage – or into the water where perhaps a bull trout hung. Esau-trout – trout-Esau. God, how he envied him his primitive talent for self-erasure, if it saved him from melancholy, from flesh and spirit pain. Did he achieve oneness with eternity? – what an overblown way to explain sun-warmed stupor in which half-thoughts and fragment dreams were projected against no time, lighted up, shaded and faded and vanished to light up again. Not too much different from the steers and cows with absently moving jaws – or the bull trout – or the fungus.

A little girl in a red kerchief and purple woman's skirt was helping Esau to his feet, then back up along the trail. All the same – he did envy him!

Opening day of the school term, the child who had helped Esau was the first to show up. By ten o'clock she was still the only pupil in the schoolroom. She sat in the last desk of the left-hand row, the farthest from him. When he asked her where the other children were, she lowered her head, black hair curtaining down, so that all he had of her was the twinkle of rhinestone barrette, the pale crease of her hair part. He turned away, wrote down addition and subtraction test arithmetic on the black-board, lines from the Grade Two Reader for them to copy so that he could assess their writing and printing.

When he had finished and turned round, he caught the flick of her eyes before she lowered her head again. Ten o'clock! One out of thirty-five! For all their helpful information, Fyfe and Sanders and Sheridan hadn't told him to expect this! Why not? A deliberate omission? Just what was he to do now?

He stood it for ten minutes more. Since he was not going to achieve oneness with eternity, and since it was obviously ridiculous to wait for pupils who were not coming . . . What was wrong with their parents! Or – was it the parents who were keeping them away? So – if they wouldn't come to him . . .

At the first cabin he knocked – got no answer – opened the door. Esau Rider. He said good-morning to the old man by the stove, got out again. At the next cabin his eye caught a flirt of movement by the wood-pile; he was just in time around it to grab the shoulder of a crouching boy.

"Why aren't you in school? Where are – you any brothers – sisters? Where's your father – your mother?"

The boy would not look at him.

"Now – you get going – that school – fast as you can!" He gave him a push; the boy staggered a few steps, caught his balance, then ran half bent, elbows pumping, into the spruce behind the cabin.

Well – he'd gone about that one wrong. Next time – different. But at the next cabin, there was no child – no adult. Nor at the next. At the next one he did not knock, pulled open the door and stepped inside, to face an Indian bare to the waist, seated cross-legged on a red-and-white cowhide. He was rolling a cigarette. A woman, stooping to put kindling into the stove, turned a startled, round, fat face to him. Beyond the stove, on a stool, sat a young boy.

"How old is he?"

The man was still holding the cigarette up to his mouth, tongue half out to lick the edge of the paper.

"Supposed to be there over an hour ago!" Lower half of the child's face looked as though someone had thrown a handful of strawberry jam at it.

"Get up!"

He didn't move.

"All right!" He walked past the mother at the stove, lifted the child off the stool, gave him a shove towards the open door. The boy stumbled ahead a few steps, then backed up exactly the same number. Carlyle grabbed a handful of denim shirt collar; with the other hand he took the boy by the faded seat of his pants. He marched him out at a stiff-backed and protesting angle, then prancing through the yard, down the rise, across the schoolyard.

Still holding the shirt, he opened the door, pushed him inside. Two! When he closed the door and turned around, Archie Nicotine was standing there.

"Trouble, Sinclair?"

"Not – now."

"Hey-uh."

"I'm rounding every one of them up – if it takes till dark."

"It might. They won't be in the cabins any more now."

"I'll find them."

"Not if you bust in on them. You got to go quiet – try the bush – these kids are good hiders, and that's the whole situation."

"Thanks."

"Don't bother my place. . . ."

"I'm not making any exceptions!"

"I got two girls – one Grade Three – one Grade Two. . . ."

"And why aren't they in . . ."

"They are stookin' on the Turkey Track with Mrs. Nicotine, but that will be finished tomorrow and then they'll be in your school."

"I see."

"If the bush is no good – try the tree."

They were good hiders, and they were high climbers as well. The branchless lower trunks of the trees were the most difficult. He used the caution Archie Nicotine had advised, found that hearing, not sight, gave him first clue of a truant child. Through the faint wind-wash of boughs he would hear a high giggle, a poorly repressed snort.

When he returned to the school with two more, he found the original boy and girl were gone. He locked the doors. By one o'clock he had rounded up nineteen. He had done no teaching, nor did he know what he could do with them now that it was an hour past lunch time. He couldn't release them for their meal; he couldn't leave them and go for his. He resolved the dilemma by cutting and spreading forty slices of bread with strawberry jam. They ate them and drank their cocoa at their desks.

In a sense he had accomplished something; they were in the schoolroom. Only. He could not get an answer of any sort from any of them. They simply sat at their desks, the only communication with him at his desk, a vaguely oriental spice-sweet laced bitterly with willow smoke, the rawness of buckskin. He couldn't mark their attendance in his register, for he couldn't match up a name with a child. When he let them go at four o'clock, he felt very tired. He was also resolved; if he had to yank them out of every goddam cabin and goddam tent, climb every goddam tree in the goddam province, they'd come to his school and they'd put in their time in his school!

The next day he bagged thirteen; with three who had shown up more or less voluntarily, he had a silent attendance of sixteen. He now knew three of them: Victoria Rider, old Esau's granddaughter, Maxine and Maureen Nicotine.

After the third morning of spooking them out of cabins, tents, wood-piles, bushes, trees, he decided to talk with Ezra Powderface. The minister must call the parents together for another meeting. He and Ezra would explain to the parents – put an end to this endurance contest. Worth a try.

But before he'd left for Ezra's cabin, Archie Nicotine was at the door.

"Somethin' I needed from the dispensary – white liniment. . . ."

"Can't it wait till I've seen Ezra Powderface?"

"Just for Mrs. Nicotine – you got to stoop a lot doin' that stookin' – her back."

"After I talk with Ezra." He went past Archie and out the door.

"Hey-uh." Archie began to walk along with him. "You aren't gonna wear them kids out, Sinclair."

"I know – that's exactly why I want to talk with Ezra."

"What for?"

"I thought if he held a meeting and I had a chance to explain. . . ."

"You can do a lot of explainin' to these people and it don't come to very much at all. Meetin's invented by the Indians."

"Were they."

"Hey-up. Already there's a petition goin' around."

"What about?"

"You."

Carlyle stopped. "Me!"

"Grabbin' Gatine Lefthand rough by the seat of the pants first morning. Harold has got sixty names on it."

"Sixty names for what?" He could feel his face hot.

"To leave us and get another teacher."

"No!"

"I said us Indians invented the meetin' – we didn't invent the petition . . ."

"Hell – I haven't even started to teach their . . ."

". . . we always got that natural. Harold got sixty names on that petition – but he got Pete Snow and they signed down all the sixty names themself. Most these Indians spent most their time goin' to meetin's – gettin' up petitions – so it don't mean nothin'. Just Harold tryin' to even it up."

"Even it up?"

"You grabbin' his boy like that. The petition just come a little sooner than I thought, but I come to a conclusion – you're the teacher for Paradise."

"Thanks."

"If Ezra holds a meetin', they'll come – they'll listen to you. They'll think inside there they'll send their kids to school. . . ."

"That's what I hope."

"It isn't natural to do that. These people love their kids and they hate to see them suffer, you understand, so they'll slide back and you'll just end up the same way."

"Climbing trees."

"Hey-up."

"So?"

"Try the belly."

"How?"

"One time they get paid treaty money – another time some of them get paid wood cheques – another time after – calf cheques – there's all kinds cheques – family allowance – or if their grampa – gramma stayin' with the young ones – try the belly."

"Just how would you – would I . . ."

"Nobody's got any right to hold back stuff from these Indians. Hasn't got a thing to do with sendin' the kids to school – has it?"

"I wouldn't know."

"I don't know your inside – I only know my own. Red. You got white in there – white conscience – different."

"Maybe it is – but those children have to go to school."

"I agree."

"Then how should I . . ."

"Try the belly."

"Mr. Sheridan . . ."

"No. You see Fyfe. Fyfe is Ottawa. Sheridan's just Sheridan."

He had intended waiting till Saturday to make his trip into the city, but it did seem silly – keeping the school open for even one day more until he had talked with Fyfe, found out if he could use an economic lever on the children's parents.

Fyfe listened without comment as Carlyle told him how impossible the attendance situation was; then Carlyle asked for department support in making the payment of cheques contingent on school attendance.

Fyfe sat back in his swivel chair.

"There's no point in going on this way," Carlyle said.

The supervisor nodded.

"I don't intend to."

"A thing like that – is entirely outside the power of the department. We have no right to withhold their cheques."

"I know."

Fyfe straightened up in his chair. He leaned across the desk, adjusted the calendar pad, picked up a pencil. He bounced the rubber end against the desk top several times.

"Aye-he."

When that seemed all he was going to get, Carlyle said, "Nothing was said to me about the difficulty I'd have with attendance."

"No – no."

"I would have appreciated it."

"Mr. Sinclair, I am no great believer in the maxim that the desirable end justifies the unjust means."

"I didn't come here to discuss general rules or maxims!"

"Sometimes I've thought the main trouble has been too great a paternalism. This alone could explain why we're at least a generation behind our neighbours to the . . ."

"Why didn't you – tell me – what I'd run into?" He knew it had come out rude.

"Are you sure you're comfortable there, Mr. Sinclair?"

"I'm comfortable. You haven't . . ."

"Ever since coming in – you've been fidgeting. . . ."

"And ever since I asked it – you haven't answered my question."

Suddenly Fyfe bared the tips of his dentures in a careful smile. "I wanted you for the Paradise School badly. At any cost – even if I had to be – well – if I did not mention some of the harsher aspects of reserve teaching." He dropped the pencil on the desk top, leaned back in his chair. "I'll go along with you."

"What?"

"On the cheque business. I hope it will work. It ought to."

"Well – thanks."

"I'll come down Monday – make the cheque announcement then." Fyfe got up. "Mr. Sinclair, you've been uneasy all through this visit."

He supposed he had seemed to be; God knew, he had been upset enough about the attendance. But now that Fyfe had mentioned it several times, he realized that there had been something else bothering him. "Mosquito – deer-fly bites. I've been doing quite a bit of fishing. . . ."

"Oh yes. I don't like to be indelicate – but – eh – those insects don't usually get at – eh – where you've been scratching."

"Sanders and I had a swim in the beaver pond."

"His visit was a couple of weeks ago."

"Yes."

Fyfe walked with him to the door. "Let them know I'm making a special trip down."

"I will."

"I don't think it's mosquito or deer-fly bites, Mr. Sinclair."

"Huh?"

"There."

"Oh."

"Very early – when I first went to work on a reserve – I found – eh – a ring of green ointment around each ankle and each wrist made a perfect barrier."

"What!"

"They'll not cross it. And I'm sorry – that's another eventuality I failed to tell you about."

He was swarming with them. There was a supply of green ointment in the dispensary. He shaved himself and applied it generously that night.

Fyfe kept his promise; he came down to Paradise; he made the announcement about the new department policy on cheques. In the next week there was a voluntary attendance of fifteen, more or less. With Fyfe's next trip and the actual withholding of several cheques, there was not – for the rest of the month – one single inexcusable absence.

The fine weather had persisted through September, clear gold-and-blue days, chilly at the morning edge; there were no nights without frost now. He saw Old Esau less frequently on his rock by the suspension bridge. Each school morning at five to nine, he rang the hand bell, the TIN-TID-DIT-TING-CLING ringing trivial down the shallow valley. He began the morning classes always by chalking up a sentence from their readers for them to print and to write. While they worked silently with heads lowered over scribblers, he would stand by the open door at the back of the room, for the collective smell of their bodies took only moments to assert itself. Against his will he found himself – unconsciously – breathing shallowly.

At recess they found their own boy or girl pole, the girls' over towards Old Esau's cabin, where they sat cross-legged on the packed earth, playing some wild sort of jacks with willow sticks, the boys' on the river side of the schoolgrounds. Several would crowd into the boys' toilet with an old wash-tub, beating it with peeled sticks, voices lifted in the cascading rhythm of the Rabbit Dance, or the swifter, more dominant chant of the Prairie Chicken Dance. Round and round the toilet bounced the others, each holding a twig to his rump, head down, elbows crooked, in a free, skipping dance till the jingle of the bell called them back into the schoolroom.

But before they began their reading class, they had their cocoa and Fyfe cookies. Carlyle had tried one himself; on its granite hardness he almost chipped a front tooth. He broke off a fragment, held it in his mouth as carefully as he would shale, cautiously testing it from time to time with his teeth. It took quite a while to soften, then gave up suddenly to spread itself between his teeth, over the roof of his mouth, and along the upper part of his gums – a gluey coat that disobeyed the tongue. He watched the children and saw that they sucked in and held before swallowing a mouthful of cocoa to aid disintegration. Fyfe's nutritious pride and scientific joy. What a hell of a means to be justified even by the most worthy end!

The reading lesson that followed always racked his patience, for he could not get them to speak above a whisper. Little Victoria Rider read no louder, but she was the best of them all. Her voice was quite husky and such lines as "SEE PUFF PLAY WITH HIS BALL" became "SUH PIFF PLEE WEEZEEZ BELL." After initial shyness she picked up speed, would race at full canter through the assigned reading and into the next day's if he didn't pull her up in time. He must get an I. Q. on the child. Joseph Ear had to be the other end of the intelligence scale, a big twelve with the jolly face of a dark buddha – hair a sable pelt fitted above his ears and down around the back of his neck – minstrel wig. Spreading fat, he sat in the last desk of the left-hand row. Carlyle could visualize under the scarlet plaid shirt male, plump breasts. Joseph Ear reminded him of Tourigny's swimming hole and Fat Snelgrove shivering half crouched with hands cupped over his inadequate privates.

145

Almost as much as the children did, he welcomed the last class of the day, when he sent them all up to the board – a box of coloured chalk to each board. Even the little Grade Ones, reaching high on tip-toe, drew excellently. With the girls it was almost always flowers: wild delphinium, buttercups, shooting stars with pointed petal heads hanging lavender, paint-brush, black-eyed susans, tiger lilies with orange throats freckled. The boys drew horses. They drew pink and scarlet and indigo parades of tractors, mowers, hay balers, trucks. But mostly horses. With blue chalk they outlined the mountains that rimmed their valley, harpooned hill-sides with the parrot green of pines and spruce, populated draws and meadows with steers and cows and calves, with moose and elk and deer. And always there were horses: at full gallop with manes flying, colts caught in stilting caprice, the stag arch of a stallion neck, bucking rodeo horses, true in mid air. When they were done, they circled off their drawings and printed large names in a corner, so that Carlyle could not possibly give the wrong one praise or confer another's blame.

They were all right: the Wesleys, the Belcourts, the MacLeods, the MacLeans and MacDougalls and Lefthands and Chinooks, the Roll-in-the-muds, the Baseballs and Ears and Powderfaces and Shot-closes and Wounded-Persons, the Nicotines and Wildmans and Educations and Snows and Bushes and Bears and Riders and Tail-feathers – Loreen and Maxine and Noreen, Altona and Alicia and Alvina, Betty and Boysie and Barbara, Doris and Donna and Dorothea, Flora and Francis and Florence, Wayne, Webster, Louise, Eunice, Delphine, Gatine, Raider and Raymond and Orville and Norville. They were lousy, but they were all right!

Especially Victoria Rider, small and slender and ten; again and again his attention was drawn to her face, pale and salient among the other dark ones. She was the only girl to take off her

kerchief in the schoolroom; unbraided, her hair caught in bar-
rettes above her ears fell in gipsy points. Her upper cheeks and
the bridge of her nose were sprinkled with freckles; her black
eyes were stark against the faintly olive skin – no Asiatic eye-
fold there.

"She can't be all Stony, Peter," he said on Sanders' next
visit.

"Nope. Her mother, Susan, is a Blood."

"I mean – Indian."

"One of her uncles is a department scout – Waterton Lakes
– seems to me he's a half-breed."

"She's Esau's granddaughter."

"Uh-huh. Jonas is his son. Pure Stony. Does it matter?"

"No."

"You sure?"

"Of course. I just wondered – why she – I mean – you can't
help it . . ."

"You should try."

". . . when you look out over the whole class and her face
stands out – her hair – when all their heads are down – it has a
different tone of black – you just wonder why."

"Well – most of them have some degree of white taint. Her
pallor isn't entirely the result of white blood. She's probably still
anemic."

"What!"

"She was – last spring – but Susan's a good mother – buys
the right groceries when she can. She promised to stick with the
cod-liver oil. Victoria'll be all right – if TB doesn't get her."

"Oh."

"She smart?"

"Damn right, she is."

"Your crabs cleared up all right?"

"Yes."

"That's nice. A ring of green ointment . . ."

"I know – Fyfe told me."

"You regular?"

"Hey – just . . ."

"I'm your doctor now. If you've got Weesackashack's revenge, the bismuth hydrate's in the . . ."

"I know."

"I saw her first."

"Victoria?"

"Yes. Susan's a pretty handsome woman."

"Yes, she is."

"I give Victoria special attention – her Schick test is positive – her Wassermann's negative. Good. Oh – Gatine Lefthand – he at school today?"

"No. I think they – the family's been away – one of the ranches – fencing. Gatine's face . . ."

"Catch it next time – staph infection – is it very bad?"

"All over his upper lip – down one side of his chin."

"Tell me sooner next time, will you?"

"Sorry – I will."

"No great harm – it's highly infectious – between now and the next visit he may give it to Harold."

ELEVEN

IT WASN'T TILL THE LAST WEEK IN OCTOBER THAT THE Reverend G. Bob Dingle managed his first visit to Paradise. He drove down with Peter Sanders on a Thursday afternoon. Just after he had released the children, Carlyle saw the car next to his own across the bridge, then, coming round the corner of Esau Rider's cabin, a tall and hatless man carrying a club bag. He saw Carlyle, dropped the bag, and came to him with out-stretched hands.

"Mr. Sinclair – Mr. Sinclair!" The minister took his hand; he did not shake it, but held it firmly between both of his. "I'm so sorry I haven't been able to get down sooner." His dark eyes under the grey hair searched Carlyle's face. "I came down with Peter – he's on his calls now – Harold Lefthand's I believe – young Gatine – impetigo. And how are they?"

"Ah – they?"

"My children – yours now – or I should say – yours as well." Irrepressible good spirits welled through his speech. Although he could feel the perspiration growing between their palms, Carlyle did not know just how to withdraw.

"And I'm sure you're all settled down now – I hear you are – and doing great work. The children – all well?"

"I think so, Mr. Dingle." Perhaps if he let his own hand go loose, it might end the clasp.

"God – be praised!" He said it loudly, his head back, stress on the "God" followed by the "be praised" almost as an afterthought. Mr. Dingle didn't seem too concerned that He be praised right here by Esau Rider's cabin at this moment, but when there was more time for it – the Almighty understood; He too was a hearty sort of person, who did not organize His time too well.

But Dingle was still holding his hand, their palms and fingers now quite warm and tacky. Carlyle began to pull his hand away. Mr. Dingle retained it more firmly, put his other arm over Carlyle's shoulder, began to propel him towards the school door. "We'll just go right in and see them, for I've missed my girls and boys – it may be selfish, but I hope they've missed me too. You and I will just . . ."

"It's after four now, Mr. Dingle. . . ."

"Oh – well. . . ." He laughed, and as he did, he took his arm from Carlyle's shoulder, freed his hand. "Then – we'll just take my bag in – Peter and I would like to stay overnight. . . ."

"Of course." He kept from wiping off the alien moisture, cooling.

"And see the children tomorrow."

In the kitchen, while Carlyle put on the tea kettle, sliced some bread and buttered it, Dingle explained his delay in getting down. He had spent a wonderful summer in the Okanagan at the Nokawamish Summer School of Youth Training For Christian Leadership, had been called to New Westminster to supply at Bonnyview United – only for two Sundays – and the first Sunday he had taken his text from the Epistle of Paul to the Philippians – Chapter Two – verses one to and including thirteen. The second Sunday he'd gone to Matthew – Chapter

Twenty – verses one to sixteen. There had been a third and fourth and fifth Sunday, for the regular minister had taken a turn for the worse and died. It had been a fruitful experience, Mr. Dingle said, and a fine congregation, but not one bit finer than his own red one. At the end of his five weeks he had known beyond any doubt that this was – for him – more than ever – the Lord's Vineyard – even though the grapes were wild ones.

"They're good people – gentle – happy – just children. Mind you . . ." He held up his hand. "No milk, thanks – I haven't got used to canned again after all these weeks – in the schoolroom you'll find it difficult to get them to say 'please' and 'thank you' – actually – in Stony they haven't any expression for 'thank you' – when you give them their cocoa and Fyfe Minimal Subsistence Biscuits – you'll find them crowding in – pushing greedily – getting second cups before all have had their first one. I've tried – not too effectively, I'm afraid, to correct that. 'Grabbing's for dogs and beasts,' I've told them again and again. Now – they haven't 'thank you' as we know it but they have another expression virtually the same. '*No-watch-es-nichuh.*' 'You please me very much.' Isn't that nice?"

"Yes."

"Just as good as 'thank you' – you'll have to keep after them about 'please' and 'thank you.'"

"I will," Carlyle said a little louder than he'd intended.

Through supper Mr. Dingle did most of the talking; several times Carlyle noticed that Peter's attention was steadily on him rather than the minister. For a long time the doctor said nothing, then, "Carlyle has almost perfect attendance now."

"I know – I know. Always a problem. I only wish the spiritual ones could be settled as smoothly."

"Use the Sinclair method," Sanders suggested.

Mr. Dingle laughed. "Oh, no. I'm afraid – with my work – coercion would only defeat the end." He turned to Carlyle. "Peter doesn't really mean that."

"But I do. I don't see why you couldn't use Car's lever. . . ."

"No – no."

"Pry them economically."

"No real gain," Dingle said. "A hollow victory. Oh!" He threw out an arm, laid a hand on Carlyle's wrist. "Not yours, Carlyle! Not at all! What you've done already is very real. I only wish I could have done as much when I had the school. I did not. You did. And I know you're going to keep on doing wonderful things for them." His hand gave two quick and comforting squeezes, then released Carlyle's wrist. "We can't buy souls." He slid his empty tea cup over towards Carlyle. "Just half a cup, please. No more than we can buy – ah – grace – humility – or sell – no more than we could buy and sell love."

"Uh-hah!" Peter gave his short almost-laugh.

"All right – all right, Peter. I'm perfectly aware that it's tried – in a profession even older than your own – but it isn't love, is it?" He turned back to Carlyle. "Buying it, selling it, corrupts – a travesty. Just sugar, thanks – one. Besides – there's no need really – you know they attend services regularly. We can't complain about their church attendance. Those fine old missionaries . . ."

"Probably used a few levers on them," Sanders said.

"I don't know. But I do know – we don't now. I don't. You know that, Peter."

"Yep. What about grabbing hold of girls?"

"Well – I'm sure it's not what it once was."

"I think it is."

"You're wrong, Peter." Dingle lifted his cup, returned it to the saucer. "I'm no cynic – man progresses, I have optimistic faith in that. He goes on – he goes up – century to century. We are lucky – you and I and Carlyle – to be able to help these people in that progress."

"They haven't progressed."

"You know they have."

"Hell, I do!"

"Come now – their life span is longer. . . ."

"And the quality of that life – compared to a hundred years ago – no, sir! And by the way – how many marriages have you and Ezra got on tap?"

"Since you ask – three."

"Great."

"What Peter is getting at," Dingle explained to Carlyle, "is that a great number of them are not married – in the Christian sense."

"Just in their own," Sanders said. "They think they're married, even if the Reverend Dingle and Powderface don't."

"That is not fair, Peter."

"Sure it is. You see – even though they've progressed over the past century – they still seem to stick with some of the old backward customs – like the fine old Stony Institution of trial marriage – maybe even two or three trials. What makes it tough to get them to see the light is – it works out pretty good – when they hit on the right combination it persists – they remain faithful – even monogamous."

"I said you weren't fair because I know as well as anybody – the moral implications of – of their blanket marriages are not what they would be for us – for white people. And I feel quite strongly that now they've accepted Christianity, it's only right there should be some outward evidence . . ."

"Besides church attendance."

". . . that they've had that change of faith."

"Look, God – no levers."

"That's right. I know many of them have been faithful to their pagan – ah – arrangements. How much better if they had been sanctified before God."

"Yours."

"Yes."

"Christian."

"Yes."

"Mmmh. Some of my best friends are married."

"It's very easy, Peter, to score debate points if you don't care."

"But I do."

"Not enough to admit that their wild – cruel God – their demons – Wendigo – Wizard – Weesackashack – can never be equated with a Christian God – Christ. I see fine things in these people – marvellous qualities and customs – little things – why – Old Esau once told me – explained to me how they referred to their wives if they were on in years – not as 'old women.' Even if she is old, her husband says, 'the woman I grow old along with.' Isn't that a nice way of saying it?"

"Yes," Carlyle said.

"Yes, it is," Sanders said.

He'd given Dingle his bed; Peter had the spare room; he slept on the couch in the kitchen-living-room. They had breakfast together; Sanders left on his calls; Mr. Dingle went into the schoolroom with Carlyle. The children seemed mildly interested in seeing him again, followed him raggedly in the Lord's Prayer, then – for Mr. Sinclair, Dingle explained – sang "Bringing in the Sheaves" in Cree. He admonished them to work hard for their unselfish new teacher, whom they must not disappoint. He turned the class over to Carlyle, sat at an empty desk near the back until recess.

"Now I must leave you," he said when the children had gone out. "See Ezra – some of my other Paradise friends. *No-watch-es-nichuh*, Carlyle."

At noon, Peter was in the kitchen when Carlyle came in from the schoolroom.

"Where's Mr. Dingle?" Carlyle said.

"I thought he was in with you."

"Not after recess. Said he had to see Ezra – others."

"Hope he doesn't hold me up. I want to get back to Hanley early."

"He's a fool."

"That's right. What you got for lunch?"

"Chili – fruit cocktail. He taught those children how to sing 'Bringing in the Sheaves.'"

"What's wrong with that?"

"In Cree?"

Sanders gave his short, aborted laugh.

"Stony's not so nice as Cree."

"Well, it isn't."

"More guttural, he said, and learning all the verses of 'Bringing in the Sheaves' in lyric Cree might soften their speech. I cannot figure out – what he was doing – for the two years he was supposed to be operating that school."

"Poor G. Bob Dingle," Sanders said.

"Why do you keep saying that?"

"Oh, I guess I feel sorry for him. Don't you?"

"No."

"Really?"

"And you don't either," Carlyle said.

"Oh, yes, I do – can't help it. Anybody who's totally inca-pable – it must be just awful to be a person like that."

"Worse for anyone depending on him."

"I don't know – no – worse for him."

"He doesn't seem to be suffering much."

"How can you tell? How can anyone tell about another? They didn't give me a suffering yardstick to use on other people – just myself. All I can do is twin my pain with the other guy's – if I were Dingle I know it would hurt." He looked at Carlyle without saying anything, then, "You know – you're a hard man."

"Am I."

"I think so."

"The chili's at the back in that pot," Carlyle said.

"A real tough teacher."

"Perhaps you have to be – in this work – in yours."

"Nope. It isn't a professional matter – it's a life matter."

"Whatever that means."

"Just that I'm not a Puritan bastard."

"But I am."

"I suspect it."

"So they did give you a yardstick after all."

"Hey-up. We drinking breakfast coffee?"

"No. I came out and started fresh."

"I always say – a Puritan who catches crabs can't be all bad."

That Sunday, on a personal invitation from Ezra Powderface, Carlyle attended the morning church service held in the long dance tent above the agency building; it was a chance after two months to meet his children's parents again, and possibly some who had not been at the initial meeting.

Ezra opened the service with "I Have Reached the Land of Corn and Wine," then made the announcements: a meeting of the Paradise Valley Ladies' Auxiliary in the cabin of Judy Roll-in-the-mud, for the purpose, to Carlyle's surprise, of forming· a Home and School Association. Now – who's idea was that? Perhaps something that Dingle had taken a run at before he'd left for the Nokawamish Summer School of Youth Training For Christian Leadership. Not a bad idea.

Ezra was glad to see Lucy Baseball in church with her parents and not up in the bush where she might be if she had not listened to the Voice of the Lord. There was a faint snickering from a back corner of the tent. Lucy wasn't one of his students. The giggling broke out again. Ezra looked over in that direction. The irreverence was quenched.

"Next Sunday there will be Sabbath again – God willin' or not. Also baptizin' as the Reverend Dingle asked me when he was here Friday. I want all your infants brought here. I'm gonna baptize them."

After the Lord's Prayer, then another hymn, Ezra stood up with his limp leather Bible.

"The Gospel accordin' to Saint Mark – Chapter Five – verses one to an' concludin' fourteen." He opened the Bible at the place his thumb held, lowered his head.

"'And they came over onto the other side of the sea.'" He looked up. "That's the Sea Galilee." He looked down. "'Into the country of the Gadarenes. And when He was come out of the ship, immediately there met Him out of the tombs a man with an unclean spirit, who had his dwelling among the tombs; and no man could bind him, no, not with chains.'"

Again Ezra looked out over his congregation. "He was crazy and he was camped in a graveyard." Back to his text. "'Because that he had often been bound with fetters and chains, and the chains had been plucked asunder by him, and the fetters broken in pieces; neither could any man tame him. And always night and day, he was in the mountains, and in the tombs, crying and cutting himself with stones.'

"This man had entered into him the Wendigo inside him – so people was afraid of him and they knew the next thing he'd be eatin' them to feed that Wendigo inside there so they tried to picket him only he pulled it up out and away he went with the peg draggin' and he broke their picket chain too. Can't tie up the Wendigo.

"'And when he saw Jesus afar off, he ran and worshipped Him. And cried with a loud voice and said, "What have I done with Thee, Jesus, Thou Son of the Most High God. I adjure Thee by God, that Thou torment me not." For he said unto him, "Come out of the man thou unclean spirit." And He asked him, "What is thy name?" And he answered, saying, "My name is Legion; for we are many."'

"That was the Wendigo talkin', and worried too after he heard Jesus tell him to get out of there. He been pretty comfortable in that warm belly there – don't wanted to be spooked out of there. So here's what Wendigo said next out of this crazy man: 'And he besought Him much, that he would not send them away out of the country. Now there was there, nigh unto the mountains, a great herd of swine feeding. And all the devils' – great bunch of Wendigos this man had inside him there – 'and all the devils besought Him, saying, "Send us into the swine, that we may enter into them."'

"Well, Jesus did that.

"'And the unclean spirits went out, and entered into the swine; and the herd ran violently down a steep place (they were about two thousand) and were choked in the sea.'

"Two thousand – maybe all the Jerusalem Wendigos when Jesus come ridin' by. Jesus knew it. Jesus He climbed down and them two thousand Wendigos He said, 'Up outa there – get outa that! I got My apostles with Me today an' we're herdin' Wendigos outa this man's soul. HAH-RAH-HOOGH-YOU! Apostle drags an' apostle swings an' Me for the lead – WHAH-HAAAAAH-HOO-NOW! We got our long lasso ropes with knots in their ends – out you get – move fast now, for We don't mind devil shrink an' this man's got the cross an' crown – not the fork on his flank! HAH-AAAW – HAH-AAAW – HAH-HIPEEEEEEE!'

"Out they come, leatherin' both sides an' belly to the ground an' their tails was high – cow devils an' calf devils – bull Wendigos an' steer Wendigos with their eyes blazin' an' their noses breathin' white fire like lightnin' round the mountain top! Some of them started back inside that crazy man, but Mark an' Luke an' Matthew was there on their cuttin' horses, lassos flyin', heelin' them calf devils by both feet. And into the swine on the full run, steers an' bulls an' cows – two- an' three-year-olds – some of them crowdin' four – five – into the same pig at the same time then gettin' shoved out an' each findin' a pig of his own for himself!

"Then – like the Bible says – that herd pigs stampeded – 'way they went in a cloud dust through buck brush an' jack-pine – down the draws and over the side hills with Jesus an' His apostles hard after them till they come to this cut bank at the edge the Sea Galilee. Hundred-foot drop right down into that sea. Over sent the lead pig and into the water below – CHUH-MUCK! And after him come the next one – CHUH-MUCK!"

Carlyle felt a thrill of appreciation course through him.

"CHUH-MUCK!"

How right! What a satisfying sound of completion – for demented Gadarene swine – for a rock – for undercut earth with grass, bush, roots and all reluctantly leaving the parent bank to drop with a gulp into the river below!

"CHUH-MUCK – CHUH-MUCK – CHUH-MUCK!"

My God, he wasn't going to do the whole two thousand of them!

"CHUH-MUCK – pause – CHUH-MUCK – pause – CHUH-MUCK!"

Carlyle began to count. Ezra stayed with it for fifty chuh-mucking pigs, then called for the next hymn.

When it was done, members of the congregation stood up one by one to speak in Stony; one woman seemed quite moved, starting very faintly at first, with her hand cupped before her mouth, her voice growing stronger and stronger and thinning to a high keen. It was during her testimonial of faith or hope or despair that the snickering exploded again. Ezra raised a hand to silence the woman, then pointed towards the back of the tent.

"There is the devil corner," he announced. Heads turned to the back. "Every church got one of these devil corners. So there it is and there's his young people in it. Look upon them – the scoffers – the unbelievers – the hypo-pricks!"

The startled faces of some young boys in the back lowered. Ezra nodded. "Go on now, Judy," he said gently. "Finish it up and then we'll have 'Though Your Sins Be as Scarlet' and that will be all for this service."

TWELVE

THOUGH HE HAD TOLD HIMSELF HE WOULD GET USED TO IT, the smell of the schoolroom still bothered him – more than he was willing to admit. He had refused Dingle's suggestion that he keep Lysol in boiling water on the school stove, and actually – though it sometimes came to him in a wave when the children were restless – the smell wasn't all that bad when the doors and windows were open. But with winter and the stove going all day, moccasins wet with melting snow, the raw smell was no longer a minor irritation like a hair in the mouth. It upset – it smothered – it harried him even in his own living quarters.

Early in December he began to keep a kettle on the pot-bellied stove, brought it to a full boil before they'd taken their seats at nine – tipped in a tablespoon of carbolic. The forthright bitterness very nearly masked the smell. He renewed the anti-septic each recess, after he'd thrown open the windows and the door to winter air, again at noon and after four. He told the children it would kill the germs, which didn't seem to be news to them. The Reverend G. Bob Dingle must have told them the same thing.

Almost every morning now he kicked his way through drifting snow to the wood-shed, had to shovel the school door clear.

All the way out to Pile of Rocks the Valley road was blown in, and there were no more visits from Sheridan or Fyfe or Dingle; for the whole second week of December the phone was out, but before it had failed, Peter had got word to him that he wouldn't be down again until after Christmas – unless there was an emergency. "And they have an inexhaustible supply of that." Before his car had drifted in, Carlyle had checked the anti-freeze – effective to fifty below – carried the battery across the suspension bridge and into the agency house.

Strangely – for he had always hated the restrictive tyranny of winter – his isolation did not bother him at all. He read more than he had since his university years; he corrected exercises, made up lesson plans; radio reception was successful off and on, so that he got as much CSFA news as he cared to have. Often, before bed, he simply sat for hours, the mantle lamp hissing, the winter wind throating in the chimney, the stove-pipe cherry. And there were callers – to use the telephone – to get something from the dispensary – just to visit.

He remembered and ignored Sheridan's warning not to let them come to the house often and unnecessarily. Esau Rider called most regularly, always wearing his blue councillor's coat, double-breasted, with silver buttons worn to thin lozenges by years of polishing. At first there had been a hard reason for visits: a cup of bacon fat, salt, a little sugar, an armful of wood. They did creep up on you. Esau accepted fine-cut tobacco for his pipe with its stone bowl pale green. He stayed to smoke it, his socketed eyes staring straight ahead; with his skull face it was a little like playing host to laconic death. The red royalty of his dignity was flawed slightly with self-pity.

"The poor old man. All alone you see. Summer now not so bad. Winter – aaaw – all alone you see – deep snow. Poor old man." He slapped his knee. "This knee."

He did limp all right. Arthritis – an old injury?

"Not the meat."

"Accident, Esau?"

"Long time."

"Horse?"

"Walkin' Sticks. The bone you see. By the Walkin' Sticks."

"You mean – you want crutches?"

"Wheesh – right there." He slapped the knee again. "Poor old man. White man was holdin' calf for brandin' – by that Walkin' Sticks – oh, poor old man – let go calf – that's no good. Broke."

"Calf broke your leg?"

"Hey-up. Calf white man let go."

Fyfe had told him that Esau had once been a fine cow man; indeed he had lived off the reserve for many years, working for ranchers as far south as Waterton Lakes. And looking at the small, sinewy hand that held the pipe bowl, Carlyle remembered Sanders telling him that Esau – if he hadn't been Stony – might have been a surgeon, that he was able to do an intra-uterine dissection of an unborn calf to save a heifer mother. Often had.

"He can't chop. Poor old man you see. Judea's boy, he say yes. I tell him good to help old man. He doesn't do this at all you see. He promise me. Well?"

The word hung on the air between them. "Do you need some more wood, Esau?"

"Can't chop the knee. The boy promise. He doesn't do this you see. Sticks cook the pork steak."

He loaded his arms for him. After that Esau did not ask for wood again, yet Carlyle saw no pile grow near the old man's cabin. Then one morning he noticed Esau at the agency woodpile, helping himself – with some regularity, Carlyle supposed. Poor old man.

"How old are you, Esau?" he asked one evening.

"Aaaaw – don't know yet."

"Not so old as Jonas One-Spot."

"That time – treaty time – agent saw me. He's dead. He saw me. He say – very little then. Few steps – fall down."

1878. Carlyle did some mental arithmetic. "Then you're about seventy – seventy-two at the most."

"Hey-uh." Esau could not be less interested in the number of years he was through with.

"Jonas is almost ninety – Ezra told me. He's blind but he gets all over – saws his own wood – hauls his own water."

Esau said nothing, drew on his pipe, exhaled. "White man didn't break it – Jonas's knee."

"I guess not," Carlyle said.

Esau sniffed deeply. "Strong."

"What?"

"Smell strong."

"Oh – that's for the germs, Esau – it kills the germs – ones in the air."

"Hey-uh. White people smell too."

"Do we."

"Hey-uh."

"How do you mean, Esau?"

"To us people, you see."

"We smell to you."

"Cow."

"I don't . . ."

"Quite strong."

"Oh – milky. You mean we smell milky to you?"

Esau lifted his eyes to the damper on the stove-pipe, stared for several deliberate seconds. "Hey-uh." It meant no. Then he said "*no-watch-es-nichuh*." Which was rather charitable of him,

Carlyle thought contritely, after the dig about Jonas's independence. "You please me very much."

He discontinued the carbolic.

The third week in December a wind was born gently during the night, but by morning it had grown to a washing roar; the eaves of the agency building were dripping, the snow shrinking under the mild breath of the season's first chinook. Like sorcerers' green arms, spruce and pine branches made passes over the melting magic; white voodoos at each cabin were changed back into wood-piles; Carlyle's car, the Valley road were made to appear again. The day before Christmas Ezra Powderface called to invite him to services in the dance tent. Christmas eve it began to snow again. Christmas morning he had just finished breakfast when Susan and Jonas Rider, with Victoria, were at his door. Susan carried a flour sack, from which she took a white doe-skin shirt with yellow and orange butterflies fluttering over the shoulder yoke, purple shooting stars formal on breast pockets and cuffs. She handed it to him.

"Merry Christmas, Mr. Sinclair."

He was utterly unprepared for the gift – either emotionally or with one of his own for them.

Susan had turned to Victoria. "Okay – give it him now."

Victoria brought her hands from behind her, held out slipper moccasins to him.

"She made them," Jonas said.

He did the best he could – thanked them – invited them to have coffee. Before they had left, Magdalene and Peter Powderface came with gauntlet gloves beaded in orange and blue and white. By ten o'clock the kitchen was filled with visitors, and he had more skins than Cro-Magnon man.

Archie Nicotine drove up in a bob-sleigh pulled by a woolly bay team, his Christmas present to Carlyle, a lynx hide.

"Put it down beside the bed," he said. "With the bare foot in the mornin' it's nice to step on it. A merry white Christmas to you, Sinclair."

All climbed aboard Archie's bob-sleigh, jerking with abortive starts as the half-wild team lunged and reared back in their harness. Passengers sat buttock by buttock on the sideboards, leaning in towards the centre of the straw-littered floor of the sleigh box, Carlyle opposite Old Esau with his death's head festive under a red toque pulled down over his ears. Shaking with palsy, Jonas One-Spot, his clouded eyes fixed, a wild smile showing toothless gums, perched on the centre of the tail-gate.

With a shout the team hardly needed, Archie slapped the reins. They took off with a magnificent lurch. Jonas went back into a gulping somersault that landed him seated deep in the snow. The others shouted to Archie, who must have thought they were cheering him on, because he swung the lines in a wide looping arc, brought them down across the rumps of the terrified horses. With panic energy they convulsed into a clumsy gallop. Carlyle saw Jonas get up, daylight showing between the spraddled old legs, half bent. Archie looked back, leaned against the reins, and in only a quarter of a mile had the team pulled down. When Jonas had come up to them, outstretched hands took him under the arm-pits, lifted the age-light body straight up and into the sleigh box.

They were away again, runners hissing, the galumphing team steaming, bells hanging them with a second, loose harness of sound. Now to one side – now to the other – the sleigh box canted, almost tipped as they came up onto the first bench, achieved balance again, if not chariot speed, past cabin after cabin exclaiming blue smoke through still air. Here a woman, her skirt like Stuart blood against the snow, shaded her eyes and watched them go. Here a door burst open, spilled children out like puppies from a basket. There a man looked up from his buck-saw, stilled and angled in a half-cut log bridging the saw-horse crosses. First the rump-bumping team, then the sleigh, pitched down a bank and over frozen Beulah, then up and out of her and into utter illumination, to run along tinsel strands of barbed wire sparkling from post to tilting post toadstooled with snow.

Archie sawed the team to a halt.

"We have arrived."

Inside the giant dance tent ambient with canvas-filtered light, redolent with pine and spruce and fir boughs, smouldering with wet buckskin, Carlyle was led by Ezra Powderface to the car seat of honour between the Christmas tree and a crèche woven from red willow. He realized he was sweating, then saw heat waves rising from the inverted wash-tub in front of him, a stove-pipe lifting to the smoke hole above. There was another at the other end of the tent.

Joseph Ear and Norville Shot-close staggered past, each with a box of apples, then Gatine Lefthand with his face healed up for Christmas, carrying a clinking case of pop. There were baking-powder tins set out along the tent walls and, as well, a dozen tins of fine-cut.

"Quit that!" Ezra stopped Joseph Ear in the act of prying open the apple box. "All that stuff's for after church."

The short service opened with "Silent Night" in Stony; Ezra made the major announcement first: that there was five hundred pounds of department-confiscated elk to be handed out, then that the fine-cut, the pop, Christmas candy, apples and oranges were the gift of Mr. Fyfe to them; the toys for the children had come again from the Shelby United Church Couples Club. Ezra stayed pretty well with Matthew and Mark for the story of the nativity, except for more precise detail: the three wise men were mounted on stud camels seventeen hands high; when they fled the cruel Bethlehem Wizard, Mary carried Jesus in a moss-packed *yo-kay-bo*; Joseph with his snow-shoes broke trail for them.

The final hymn done, Ezra stepped over to Carlyle.

"Mr. Sinclair – I think they would like you to say something to them. I will interpret it for you."

Carlyle stood. What could he say to them? He looked out over their dark faces in the illuminated tent, Jonas smiling, Esau in his red toque, all of them looking up to him. He saw Magdalene Powderface tip her face back and away from her baby's hand like a moth at her mouth and cheek. He felt his throat stiff, and he knew that if he spoke, his voice would betray him. He waited for the emotion to subside.

"I came to live with you last summer . . ."

"That's plenty at a time," Ezra said, then translated it into Stony for him.

". . . for myself."

"Because I lost my wife."

"And I lost my baby daughter."

"Before she could be born."

"You have helped me."

"I will try to help you."

"I have no daughter."

"I have no son."

"I will do all I can."

"For your daughters and your sons."

"That's all."

"Merry Christmas."

He sat down on the car seat in a storm of clapping.

That night, just as he dropped off to sleep, he wished that he had thought of saying *no-watch-es-nichuh* to them. Through the open bedroom window came the sound of the dance drum, just a soft nudging at the edge of the Christmas night.

THIRTEEN

It was hard to understand why the water system had been giving him trouble. There was a big spring run-off, so that the concrete reservoir up on the second bench, fed by the chill weep of Beulah springs, must be slopping full. Two-inch pipe dropped almost two hundred feet to the agency building, a beautifully efficient gravity system – at least until early in June. He hadn't taken the first faltering too seriously, and indeed it had recovered quickly. The water system bore him no ill will – not like the telephone line, which didn't give a good goddam whether it served him well or not. Ever since he'd come to Paradise, it had hummed and whined and annoyed with pelleting static – viciously and deliberately elliptical. For two weeks – off and on – something bothered the water line. It gave up on a Saturday morning.

When he twisted the tap to fill his dish-pan, the flow came full enough, but without force. He turned the tap completely on; the water contracted to a clear string. It piddled, then dripped reluctant drops. Finally – nothing. Damn it – he'd have to check out the line – could be anything – a frost burst – corroded elbow – anywhere between the reservoir and the house. If only he'd attended to it when it had first begun to act up – before the damage got . . .

From far off there came a travelling rapping, several nearer knocks, a hard hiccup, a cough, and then one gassy, wet explosion worthy of a sperm whale surfacing. In a fierce rush the water hit the bottom of the dish-pan; the rebound fountain had soaked him before the tap could tame it. He should have known the water system wouldn't let him down. Pressure must have finally overcome the line block.

The water in the white dish-pan was tea-coloured; shredded debris floated there; one true lump was bobbing. He captured it, lifted it out. It couldn't be; it simply could not be! It might have made it down the length of the two-inch pipe, but not through the tap! He stared at it in his palm – not the black jelly-bean of rabbit or elk or deer or mountain goat or sheep, but one small and perfect clove of horse manure! Shee-yit!

Up on the second bench, a tent was pitched near the water reservoir; the lid planks were scattered over the ground. A wall-eyed pinto was picketed near by, the chain just long enough so that, as he grazed, his rear could have passed the reservoir at precisely the right moment. God damn it! God damn them! Then he saw a boy come out of the tent flap. Gatine Lefthand; in the entire band the one man too lazy to haul his water from Beulah or the Spray – Harold Lefthand! Pitched his spring camp right next to the water supply.

He saw Harold then – coming round the tent, a bucket in one hand. Carlyle waited for him, but Harold saw him, angled off to the left towards Beulah, as though that had been his original intention.

"Just a minute!"

Harold kept on going.

"I said – hold up!"

Harold stopped. Carlyle went over to him.

"What the hell do you think you're doing!"

Harold set the bucket down on the ground, "Water my jingle horse."

"Who gave you permission to take the top off that water reservoir – use it?"

Harold had taken a tobacco package and papers out of this shirt pocket.

"That is the agency water supply!"

Harold tapped fine-cut into the creased paper. He replaced the package in his shirt pocket.

"You've contaminated it!"

With careful thumbs Harold rolled the cigarette away from himself.

"With horse shit – God damn it!"

Harold licked it.

"Not just my water – all the children drink it too!"

"You got a match?"

"I said – you've fouled up the drinking water."

"I said – you got a match?"

"And I say – get your goddam tent down – clear out of here! After – you get that goddam lid back on that goddam reservoir – ever again you foul up my water . . ."

"Ours."

"Huh!"

"Indian water."

"The hell it is!"

"Hey-uh – I guess I did have a match."

Carlyle heard a movement behind himself. He turned. Archie Nicotine. He turned back to Harold. "Lefthand – get cracking!"

"Trouble – Sinclair?"

"Yes – mine! Unless Lefthand gets his camp out of here – replaces that lid on that reservoir – it's his!"

"Maybe I could help. . . ."

"I told you – it's my affair, Archie."

"This reserve is our reserve," Harold said. "I belong to this band on this reserve. Anywhere I want on our reserve – I camp."

"Lefthand – you are making two very bad mistakes . . ."

"He's right, Sinclair," Archie said.

". . . first one when you took the lid off that reservoir and began helping yourself to agency water . . ."

"All Indian," Harold said. "Buildin's too."

". . . second one is now! And you're going to unmake those mistakes!"

"That school is Indian too," Harold said.

"Right now!"

"Hey-uh." It meant "no."

"You refuse!"

"Hey-uh." It meant "yes."

"Maybe there could be some kind of way to settle . . ."

"I said this is between Lefthand and me!"

"I just thought . . ."

"He don't order me," Harold said. "He's just teacher."

"Maybe you better do what he says, Harold."

"He's just teacher," Harold said.

"You get your water from the river like all the others! Don't you draw one more drop from . . ."

"He's right too, Harold."

"I'm still usin' it."

"No."

"You're not the agent."

"Right, I am not! But I am the man who is about to kick the living . . ."

"That wouldn't be right, Sinclair."

"Archie – his horse fouled my water!"

"I'm usin' it," Harold said.

"That isn't right, Harold. Everybody can't camp here close by the water. . . ."

"Nobody's camping by the . . ."

"I'm camped," Harold said.

"Maybe we take it up with the duly elected band council and they can bring down their decision – democratic," Archie said.

"He's moving right now!" Carlyle said.

"Fuck the band council," Harold said.

"Hey-uh." Archie's eyes glittered. "Now I am waitin' to hear you say further, Harold."

"Get out!" Carlyle said. "Right now!"

"Anybody else, Harold," Archie said. "I'm here, you understand."

"Fuck Sinclair too."

"Hold on, Sinclair!" Archie had grabbed his arm. "These people don't use the fist!"

"I do!"

But Archie had got between them. "You got to be civilized and that's the whole . . ." A sudden convulsive movement threw Archie backwards and up against Carlyle's chest. Archie's pointed riding boot took Harold Lefthand precisely in the crotch.

Harold clutched at himself. He staggered a few steps. He dropped to the ground. He drew up both knees.

"Now it may take a while before you will be able to do that to the band council."

Harold's breath hissed as he drew it in again and again through his teeth.

"Or Sinclair."

Carlyle looked down at Harold's face, muddy with agony. "My God, Archie!"

"He was right you understand."

"You shouldn't have . . ."

"I didn't like to interfere."

Harold whimpered.

"This here water comes out of Beulah springs," Archie said, "and no fed'ral gover'ment put them there."

"He's got to have medical attention!"

Harold's whimpers were short ones – almost interrogative.

"He has to get to hospital!"

"Hey-uh," Archie said. "You want the hospital, Harold?"

"Aaaaaaaw!" Harold said. Some colour had returned to his face.

Archie spoke in Stony – evidently a question. Harold answered in Stony – the first words he'd spoken since receiving the kick in the testicles.

"He says he refuses treatment," Archie explained. "Also he repeated what he said about the band council and about you, but he don't seem to mean it so much this time."

"Maybe he should be helped. . . ."

"This whole reserve is in the band's name," Archie said. "All the buildin's belong to us Indians. That wasn't right – you quarrellin' with him. . . ."

"Just a minute – that filth and contamination . . ."

"Ai-ai!" Harold had made it to his feet but he was having difficulty in straightening up. Still holding himself he began to walk towards his tent. Carefully.

It was then that Carlyle saw the knife in Archie's hand.

"My God, Archie – were you going to stab . . ."

"His."

"His!"

"Hey-uh. He pulled it."

"I didn't know – I didn't see – oh, Archie!" He suddenly realized he felt sick – quite weak. If it hadn't been for Nicotine!

"You don't have to worry about the water no more, Sinclair. Evened up now."

His legs and arms were trembling, but now he was feeling a warm rush of gratitude. "Oh, Archie!" How could he ever thank him enough! He remembered then his conversation with Dingle in the classroom last fall. "*No-watch-es-nichuh.*"

Archie's eyes glittered. There was a sudden and involuntary thrust of the knife. "What you say that for?"

"Thank you – you please me very much."

"*Ish-ny-ish.*"

"What?"

"You got the wrong one. *Ish-ny-ish.*"

"But – Reverend Dingle . . ."

The opaque black eyes softened with corner wrinkles. Archie grinned.

"He got it wrong too."

"*No-watch-es-nichuh?* What does it mean?"

"I guess somebody give him the wrong one."

"But – then what's *no-watch-es* . . ."

"Bull shit."

"Now wait – I want to – I asked you a civil . . ."

"That's what it means – bull shit."

He had a pretty good notion who had given G. Bob Dingle the wrong expression.

The incident wasn't easily forgotten; his mind returned to it again and again in the next few days. Each time he felt a little more helpless. What could he expect from Harold Lefthand now? When? It was like having your back unprotected and knowing that a blow might come at any moment. He wouldn't even know when it happened – a rifle crack as he was walking across the suspension bridge to his car – on his way to the woodpile – maybe even when he was sitting in the kitchen by a window. A week later Archie referred to the matter.

"All even now, Sinclair."

"What?"

"Harold Lefthand. Your water made it even for him – grabbin' his kid last year."

"But what about kicking him?"

"That wasn't you. Me."

"Oh."

"With you he made it even."

"When he took the top off – his horse . . ."

"Not the horse – him. How long that water wasn't workin' good?"

"Several days – couple of weeks."

"Hey-uh."

"Just a minute – do you mean he deliberately . . ."

"You grabbed Gatine – Harold made the petition, but it didn't work. Spring – he camped up there. . . ."

"Are you telling me – it wasn't accidental?"

"Whenever you turned on that tap he evened it up with you a little bit more."

"Deliberately!"

"Hey-up."

"But – what about you? If you kicked him – then you've got to be careful."

"I don't. We're even too. You and Harold even. Everybody evened up, and that's the whole situation."

He suspected he had just been given an important insight. Harold Lefthand did not care at all whether or not Carlyle knew that the horse manure had been deliberately flipped into the water supply. It was enough that there was an evening-up, that Harold had done it, that Harold knew it. Nor did it matter to Archie Nicotine or to anyone else in the Stony community whether the Reverend G. Bob Dingle ever found out that for ten years or more he had thought he had been saying "you please me very much" when in fact he had gone his sweet and joyous rounds saying "bull shit." What impersonal justice! He had no intention of saying anything about it to Dingle – of hurting him – or of spoiling the objectivity of that justice, though he might mention it to Sanders – who, for God's sakes, probably already knew.

But he was unable to keep from asking Archie, "What did you have to even up with Harold Lefthand?"

"It was personal, Sinclair – kickin' him in his blueberries was the right way to do it."

By July there were no more night frosts; Spray and Beulah cleared and subsided; Sanders came down almost weekly, and they coursed the stream-banks together, the back cast of their lines whispering high behind them. Taut line communication with fighting rainbow seemed enough for them; they seldom spoke to each other, each in his own solitude throughout the smooth mornings and afternoons. They were not the only anglers along the Spray, for an osprey often flew over them in high reconnaissance. Peter said it had fished this stretch as long as he had, that if it was successful it always came back with its catch to the same dead fir spar out over the Spray.

It was remarkable how the metronomic regularity of the fly rod back and forth, the rolling out of line and leader to drop the fly, the hours of reading the water surface, vacuumed the mind clean of the finest dust of thought. And when he took attention from the water, rocks and trees and opposite bank were no longer fixed. They drifted sideways, and he himself was part of the magic land flow – grassinclair – cloudsinclair – sinclairrock. . . .

"He's got one!"

Sanders, kneeling by his creel, was looking up the river. The fish was still flipping in the osprey's claws as it came to rest with wings upstretched, on the fir branch across the river from them.

It shifted uneasily; yawned its wings, talons clutching branch and fish as well. It began to eat.

They did not fish until it had finished, and when it had, it seemed to gather itself together, the body hunching and contracting.

"Magnificent!" Sanders exclaimed.

The stringing whitewash slobbered – floated down to join the river flow.

FOURTEEN

When he looked back over it, he realized that he had spent his first year of teaching in Paradise without lifting his attention from the schoolroom – that his confrontation with Harold Lefthand up on the second bench had been the beginning of a change in perspective for him. Several times between the suspension bridge and agency he had passed a small skeleton; the pelvis had been furry at first, then quite smooth, as maggots and other insect undertakers practised their crawling trade.

"The bulls," Archie Nicotine said when Carlyle mentioned the calf skeleton to him. "Last year they got in with the cows – too early. Lot of February calves out of it – all those calves didn't make it."

He was no cattle man, but it was evident to him that the agency stock was inferior to that on neighbouring ranches. There were too many peak-rumped cows, line-backed steers; good breeding didn't produce ox-like beasts, all bone. Also – any fields he'd been over had been grazed right down. He mentioned it to Sheridan on one of his visits.

"Horses. They've all got at least a dozen – so – naturally – overgrazed."

"Why?"

"Hmh?"

"I wondered why they have . . ."

"Lot of things a person wonders about in Indian work. Indians love horses."

"I know – but – I understand a horse eats as much as a cow and a half – the horses don't bring them . . ."

"Economics hasn't a thing to do with the number of horses an Indian keeps. Agricultural matter anyway."

"I know that."

"Then you probably know as well – from the time you've spent with them – in the school – that an Indian does as he damn pleases."

"I understand – Moon was telling me . . ."

"Moon is not with Indian Affairs."

"But he is a pretty fine rancher."

"Perhaps."

"He says – summer fallowing – sowing grass – would double the hay and feed."

"I'm sure it would."

"Then why . . ."

"No problem at all – on his own lease."

"I don't see what difference there is between the Turkey Track and . . ."

"Perhaps it's because you haven't spent thirty-five years working with Indians. Who makes them do it? It's tough enough to get them to sow the oats they do. Seen any gardens?"

"No."

"Have you taken a pig or chicken census?"

"No, I haven't."

"Up at Hanley the odd one has planted potatoes – beets – turnips – in cut and covered sod. I have yet to see one of them out there with a hoe. All they get is grass – weeds."

"But – milk cows – their children . . ."

"My God, even Moon doesn't keep milk cows. None of these ranchers – or pigs or chickens for that matter. Yet you expect an Indian – a cow has to be milked daily. How can they look after a cow when they move off the reserve to fence – hay – stook. . . ."

"If it were – if the reserve were run – if it supported them, they wouldn't have to move off to work for . . ."

"Oh, yes, they would. What happens to the cow that has to be milked every day – chickens to be fed – eggs gathered – gardens hoed – when fair and rodeo time rolls around? These people have to move around."

"You make it sound pretty hopeless."

"I don't make it that way – they do! Without any help at all from me! It's taken me thirty-five years to learn that – to teach me what can be done with them and what can't be done with them!"

"That Sanders' attitude?"

"I don't know."

"Fyfe's?"

"I speak only for myself!" He looked at Carlyle. "But I do it from experience – thirty-five years of it – as an agent!"

It had been a rebuking reminder – no doubt about that. "As an agent!" Sheridan was telling him that he was in charge of Hanley and of Paradise Valley. The angry message was not one bit different from that of Harold Lefthand by the water-supply reservoir. "He's not agent. He's just teacher." And the teacher had not been minding his own business. Why did the man have such ready resentment? If Sheridan had shown some interest in the school – and he had not in the whole year – it wouldn't bother him!

A week later when he came down, Sanders suggested they give the beaver dam a try – an unusual preference, the pond rather bland after the fast, white anguish of the Spray. It meant

going to finer leader, more exact flies, but it wasn't more chal-
lenging really, for the trout were all smaller and mostly brook,
and therefore innocent. They plucked pretty consistently at a
tiny, dubbed nymph – muskrat belly fur – with a red tag.

Sanders gave up early, came over by Carlyle. "You still keep
that elbow high, don't you?"

He saw that Sanders had taken down his rod. "Got your
limit already?"

"Nope." Sanders sat down.

A greenhead planed over them, splashed down to ride the
water under the opposite bank.

"He's all right," Sanders said. "You shot gun?"

"No. Just fish. That's what I'm trying to do now."

"Uh-huh. Idea isn't to flail the water – if you kept your
elbow down . . ."

"I manage all right."

"That's nice. I hear you had an exchange with Arthur last
week."

"You heard from him?"

"Ah – yes."

"What about him?"

"Arthur – oh – smokes too much – I keep telling him all
about emphysema."

"He got a little hot." Carlyle laid his rod up against a willow
bush. "When I asked him a few questions – he didn't seem to
think they were school matters."

"Were they?"

"I thought they were good questions – not too far out of
line." He sat down beside Sanders. "In a way they concern my
children. I had a right to ask them."

"What questions?"

"Didn't he tell you? Why the grass was overgrazed – why the
calves came early last year – most of them perished – how come

so many peaked-assed cows – what was wrong with sowing grass. He got angry."

"Good going."

"Upset enough to mention it to you."

"Well – yes."

"Maybe I have a lot to learn about Indians – maybe I'm not a cow man. . . ."

"Maybe you're tactless."

"Maybe."

"Thirty-five years . . ."

"He told me that – several times."

"Arthur's been a capable man."

"I didn't say he wasn't."

"That isn't important – he felt you did. He came to Hanley twenty years ago – has a good record with the department – not brilliant – but good. Hanley Wolverines."

"What?"

"Baseball team. Eastern slopes champions three years in a row – those kids really knew baseball – not just batting and pitching and catching – all the terms – kill the umpire – he's got a glass arm."

"What's that got to do with . . ."

"Arthur has spent thirty-five years fighting his way through red tape – paper – department and Indian apathy. He has suffered inattention – been a minor cog in the civil-service machine – too long unnoticed – spit in the wind. Now – Arthur is very tired. He retires next year."

"With his glass arm."

"How would you like it? After thirty-five years it doesn't matter whether you lived or died – or retired – all comes to nothing. You could have been added – subtracted – divided – multiplied, and the result would have been exactly the same – except for one thing – those champion Hanley Wolverines. Arthur bought them their first bats, balls, gloves – catcher's mitt – himself – on a department salary. He went out the way they went out with their begging letters – he went to the town business men and begged uniforms for them."

"So – I shouldn't have asked questions."

"Of course you should have. I'm only explaining why – when you asked them – you ran into hostility. He has the right to it. And when you've got your glass arm – and they throw that banquet for you and give you your gold watch – you'll have the right to it too – thirty-five years from now."

"That's what I like about you people – you're so encouraging."

"Antidote to Dingle." The mallard drake took off in slapping flight. "He hasn't."

"What?"

"Glass wing. Out the Valley road – you must have noticed the sloughs this year. It's been a dry summer, you know."

"I've noticed that."

"Low – shrunken – a lot of them have disappeared entirely. Migratory-bird season opens next week."

"I don't hunt."

"They've issued warning to hunters – be careful."

"About what?"

"Watch for listless ducks. Don't pick them up. Make sure you get the one you dropped."

"Why?"

"Warm water – exposed and rotting vegetation – botulism – they get weaker and weaker till they can't take off any more. And that's just what you've joined, teacher – the reserve-system slough – tepid with paternal help – the more you do for them the more you sap their strength. Got any helpful questions about that?"

"I don't know."

"Neither do I – neither did Arthur. But he gets a gold watch for trying. They'll give me a gold sputum cup, of course."

"Get them off the slough."

Sanders gave his short cough-laugh. "Good boy, Carlyle, go up to the front – with young Esau."

"Old Esau."

"Nope. Not the old one. That's the one Alf's Taxi calls for every month – when the old-age pension cheques come. He can't fly any more. He could once, you know. When he felt the slough piss warm under him, he took off of there, but he came back. You know why?"

"No."

"So the others could fly off too – follow him into Storm and Misty country – to the old happy days again. They couldn't. Esau gave up – Alf's taxi – ten dollars return to Shelby every month – the Bon Ton Store – back to Paradise with a taxi full of pork steaks – raisin bread – orange crush – enough to last five days, then starve till the next cheque. Poor old man, you see. Gave up. We all give up, you see. Not just Indians – all of us. There's a giving-up time for everybody – when everything squeezes right down to impossibility – no way out of it – stop doing – quit!"

"What if they'd followed him?"

"Would have been a very nice flight."

"Return."

"I don't know – maybe. There's a Cree – Chief Smallboy of the Ermineskin band – agitating. The department's even considering it as a serious possibility for them."

"It's no solution."

"All I know is – I need a green reprieve." He indicated the pond. "This is it. Almost as good as liquor. When were you last into the city?"

"Month ago."

"Noisy, eh?"

"Yes."

"Hell of a lot noisier now than it was a year ago – before you joined us?"

"I guess so."

"I'll tell you something – every year it's going to get noisier for you – and it is not life noise – wind or water or leaf or bird or man – machine noise – it is one crowded, noisy, concrete and glass and plastic and asphalt slough! Whenever I get too sorry for these people, I just need one trip in there to straighten me out. These Stonys are aliens, but what are they alienated from, huh? From the rest – from the real aliens – that concrete and asphalt doesn't sprout and turn green in spring for them – those high-rises don't bud and leaf and turn and drop – that is one rigid, frantic, son-of-a-bitching slough!"

"All right, Peter, but I'm not joining you and Old Esau. It'd be a great trick if you could do it. I don't think anybody can – just the osprey – rainbow – the fungus on Old Esau's rock. Our problem is – we're human and we know it. God damn her anyhow."

"Who?"

"Eve."

"Eve who?"

"Garden of Eden Eve."

"Oh – her."

"That wasn't any MacIntosh Red she picked, you know."

"I guess not."

"Early Winter Knowledge. Try one, Eve, that old serpent said to her. I can recommend it – a hard, tart, good-keeping apple. So she picked one and she tried it and she gave Adam a bite or two and right then they clearly knew – they weren't any osprey or rainbow or fungus after all – they were humans – the only living thing that could look at itself, and there was no way they could get away from it – sure blew the ass off the Garden of Eden, didn't it? God, how I'd like to hear Old Ezra do Adam and Eve."

Sanders' pale eyes looked at him for a moment. "You do all right yourself, Rev-rund." There was mild surprise in his voice.

He had surprised himself too. Five years now since Grace had died.

One August noon there came a tapping at his door. Esau Rider.

"Sinclair."

"What is it, Esau?"

"Show you."

"Come on in."

"You. Show you."

He walked with Esau to his cabin, followed him inside.

Esau pointed.

He didn't have to; it hung from the cabin ridge, in front of the stove, a spongy, orange-red mass, dripping slowly. Carlyle felt his stomach rise.

"Lungs!"

"Esau!"

The smell was strong; the flies were busy.

"Her Majesty, the Queen, he give me supper, you see."

"All right, Esau."

"He don't tell Queen I was head councillor you see."

"Who gave you . . ."

"Her Majesty don't know my father signed treaty with His Great Gramma. Poor old man you see. Maybe – another time – Queen haul guts!"

From his own meat supply he gave the old man a roast, bacon, some sausage links.

"Pork steak," Esau said.

"No, Esau."

"Raisin bread."

"Sorry. I'll get you some next time I'm in Shelby."

"*Ish-ny-ish*," Esau said.

That evening Carlyle asked Ezra who distributed the band rations. It seemed that Prince Dixon and Harry Wildman handled it for Sheridan, doling out from the storage buildings up by the barns and corral. He supposed he'd passed them a hundred times in his year at Paradise.

The next morning after breakfast he went up. He saw that the corral was down in several places, gateless, and, where it should have joined the barn, gaping for almost fifty feet. Rails were missing. He looked at the barn with new eyes, studding bared where boards were gone – not unrepaired age – the sides had been stripped.

Inside, he did not have to wait for his eyes to become accus-tomed to barn dusk. He walked over accumulated manure, saw team harness half swallowed, halters trampled in, one brass ball all that was showing of hames buried. Outside again, as he went through high grass towards the ration shed, he tripped on barbed wire tangled there, followed it for a hundred yards without a single post. There was no lock on the supply-shed door, not a shard in a window. Here too the studding skeleton showed where boards had been ripped off. Inside, a mouse trickled over the sagging floor, along the wall to his left, then out of sight behind a burst flour sack. Fyfe cookies were scattered all over. Salt cartons had uneven tide lines along their sides. There were hams and bacons hanging – starred blue with mould. He took out his jack-knife, opened the top of a burlap sack – black and mushy – rotten in his hand. He doubted there was an edible potato in the lot. Frost.

He visited the ice-house in the side of the hill next. There was no meat hung in the warm darkness rich with the smell of decay. He could not remember anyone's cutting ice during the past winter. Outside once more, he saw a man at the corner of the supply building – Harry Wildman. He asked him about the lungs given Old Esau yesterday.

"All we have left for him," Harry said. "Prince hauled them down for him."

Sunday afternoon, he spoke to Archie Nicotine.

"What's happened to the barn – corral – fences?"

"Pretty bad."

"Sure as hell are."

"Been goin' on for a long time," Archie said. "These people get short firewood, you understand. Take a post here. Take a post there. Then they need some kindlin' – ship-lap splits good, you understand. Used to be a phone line from up there too – here."

"I didn't see any."

"Hey-up. You look, you can still find wire some places. Telephone poles went – camp fires always eatin'. Sheridan was down for the treaty cheques last week."

"Yes."

"I guess he said for you to look around."

"No – I went up to see where Esau got his rotten lungs."

"That was from the lump-jaw yearlin'."

"I think it's terrible!"

"Twenty-five families, one yearlin' doesn't go so far, you understand."

"Yes."

"I guess you just found out now."

"Yes."

"I guess Sheridan said for you to . . ."

"No – he didn't."

"Summer holiday – so you aren't busy teachin' the kids – you got a chance to look around this year."

"Yes."

"Maybe that wouldn't please him."

"I can't help that."

"When he was down last week – you had a fight with Sheridan."

"No – not a fight."

"Hey-uh. These people exaggerate a lot what they hear about. Sheridan quits it next year."

"I know."

And he could never again share Peter's slob compassion for Sheridan with his glass arm – or for G. Bob Dingle!

FIFTEEN

WHEN IT WAS HIS TURN, THE REVEREND G. BOB DINGLE referred in kindly and solemn strophe to Sheridan's long and faithful thirty-six years in the vineyard. He said that it had been appreciated by red and white alike, had not gone unnoticed in the teepees or in Ottawa, in the hills, in the valleys, in the mountains, up and down the flowing waters of the Spray. Mrs. Sheridan cried. The Reverend Dingle took for his text Luke, Chapter 8, verses 5 to 8.

"And I can conclude in no better way," he said, "than with these words of your own dear people to you, Arthur – *no-watch-es-nichuh.*" Mrs. Sheridan cried. Other department people spoke their pieces, and then several councillors were interpreted by Ezra Powderface. With the exception of Dingle, all mentioned the Hanley Wolverines. At the end of the speeches, Sheridan was made Chief Standing Apart, and Chief Meadowlark of the Hanley band presented him, not with a gold watch, but an elk-hide jacket, beaded gloves, slippers, and a good-luck pouch breathing Paradise Valley sweet-grass. Mrs. Sheridan cried.

Peter Sanders got very drunk; in his tuxedo jacket, up to his waist in tepid water in the bathtub in Fyfe's room, he sang the "Volga Boatman." He got himself lost in the hotel corridors, was found in a broom-closet by the third-floor chambermaid coming on duty at six the next morning. Even for a broom-closet Carlyle had thought it a little crowded in there.

Early in March, two weeks after Sheridan's retirement banquet, he fought snow-drifts out of Paradise Valley and into the city. It was a Saturday, and Fyfe had him to lunch in his Meadow Lark Park home with its great curved conservatory; it had been quite lovely under the frost-rimmed glass, benevolent with sun and humidity and orchid fragrance. He had added the conservatory, Fyfe explained, after Mrs. Fyfe's death almost fourteen years ago. Most of his mature plants had been raised from seedlings under controlled light; two years before he had started breeding his own.

Fyfe congratulated Carlyle on his three years with the department. He said that he was recommending administration of Paradise Valley be separated from that of Hanley and that Carlyle take over the duties of agent as well as those of teacher.

"I think you know Paradise needs tidying up."

"Yes."

"I have too. But – I felt it should wait until Arthur's retirement. It didn't seem fair to spoil that. In any way. Of course, officially, Arthur is not retired until July first, but I think now the banquet's over – you may – eh – consider your new duties have already started. Salary increase begins in August."

So as well as teacher: agent – judge – nurse – police – agriculturalist. He began deliberate visits to the neighbouring ranchers, talked cattle with them, asked their advice. Moon was very helpful, recommended the Indian bulls be sold for bologna, new ones bought – not necessarily bull show, registered animals – just good bulls. He suggested the Indian department pay the Indians – as he did – to cut poles to repair the reserve fences. If there was any way Carlyle could persuade them to turn more land into oats, they'd use it for their horses of course, but at least it would take some pressure off the grazing for the beef.

Fyfe came through with a pole requisition. Carlyle sent for Harry Wildman and Prince Dixon.

"How many head of cattle, Harry?"

"Uh – uh –"

"Prince?"

"'Bout a hunderd."

"All right. I'd like you to get together a crew – fix up the corral – hold-up field fence – run the cattle in. I want them counted in and out."

He made an inventory of implements, tools, blacksmith-shop contents; not a fifth of Sheridan's list could be found. He told Prince and Harry to get any help they could, to carry across the river the lumber the department had sent down, to haul it up to the barn and the supply shed, to start a nailing bee. He gave them a padlock and hasp for the supply-shed door. When he checked two weeks later, he found no boards had been replaced, no padlock on the door. Across the suspension bridge the lumber piles were noticeably lower, but none if it was stacked by the barn.

He sent Raymond Ear for Prince.

"Prince, how much do you and Harry get for what you don't do around here?"

"Twenty a month."

"We're going to fix up a lot of things around here. You and Harry are supposed to get crews together to see that they're done. It's over two weeks now – that lumber is still across the river – nobody's lifted a hand on that barn – corral – supply shed – the hold-up field fence."

"It's hard to get them to do anything, Mr. Sinclair."

"That's your job."

"They don't work so good unless they get paid."

"It'll pay them later."

"I said that to them."

"Way I've been sizing things up – I'm beginning to think you and Harry aren't doing what you're getting paid twenty a month for."

"We do our best."

"You've got to do better than you've been doing."

"Hey-uh."

He gave Harry and Prince two more weeks. The lumber across the Spray shrank more. The barn was not repaired. The hasp was not screwed to the supply-shed door and padlocked. No fencing was done on the hold-up field, nor poles put up on the corral. He spoke to Archie Nicotine.

"You people don't like work much, Archie."

"We don't make a lot of things all the time."

"That's right – like corrals and fences and repairs to barns."

"You white people do a lot of that."

"Yes – we do."

"You like to do that."

"Not any more than you people – but we know we have to. . . ."

"Hey-uh. I didn't notice any you people workin' for nothin'."

"I'm not asking you people to work for nothing – it's for your own good!"

"Easier to tell that if you get paid for it."

"You think they'd do it if they were paid for it?"

"Maybe."

"You figure you people like money as much as white people?"

"Not quite."

"Harry and Prince have been getting twenty a month. I'll pay you sixty."

"You fired Prince and Harry?"

"No, but I'd like to hire you."

"Sixty a month?"

"Yes."

"Fyfe say so?"

"I said so."

"But you didn't fire Harry or Prince?"

"I thought you might need them."

"I might. That make me a civil servant too?"

"I don't – yes – I think it would."

"What kind?"

"Mmmh?"

"Not the teacher – not the agent . . ."

"I guess not."

"Paradise Valley ager-culture-list."

"Okay."

"Eighty."

"That's quite a bit."

"Hey-uh."

"All right, Archie."

"And my men – they got to get paid too – same as by the ranchers."

"All right."

"Minimum wage. You do that – things get fixed up. And a hell of a lot of oats too."

"Pay them for putting in their own oats!"

"If you want oats."

"I don't – their horses do!"

"Our horses ain't heard about money yet, you understand."

Fyfe had objected, but finally went along with him. Almost two thousand acres of oats were seeded, spread over the reserve in plots of ten to a hundred acres. Ezra Powderface, Archie, Jonas Rider, Prince and Harry Wildman, and Mrs. Sam Bear ploughed and planted gardens. It was a wet spring; it was a wet summer; the oats and garden weeds did very well. The hay crop was magnificent. The barn was patched; the padlock went on the supply-shed door; the corral gap was closed, the hold-up field fenced, the cattle run in. There were eighty-two head. The new bulls went out to the cows at the proper time.

The first week in August, the oat crop was nodding ripe; Carlyle expected to see them any day, cutting with the agency binders; it was difficult to keep from asking Archie when he intended starting harvesting operations. The morning of the fifteenth, he noted a great deal of activity, the passing of wagons and rigs loaded with women and children, going out the back way that would take them south and then east to the ford over the Spray, below Moon's. Man after man mounted, clocked across the extension bridge. By noon he realized that an exodus was taking place. He went to the bridge, stopped the next group. It was Harold Lefthand, Orville Ear, Watty Dixon, Jonas Rider.

"What's going on?" he asked Jonas.

"Everybody to Shelby."

"But – why?"

"Rodeo."

"Rodeo! You people have your oats . . ."

"I got no oats."

"The others have! You've left it too long now! Another day . . ."

"Three days. P'rade tomorrow – then three days."

"But Archie Nicotine needs you to cut and stook."

"Boys all ridin' – calf ropin' – wild-cow milkin'. Then there's the flat races. Sam Bear always wins them stake races. We got the Paradise chuck-wagon too."

"Three days – four!"

"Prizes. There's Hartley Stampede – Bentham Pioneer Days . . ."

"You'll lose your oat crop! Archie Nicotine has to have some help. . . ."

"Nicotine left last night – he's helpin' put up the teepees on the grounds – he's in the buckin' events and calf ropin' too. I got no oats."

The parade had already started by the time he'd driven into Shelby, parked his car, and got a place on the post-office steps. Esau Rider led the Indian section; he rode a bony grey, his skull face under buffalo-horn headgear; after him came Matthew Bear, breech cloth over pink-dyed underwear, a blue, feathered cape, a crest of porcupine hair on his head, others in paint and war bonnets, Sadie Lefthand, Harold's wife, pulling a travois behind the bearded, wall-eyed pinto that had fouled the agency water supply.

When floats and chuck-wagons, the brave town band, the endless entries of tractors, hay balers, combines, had passed, he drove out to the rodeo grounds on the western edge of Shelby. He found the four giant teepees behind the chutes; he found Ezra Powderface, who promised to get the councillors together by noon at the main entrance by the midway.

But he knew it was hopeless even before he talked to them. He stood with them among the bright bubbles of balloons, shaving-tailed canaries, kewpie dolls and panda bears; he argued with them against the up-and-down music of the merry-go-round, the hoarse seduction of barkers for Crown and Anchor, Bingo, Wheel of Fortune. All the time he interpreted, Ezra's eyes seldom left the flinging arms of the airplane swings and the ferris wheel.

"They don't want to come back, Mr. Sinclair," Ezra explained in his deep voice.

"But they have to!"

Joe Wounded-Person spoke in Stony.

"He says they haven't run one flat race yet," interpreted Ezra. "Tomorrow's Indian Day – Chicken Dance contest – pony relay – stake races."

"Tomorrow's the day all those oats shell out!"

Jonas One-Spot spoke.

"Jonas says it's up to the ones planted oats – to go back. Mr. Sinclair, these people are pretty fussy about stampedes and fairs and rodeos and the like of that. Tonight there's a hundred-dollars prize for the chuck-wagon race. Sam Bear's got blooded horses in the team now, and he's sure the Paradise Valley wagon can beat the time around the barrels."

"But there are thousands of dollars' worth of oats!"

"I guess money isn't everything, Mr. Sinclair," Ezra said.

"It will be this winter!"

"Another thing," Ezra said, "there's their word they give."

"What word?"

"They get a dollar a day a head – kids too – comes to a lot – Judea here – eleven times three."

Judea Roll-in-the-mud said, "Hey-uh."

"They made their bargain. Rodeo wouldn't be rodeo without us Indian people. White people got to have them to photograph in colourful costume – can't go back on their . . ."

"With whom?"

"Shelby Rodeo Committee."

"Who are they? You know them?"

"Some. The Central Motor – hardware – Bon Ton store – he's the chairman – mayor too."

"MacTaggart."

"Hey-uh. I was talking to him a while ago on the midway."

He turned away from Ezra and the councillors, joined the slow flow of people through the midway, looking to either side and ahead for MacTaggart. Carnival smells came to him in waves – the sweetness of pink floss and candied apples like red glass, of popcorn and hot dogs and hamburgers. Half way down he saw MacTaggart coming his way on the other side. He crossed over, stopped him.

"Mr. MacTaggart."

"Have you seen Princess Grace," the electronic voice blared from high up behind MacTaggart, "the living body beautiful minus her head and completely topless, yet functioning in a normal manner!"

Recognition lighted MacTaggart's face. He shook Carlyle's hand, but his words were blotted by the loud speaker.

". . . see her blood coursing through her body by special machine! They said it couldn't be done. . . ."

MacTaggart led him away from the side-show front.

". . . Dr. Karl Schaddlemeyer, Junior, of Dusseldorf, Germany . . ."

"Carlyle – how are you?"

". . . but the delicate operation was a success! There is a special trained technician in attendance at all times. . . ."

They were in front of the house of mirrors now. "Mr. MacTaggart, I need your help."

"Sure – sure – anything I can do, Carlyle."

"My Paradise Valley people have left their oat crop."

"Didn't know they went in for puttin' in crops."

"They do now."

A dark-haired young man in Levis, his shirt sleeves rolled above his tattooed arms, appeared, bumped against one of the glass panels, turned and groped away.

"How can I help?"

"They've left it to shell out to come to your rodeo."

"Yes?"

The tattooed man was back again; he had ear-rings.

"If it does, you're responsible."

"I am?"

"Your rodeo committee."

A very small boy came up against the glass, fell, began to cry; a man appeared and behind him a woman; they picked the child up and turned around.

"I want you to help me get them back to harvest their crop."

"Aren't you being a little hard on us? You know our rodeo committee – when you taught here . . ."

"I don't teach here now – I have a different perspective – I see it – I want them back on the reserve before it's too late!"

"We have Indian Day tomorrow. We have a whole program of events planned – advertised. . . ."

"And their crop goes to hell so you can trot them out in beads and paint – forget them till next year!"

"Now – look . . ."

"You said you'd help me."

"In reason."

"It's a serious matter – two thousand acres of oats. . . ."

"Don't have to tell me that. I have a farm too. I bought the Taylor place. I was hailed out last week. What is it you want me to do?"

"Get on the public-address system."

"Yes?"

"Tell them to strike camp – head home for the reserve – that there's no point in their staying."

Two girls had appeared; one of them ran her candy apple up against the glass. It dropped off the stick.

"Tell them – you appreciate the part they played in the morning parade – you'll welcome them back next year. . . ."

"When their oats are shelling out again."

"No – next year you are scheduling your rodeo earlier – when it won't clash with the oats."

"Pretty rough."

One of the girls was Martha Bear – the other who had destroyed her candy apple was Victoria Rider. With hands out, they turned and, bumping each other, groped away.

"You tell them," Carlyle said, "that it is an official order from the Department of Indian Affairs!"

"It is?"

"No. But I've got to get them back! They've helped your Shelby rodeo every year, haven't they? I think it's fair."

"All right, Carlyle. One hour. I'm chairman of Shelby school board now. Any chance you might be coming back to . . ."

"No."

"We're looking for a principal. I understand Sheridan retired."

"Yes."

"You took over."

"Just Paradise Valley."

"That's nice. You ought to do well at it. Way these kids are getting, you'd make us one hell of a good principal too."

". . . you'll fall in love with Phillip-Phyllis – two heads on one little body – seen in over seven hundred colleges and universities! One heart – one set of lungs! You may ask the trained nurse always in attendance questions, but please refrain from smoking or loud talking!"

He stayed in town until the last outfit had left, went down town for lunch, then took the road west. Ten miles outside Shelby, he caught up with the ragged line of returning Indians. He slowed down, waited for them to pull over to either side, drove through the gauntlet of eyes glittering. Some called out in Stony; a rock bounced off his rear window.

Long after he had got back to Paradise Valley and gone to bed, he heard hooves on the suspension bridge, the clink of harness and creak of leather outside his bedroom window. In two days they could cut the oats, then take their time about stooking it.

The binders did not go out the next day – or the next – or the next. They were letting the crop go – deliberately – to show him. But it didn't discourage him as much as it should have. He knew that next year, there would be no sullen pride – they'd plant their oats, but there'd be no need to even up with him.

SIXTEEN

It had been the latest spring of his four years in Paradise, true winter from mid November, almost without chinook through to late April. Bad for man and beast, Moon said, stacks shrinking as, day after day, hay had to be hauled to cattle unable to get through crusted snow to grass. Archie with Prince and Watty and Orville had turned all the agency herd into the hold-up field so that they could be more conveniently fed. Thank God for the good hay crop!

The Nicotine and the Rider and Mrs. Bear gardens had done well. Early in September Archie had come to Carlyle with concern.

"What the hell we gonna do with it, Sinclair?"

"Do with it?"

"Hey-uh. Carrots – potatoes – beets you got us to plant. I'm up to my ass in turnips, you understand."

"Great – store them."

"Where?"

"Why – ah . . ."

"We got no place for all this. Not like hay or green feed – can't stack outside, you understand. We already had frost – light – it's all gonna freeze on us."

"Get it inside."

"Hey-uh. I'll tell Mrs. Bear and Mrs. Nicotine and Mrs. Rider that – all inside."

"That's right."

"Keep the vegetables nice and warm in there."

"Yes."

"You got the forms?"

"Forms?"

"Right-number forms – make-room-for forms they can make out and you can send down to Ottawa."

"What are you . . ."

"Got to make the forms to run the kids out of there – gramma – grampa – everybody outside."

"Huh!"

"Sinclair – those cabins – shacks ain't big enough now for all the people, so there's no room for vegetables too, and that's the whole situation."

"Oh. Well – I guess there's got to be a root house."

"What's that?"

"Cave – in a side hill."

"Hey-uh."

"Stored vegetables won't freeze."

"You got the plans for one of those?"

"I think if you took a look at Moon's you might get a few ideas."

Archie had. With the tractor and an improvised blade bolted to the farm-hand attachment, the very minimum of pick-and-shovel effort, a root house was dug out behind Archie's cabin. All the Rider and Bear and Nicotine vegetables went inside. With hard winter, more and more of the band called to get a few turnips or potatoes or carrots or onions. Archie charged them against future earnings, scratching their accounts on the root-house door with a nail. Carlyle's dispensary did a roaring trade as well – in diarrhoea mixture – as adult and infant stomachs, familiar with beans and bannock and elk, cramped on the steady diet of foreign and health-giving vegetables. By the first week in December the root house was empty.

In April the chinooks began to breathe steadily down from the mountains, shrinking the deep drifts, rotting the Spray and Beulah ice, but the falls above the suspension bridge held in a frozen cascade of cream and emerald, and the children at recess and after school still slid down the steep side below the bridge, sullied with coal-like shale. They coasted face-down on pieces of cardboard, galvanized tin, or home-made sleds, toes dragging, almost to the opposite bank of the Spray. The day that Carlyle warned Archie the honey-combed ice might not hold up the agency truck, Martha Bear and Victoria Rider went through, were fished out by Gatine Lefthand and Raymond Ear. They steamed before the school stove, were almost dry by three-thirty.

Victoria was nearly fourteen now, a year older than her close friend Martha Bear; yet Martha looked two years older than Victoria. These were the two who had often brought flowers up to him at his desk. Victoria had become the special one, her hair, her eyes, her skin still startling him in unguarded moments when he looked out at the class.

She had lost much of her shyness, but he was still very careful with her, remembering the arithmetic class when he had asked her to go to the board and do an addition problem he knew she had been capable of for months. For twenty minutes he had waited for her to do it; she had simply stood – alone at the board – holding the piece of chalk he had put in her hand. Head hanging, hair mercifully hiding her face, she twisted and turned the chalk as though she could worry it right through the black-board ledge. It broke, fell to the floor in bits. She whirled with hair flying, pelted past her desk, out the door, across the schoolyard. She stayed away from school for three days.

She had taught him his own important lesson; now he never brought her or any of them up to the board alone; they came in twos and threes and whole grades, sliding one moccasined foot reluctantly ahead of the other. For reading he had them stand around his desk, with faces over tilted books, the girls leaning and swaying as though the chinook of shyness moved their heads together and apart.

But for all their progress in reading and in arithmetic and writing, he knew he had a long way to go with them. Except for Victoria, he really had no bridge between himself and them. He could not know what went on inside their heads – behind the eyes that refused to hold his. He had no way of telling whether he was under- or over-estimating them.

"God damn it, Peter – I can't really tell if a kid's bright or dumb! He could be Einstein and I wouldn't know it because he doesn't understand or speak English!"

"Just have to wait till he does."

"Too long – maybe too late! If only they'd speak it in their homes – at recess – they won't – they won't – not on the playground – not to each other. I can't tell if the words mean anything to them – they can memorize the look of them – sequence of letters. . . ."

"How good's your Stony?"

"Huh?"

"It's not a one-way street you know."

"No. I've considered it, but – no. What I have to do is – realize that I'm teaching them a new language – first; the spelling and reading come after."

"Be a nice gesture anyway – you know – learn a few expressions. . . ."

"No – I'll stay the only one of the reserve that they have to speak English with. And then there's that goddam drum."

"What about it?"

"I don't have to tell you – you're up against it as much as I am – right from birth they've got that drum . . ."

"You're not going to take that from them?"

". . . with their mother's milk – every week – every month – every year – last time I was up there – the Chinook baby's head over Louis's arm – the one that was pounding with the stick."

"Christ, Sinclair – let them keep their drum at least!"

"I tell you – it's what we're up against."

"Maybe. But it is theirs."

"That makes it all right."

"It is – at least – one thing we didn't give them – along with the D. T.'s – TB – V. D. The drum is beautiful."

"It's lobotomy."

"Maybe. But their own kind."

"And you recommend it."

"Sure – if the torment's too great I do – every human's entitled to a dram of Lethe now and then. Just take your pick – liquor – drum – Dingle – Esau's Storm and Misty magic – your own. . . ."

"What's mine?"

"I don't know. Maybe you don't. It is very interesting though – that you came to Paradise. Maybe it's Esau's."

"Green lobotomy."

"Hey-up."

"*No-watch-es-nichuh.*"

One afternoon late in March Susan Rider visited him; he waited, as he always must with them, to learn why she'd come. He poured her tea, buttered some slices of bread. When she'd finished, she still hadn't told him the purpose of her visit, sat with her head bowed, unceasingly running a finger-tip along the edge of the oilcloth. Finally she got up, and only then did he realize she hadn't eaten all the bread. The hand that held the side of her skirt also held slices.

"Susan – what . . ."

"I wasn't very hungry. I'll take it home for Wesley."

"Haven't you any – how are you for supplies?"

"I put the calf money into oatmeal. We got porridge – Victoria brought home Fyfe cookies too. She didn't miss a day at school all winter. Pretty soon there'll be some Fyfe elk."

Fyfe had promised a truck of confiscated elk, but there had been some hitch in the department machinery, and it had not yet come down. The telephone line was working; he caught Fyfe just before the office closed for the day.

"What about that elk?"

"The next trip of the truck," Fyfe said.

"When's that? Next week – next month?"

"Thursday – a special trip."

That night he heard the drum, its cadence beating clear through the cold and crystal night. He wondered how any of them had the energy to go through the Prairie Chicken dance. If there was only more he could do for them! He couldn't feed them all out of his own supplies! Dear God, if only he were the richest man in the world – if he had all the money in the world to feed them with! And he hated Ottawa – the slowing and narcotizing routine – the impersonal red tape that formalized hunger and sickness and death. God – how he hated it!

The truck did make it on Thursday as Fyfe had promised. Sanders came down too.

"Archie Nicotine wants you to call."

"That'll be a ride into the city," Sanders said, "or his mother-in-law."

"Lucy Baseball."

"Yes."

"What's her . . ."

"I suspect diabetes – so – a sample of urine from Archie Nicotine's mother-in-law – if she has to go on insulin now won't that be the balancing act of the century! Did he say she was thirsty and tired and itchy again?"

"He didn't say."

When he came back from his calls, Sanders seemed depressed. "They skate so goddam close to the edge – especially the old ones – especially the little ones – especially all of them! I give old Jonas about even odds he makes it through the winter – and Sally Ear and Mary Wounded-Person – and the Peter Powderface baby."

"What about Archie's mother-in-law?"

"Tit scald."

"Lucy Baseball!"

"The cows – from sun reflection off the snow."

"And what's your remedy for that?"

"I told him – since he's got them all gathered in the hold-up field – feeding there – he put out the hay in one area – and straw to – uh – cut down the snow glare on their tits."

"Clever."

"Well – actually I didn't tell him – he said he had come to a conclusion, and he asked me if I thought it would work."

Old Jonas One-Spot made it; Sally Ear did not – nor did Mary Wounded-Person and the Peter Powderface baby. Esau Rider had wintered well; his knee bothered him badly, but he had his remedy for that: a fire stoked by Susan and roaring in his stove from morning till night, its furnace heat striking right through to the heart of the bone.

Attendance at school was more spotty now that families began to move off the reserve to work for neighbouring ranchers, but there had been discing done first, more oats sowed than last year.

By actual count there were twice as many gardens planted. Fyfe had congratulated him, but it was hard to keep satisfaction from weakening. It was hard to get used to the refusal of both children and parents to look into his face; every eye-flick and sly withdrawal sapped his confidence. And they certainly got out of their cabins and into tents with alacrity. Their cabins were no hell – just log shacks actually – but all the same . . .

"Tent isn't stuffy," Archie said.

"No – I guess it isn't – but those cabins are a long way from being stuffy, Archie – any of them. Cardboard on broken windows – see light through where the chinking . . ."

"Houses are stiff and they're kind of stuffy. Kids get colds and coughs out of bein' stuffy."

"Get more out of sleeping on damp earth."

"Hey-up. I know. I slept in houses – cabins – in bunkhouses lots, and I couldn't sleep worth a damn. It's like a heavy weight down on top of your chest so you can't breathe good and loose."

"I don't think . . ."

"We can't get used to it."

"You could – if you tried."

"Hey-up. A man can get used to anything."

"That's right."

"That's what he said."

"Who said?"

"Fellow wore an elk turd under his hat for thirty years."

Early in September, when he looked through the west windows of the schoolroom, he noticed that Victoria was not with the other girls in their part of the grounds; then he saw her standing apart and watching the boys in their Chicken Dance, bouncing jaunty around the old wash-tub. Each recess for the week she stood in the same spot. The beginning of the next week, he did not see her with the boys or the girls – at first – and then he saw her at the end of the Chicken Dance train, her head forward, face turned upwards, her right hand holding a twig to her rump for prairie-chicken tail-feathers. Her elbows were crooked into quivering wings.

He slammed from the room. He grabbed her by the shoulder and yanked her out of the dance circle.

"No more of that!"

He saw fright in her face.

"It's not for you, Victoria!" He had released her shoulder now. The dance had stopped; the others were watching. "I don't – you – Chicken Dance isn't for girls!"

"Hey-uh," Gatine Lefthand said.

"I want to talk with you, Victoria."

In the schoolroom he said, "Not any more, Victoria – it isn't a good thing. I don't want you to do it any more."

"They invited me – except Gatine."

"I don't care if they did."

"What's wrong with it, Mr. Sinclair?"

What could he tell her! "It's – I just don't want you to, Victoria."

"Is there anything wrong with it, Mr. Sinclair?" she persisted.

"I don't want you to, and that's enough!"

"Shouldn't they?"

"Who?"

"The boys too."

Damn it – it wasn't all right for them either, but how could he explain! "It's all right for them – now. Not you."

"Because I'm a girl."

"I guess so, Victoria. Now – take your seat – no –" He held out the bell to her. "Ring this for me."

Her face lighted.

The next day he spoke to Susan Rider, asked her if she would permit Victoria to take over janitorial duties at the school, and, as well, do housework for him on Saturday mornings. Susan seemed pleased. With the department's five dollars a month for starting the school fire, sweeping, and his own weekly dollar, it meant nine dollars Victoria would be bringing home.

She came at nine, and when she had finished his washing, cleaning, she ate lunch with him before she went home. The meals were awkward at first; it was as though every mouthful were painful for her, and he saw that her dark eyes watched every move he made. With each Saturday she seemed to relax more.

She came almost an hour early the first Saturday morning in October, just as he had brought the porridge to a boil. Fyfe would approve of his porridge; he prepared it always the night before, tipping the meal into the boiling water, stirring, mashing any lumps against the pot side with the bottom of the tablespoon. The next morning it was a matter only of bringing it to a boil again.

He saw that she was watching him at the stove, her nostrils distended. Surely to goodness she hadn't missed her breakfast!

"It'll be done in a minute. There's lots – if you'd like some."

The distaste on her face was instant and fierce.

"Don't you like porridge, Victoria?"

She shook her head.

"Good for you."

"Smells."

"I know – porridge smell."

"It smells just like a wet sweater."

"Oh." He bent down over the pot. "By God, you're right – wet wool! There's bacon and eggs. . . ."

"Hey-uh."

"Oh, come on, Victoria!"

"Yes – please, Mr. Sinclair."

TSSSSZZZZZZZZHTEW went the saw out in the schoolyard, as it eased slowly through the log that Prince and Archie eased forward in the cradle, Gatine and Raymond pitched the chunks into the pile to one side. *TSSSZZZZZZZZZZ*-TIT-CHEEEEEW! It screamed high as the blade hit a knot. They relieved its agony by leaning back on the cradle so that the blade could regain speed. It whirled faster and faster, and the sound thinned to sustained hissing that shrieked again as the next log was pushed into it.

The fine sawdust rose like tan smoke, and the air was filled with the bitterness of resin. The watching children hooted in imitation of the saw's scream; they sneezed a lot as the dust got sucked up their noses. As chunk after chunk was negligently tossed aside, the wood-pile grew to the mountain proportion that would feed the agency's stoves for all the year to come.

Fyfe arrived with his gold-and-red-stamped brief-case, laid out his papers on the kitchen table, and one by one, the Indians came to get their cheques: the calf-crop cheque, the wood cheque for what had been hauled and cut the past three days. They were short five cords.

"What about Pete Dance and the birthday cakes?" Fyfe asked, after department cheques had been handed out to all of them.

"Nothing. Another cup?"

"No – thanks."

"He is a talented scrounger," Carlyle said.

"I know."

"Starting with Moon's – he got thirteen – asked Mrs. Moon first – explained he wanted it for little Hughie – then the next ranch and the next and the next. The birthday party grew – he told them exactly what guests were invited to Hughie's party – number of cases of pop he'd need – second-hand guitar he'd already bought for the main present. . . ."

"How many cakes?"

"Thirteen."

"I didn't know there were that many ranches in easy riding distance."

"There aren't – I think he got several in Shelby. Hughie's birthday isn't for three months yet. Um – something a little more important than Pete's birthday cakes – Charlie Cook on the Walking Sticks is angry."

"What about?"

"He says some of them are turning horses in on Walking Stick lease – you know – where the reserve touches him. Evidently they've been getting the horses out in the morning, but he says the grass has been grazed heavily."

"He see them at it?"

"No."

"You think they are?"

"Yes."

"Who?"

"My guess would be Harold Lefthand – maybe Orville Ear."

"Can you handle it?"

"Yes."

"How?"

"I suggested to Cook he get his place officially made a pound – that he round up their horses and hold them – charge them two dollars a head to get them back. He thinks it's a hell of a good idea."

"Aye-hee. Johnny Education grabbed hold Josie – ah – ah . . ." Fyfe looked down at his notes.

"Snow."

"Did he – her mother told . . ."

"He might have – but Josie's home now."

"How old?"

"Fifteen."

"Rape?"

"Mrs. Snow says so. But she's back with her people – he didn't take her into Storm and Misty – also Josie could have wanted him to – eh – grab hold of her."

"All right. Dispensary seemed pretty exuberant over the last quarter – aspirins way out of line over last year."

"Bad winter – spring and summer colds."

"You must hold them down, you know, Carlyle."

"I know."

"They'll ask for buckets of the stuff if they think they can get away with it. Are you sure it's colds?"

"Sure."

"I understand aspirin dissolved in carbonated beverages can have – eh – quite a kick to it."

"Not as much as your Drambuie or Teachers' Highland."

Fyfe gave his brief and unusual smile – just the tips of the dentures, more as though he were sucking in air. "And they do get to that more and more each year. I'm sorry to see it with this band – the isolation – they've been lucky – but more and more of them have cars now. I think I will have another cup of tea."

Fyfe's observation about the cars was right; there were several now, parked across the suspension bridge – Mark Wounded-Person's, Rod Wildman's half-ton, MacDougall Meadowlark's Hudson. Finance-company envelopes turned up in the mail regularly now; he wondered why the car dealers took chances with them at all.

"I've been giving some thought to their housing," Carlyle said. "As Nicotine would say – I have come to a conclusion – way we might improve it – that they could."

"How?"

"Well there's quite a bit of money in the band fund – it might be possible to pay them out of that – way we do with the oats – encourage them to build better houses."

"Pay them – to build their own houses!"

"Uh-huh. The money's theirs anyway. Say a man put in a foundation – cement supplied by the department – out of band funds – work it so that when he finished his foundation he'd get paid for his work – out of band funds – which he's entitled to – sooner or later. Then when he's raised his studding and framework – pay him another fixed amount for those hours of work – the balance when he finishes the interior – doors – windows. . . ."

He saw that Fyfe's head was turned slightly aside as though he were listening to himself as well.

"I think they'd build them – if it was worth their while. I'll bet they'd work on their own houses before they'd go to work for the ranchers."

"Now," Fyfe said, "that's the way I like to see things done! Practically! You outline it – send it to me – we'll try Ottawa with it!"

"I think it would work," Carlyle said. "It did with the oats, you know. I'd like to see them in decent houses."

"So would I – so would I!"

"Of course – it's a long-term deal. Something more immediate – well, by next spring – way these children play – at recess – I want a ball diamond out there – and I want sports equipment – swings – teeter-totters."

"Mmmh. Yes." Fyfe made a note. "Peter tells me he brought the X-ray unit down."

"Not much luck," Carlyle said. He was seeing them standing, staring at the mobile unit before the school; he was seeing Sanders taking off his jacket and shirt to stand before the machine in a vain effort to show them it was harmless. He had been successful with fifteen. The Rider family had co-operated.

"I want Victoria Rider to try her seven and eight together this year. Nine involves departmentals – so if she's going to pick up an extra year it's got to be this year. She's cleaning the boards for me – sweeping – starting the fires."

"A girl!"

"I've tried the older boys – it's always a mess with them. She's been doing it and doing it well since school opening."

He did not tell Fyfe that she was doing work for him on Saturday mornings as well.

SEVENTEEN

He knew that in six years he had accomplished a great deal for his Paradise Valley people. He knew that. He ran a good school by any standards; calves, yearlings, and two-year-old cattle showed their improved breeding. The annual calf crop had increased; there were stacks as insurance against a bad winter; fences were in good shape; there were over two thousand acres under cultivation. Ottawa had approved the building plan. Fyfe and Carlyle had each made his own guess-list of those Indians who might take advantage of the scheme. When they checked with each other, both lists tallied. In early June Archie had finished his forms and poured his foundation and collected a hundred dollars. He drank most of it up in three trips to the Empress beer parlour in the city; Carlyle had bailed him out three times. By July, his new house was framed, sheathed, the roof and asphalt shingles on. Carlyle took another two trips to the city to get him out of jail on drunk and disorderly charges.

Archie helped Orville Ear, Prince Dixon, Rod Wildman, Jonas Rider, and Elijah Race finish their houses. He did not drink up all they paid him; for three hundred dollars he bought a half-ton truck at Skipper Jones' Auto Mart. It ran as far as

Moon's turn-off; with a Turkey Track team they hauled it through the ford and onto the reserve, where Archie hoisted out the motor under the great cottonwood before his old cabin.

Harold Lefthand had a new house too; he had managed to make his building money go twice as far as the others by running up record-breaking credit at two Shelby stores on the strength of his building cheques to come. He hired Orville and Elijah to do his carpentry for him, collected the cheques, paid them half. The Shelby storekeepers whistled for theirs.

Early in October Fyfe arranged for a visit by municipal, provincial, and federal dignitaries, who gave formal speeches of praise, interpreted by Ezra Powderface. G. Bob Dingle blessed red and white; his text: Luke – Chapter Seventeen, verses five to ten. All visited the new houses, inspected the barn, the cattle, those gardens that had been harvested before frost. A laudatory article appeared next to Ann Landers' column on the women's page of the *Leader-Times*, was picked up by the Canadian Press. The reporter had taken as her theme: "The Vanishing Savage." She gave her readers a word picture of a model community "under the mile-high grandeur of the snow-capped Rockies" with golden crops of experimental-farm excellence and a Hereford herd sired by Grand Champions, knee deep in lush grass.

Carlyle found it a little embarrassing, and it seemed ironic to him that the most important thing of all had been overlooked: for the first time in either Hanley or Paradise Valley history, an Indian child had been successful in Grade Nine departmental examinations, and in September had begun her high school. Victoria's was the real accomplishment; the cattle, the crops, the houses were important, but the victory was not actually their own. Victoria's was.

She was not an easy child to know; he suspected the reason for that was as much in himself as in her. She was not withdrawn and cautiously careful like the others, but she did have a quiet, waiting quality. Her responses could be missed, for they were subtle as the soft nudge of a wrist pulse. And sometimes not! There had been an August afternoon when she was twelve. He had taken her into the city for Jonas and Susan, to see the orthodontist who would cap the front tooth broken by the bat exuberantly swung by Sally Ear. As they walked through the crushing flow of people, she had taken his hand and held it as they walked. For the first time two worlds had merged, and he knew it. He and she were no longer so vulnerable on this concrete and asphalt planet. The memory of her hand in his could still surprise him with the dry, sun heat of its own.

Yet he was often visited by depression, reminded of the impossibility of ever knowing what happened in their minds and hearts. So – wasn't all communication between all humans hopeless? Out of my skin and into yours I cannot get – however hard I try – however much I want to! All one could do was – wish it were possible – and know that illusion was the best that could be managed. The love illusion – possessing – being in each other – simply could not be brought off – love died instant death with each satiety. As Peter said, "a dram of Lethe now and then." What a weak bridge emotion was for people to walk across to each other – emotion swinging, unable to hold the heavy weight of communication. About as dependable as the goddam telephone line. Just illusion after all, for once the passage was made, the door was always closed. You stopped at the eyes, and you had never left the home envelope of self anyway.

She had held his hand again when they had come down the elevator from the dentist's office, and he had taken her into Woolworth's for ice cream and orange crush.

The waitress at the counter had said, "Your little girl hasn't got much to say, has she?"

He bought her a ruby ring.

Early in December Archie Nicotine had one more try at getting to Hercules Salvage for the rings and rebuilt carburetor he needed for his truck motor. The Empress stopped him. Carlyle rescued him, used the trip to the city to do his Christmas shopping. He bought Victoria a velvet dress, the lovely lavender of shooting stars.

Driving back to Paradise Valley he and Archie saw the little maroon Volkswagen abandoned just above the suspension bridge. It had been left there by the hunter Archie had trailed into Storm and Misty country, found frozen to death. Archie had frozen both feet himself in getting out. A week later the young Mounted Police constable walked across the suspension bridge. He questioned Archie in the kitchen.

"Where was he?"

"Storm and Misty."

"How did you find him?"

"By tracking."

"I mean, how was he when you did find him?"

"Dead."

There was a quick jerk of the constable's head. His mouth tightened – relaxed. "Yes?"

"On his face."

"What else?"

"Dead."

"You said that."

"When a person is dead, that's just about the whole situation."

"I would like you to try to remember how he was – in some detail."

"Covered up mostly," Archie said. "I saw one of his arms first. Part of it."

"If he was almost covered – what about his tracks?"

"Hey-uh."

"Were his tracks covered over?"

"Hey-uh. At the last."

"Just at the last?"

"Hey-uh. At the last."

"It was snowing."

"Hey-uh."

"Just at the last?"

"Hey-uh."

"Then – if his tracks were covered over just at the last and it was still snowing – then didn't you get to him not long after he got there?"

"I don't understand that," Archie said.

"If there were still some tracks showing – and it was snowing still – he must have just made those tracks – and he would have to be alive to make the tracks that weren't covered over yet by the falling snow."

"I agree," Archie said.

The constable waited.

Archie waited.

"But he was almost covered with snow?"

"Hey-uh."

"But his tracks were not."

"Hey-uh. Also he was dead when I got to him. Quite a while."

"How do you know that?"

"Some ways."

"What ways?"

"One way – covered nearly with snow."

"Yes?"

"Where he fell the last time – on his face."

"What other ways did you know?"

"The way he was stiff – all spread out and he was dead a long time and that was the whole situation."

"Yes?"

"Another way – it wasn't snowing heavy so it took time to cover him so much."

"But how did you know he was dead?"

"Mainly by him being dead."

After a moment the constable said, "You say his tracks were covered up?"

"Hey-uh."

"Well – were they?"

"Hey-uh."

"That you followed – to him."

"Dead."

For several ticks of the kettle on the stove the constable stared at Archie. "Just how – do you follow tracks – covered with new snow?"

"It's difficult," Archie said.

"Wouldn't it be impossible?"

Archie shrugged.

"Wouldn't it?"

"For you."

"Or for anybody."

"Hey-uh."

"You mean impossible for anybody?"

"You do."

"All right then – will you – can you – explain how you were able to follow tracks that weren't there?"

"I couldn't do that."

"You couldn't."

"That would be impossible – for anybody."

"But you did all the same? I'm still waiting for an explanation."

"I guess I can," Archie said. "You too."

"What?"

"Try. The whole situation is the way snow falls. It falls down, you understand."

"There was wind."

"Hey-up. With wind it doesn't fall straight down – but with wind it falls mostly down, you understand."

"Yes?"

"There was wind."

"I know there was."

"It can pile the snow and it can clear away the snow."

"Yes?"

"Some places there is something to cover over, then the snow piles on there. It doesn't pile under there. Like all that dead-fall up Beulah Creek. How do you get through that dead-fall?"

"Climb over."

"When you're tired and no strength left."

"Climb under."

"Hey-up. If you climb under dead-fall on your belly you will make a pretty big track, you understand. With your whole body. It will take one hell of a lot of snow to cover in that deep belly-track you made under there, won't it?"

Archie waited.

"I suppose so."

"That snow will cover your tracks you made in the open – but not in some other places. I would track you by now and again to where you were lying froze to death – on your face and all your fingers split open and that is the whole situation."

For the first time in the interview, the constable seemed slightly uncertain.

"Couple places I was lucky," Archie said.

The constable consulted the small notebook cupped in his hand. He looked up again. "His gun."

Archie waited.

"He had a gun."

"If he gut-shot a cow moose, I would guess he could used a gun to do it with," Archie said.

"It wasn't with him."

"No."

"Any idea what happened to it?"

"He dropped it."

"You found it."

"No."

"You saw it – did you see it?"

"No. I said he dropped it because I didn't see it."

"That doesn't seem to explain . . ."

"Before he died – somewhere I didn't see it. Back on his trail there."

"So – actually you are assuming . . ."

"When he knew it was something to carry that would cost his life . . ."

". . . still you are making . . ."

"I didn't see it anywhere around him – I didn't kick it up out when I worked to lift him and prop him against that tree."

"Why did you move the . . ."

". . . and you R. C. M. P. people didn't find it either, then I guess he must dropped it back on his trail."

"Why did you move the body?"

"Huh?"

"Don't you know you aren't supposed to move a body?"

"No."

"It is pretty generally known. Why did you move it?"

"Sensible."

"Sensible?"

"Hey-uh."

"In what way?"

"Prop him up against that tree – so he won't cover over deep – you can't find him at all . . ."

"You are not – were not supposed . . ."

". . . till next spring. . . ."

"You are not supposed to touch the body! We want to see that body first – exactly as it was!"

"By spring it would be a lot different, you understand."

"I am telling you . . ."

"High."

"Do not – ever again – touch or move – a body!"

"Next time I won't," Archie promised. "To please the R.C.M.P."

The constable stared at him for several long moments, then consulted his notebook again.

"And the spring bears," Archie added.

The constable's head jerked up. "It – is – the – law – in all cases – for everybody!"

"And ravens – magpies – bears . . ."

"You did not find his rifle."

"Hey-uh."

"By him."

"I told you that."

"But he had bruises." Again the constable's eyes held Archie's face. "You know he had bruises?"

"No."

"The undertaker reported . . ."

"Storm and Misty hasn't got those lights like the undertaker . . ."

"They were quite evident – on his head – the right side of his face. His wife – widow – his brother-in-law too – they were wondering how he got those bruises."

"Do you?"

"Do I what?"

"Wonder if he got them from his gun-butt?"

"We're checking it out for them."

"I'm sorry I can't help them that way. I tracked him down for them. Then I spoiled it."

"Spoiled . . ."

"I moved their body. Now they need a specialist."

"In what?"

"Bruises on the head and face." Archie looked directly at the constable. "I guess that's why."

"Why – what?"

"They got you to check it out. Bruises on the face and on the head and not moving the body – drinking rabbit turds in tea . . ."

"What the hell are you . . ."

"Write in that little book a question for them – what happens to a person when they fall all over dead-fall and hitting himself on his face and his head? . . ."

"Just you hold on . . ."

". . . can't feel because it is all froze – why will I waste my strength and make myself sweat to club him to die which he will anyway. Write down – it don't hurt much to freeze to death so I would not have to kill him to save him some suffering. . . ."

"Look here, Nicotine . . ."

"Gone but not forgotten," Archie said. "Every time my goddam feet itch, I'll remember him the rest my life!"

EIGHTEEN

IF THEY WERE SO CLOSE TO THE LIVING WHOLE, THEN SPRING should be renascence for them as well; yet three children and Moses Rider died of pneumonia in early May, and Sarah MacLeod and her unborn child; the Bony-Spectre finally rode up for Jonas One-Spot the night the ice went out of the Spray. Each spring death seemed to play a counterpoint to bud and sprout and rising sap and river flow. The tapping at his door increased: callers for green liniment and for white liniment, cough medicine for the baby; for the adult, ginger to make hot infusions for chills, mustard and belladonna plasters.

"For the ear-ache, Mr. Sinclair."

"Proud flesh on wire-cut the colt got – lots of peroxide, Mr. Sinclair."

"Aspirin, please, Mr. Sinclair."

"Grease for the baby sat on the camp-fire, Mr. Sinclair."

Of course there were always the smiling and giggling teen-age girls; in threes and fives and dozens they came, wanting the little, flat, cardboard pill-boxes filled with unguent of roses – usually the afternoon before a dance night. And often Victoria was one of them. Was it possible to pick an arbitrary point in growth time; say yes, up to now she was a little girl – but from now on, no. No more taking a hand on a city street – no more lupin or jack-in-the-pulpit brought up to his desk – or those maroon, spider-like flowers drooping hairy from her fist. No more bucking-horse tree or skipping or jacks. Now – this very spring – for the first time in the dance tent: make-up – lipstick right out to the corners of the mouth – rouge toned for white skin, giving her cheeks a damson blush. The freckles still there – but no braids hung and gently swung in the Rabbit or the Owl Dance, in the Montana Fox Trot. She hadn't piled her hair high in the tarty confection popular with many of them, but tong-baked curls spiralled down before each ear.

This spring was special for her. This one was the breast spring, poignant as young ferns' tight thrust through earth. She made him think of a tiger-lily; perhaps it was the freckles – or her upright carriage. In the dance tent, up at the black-board, out in the schoolyard, she stood, she moved with balanced flow up through the long arc of her legs, the waist socket of her hips, the shallow curve of her back and shoulders. And her hands – oh, her hands! Not great-knuckled and Caucasian angular – bird-boned – the grace of her grandfather Esau right through to her finger-tips. If only he could get her to take care of her goddam nails!

It was Martha Bear's spring too; a year younger than Victoria, she was a large fifteen, Matthew's young sister, Sam's daughter. For over a year Carlyle had noticed her sending boys notes in class, pushing boys, bumping boys, slapping boys, tussling with them over in the male territory of the schoolgrounds at recess time and on the way home after school. Every day for the last two weeks of May, Wilfrid Tail-feather had loitered at the edge of the soft-ball diamond.

"Her flesh is lustin' pretty hard," Ezra Powderface had said to Carlyle. "And grabbin'-hold-of time is abroad throughout the Paradise Valley now." He said he had cautioned Mrs. Bear and that she had warned Sam about it. Neither Ezra nor Mrs. Bear were optimistic, for Sam had only two interests: a black gelding, half thoroughbred, and a sorrel mare with silver mane and tail, sired by a Tennessee Walker stud out of Moon's quarter-horse mare, Rat Trap. "Winnin' stake races a lot more important to him than Martha." Carlyle could accept that; it would be difficult for Sam Bear to take seriously any threat to the trivial and questionable virginity of his daughters.

The first Monday in June, a very angry and frustrated Mrs. Bear showed up with Martha's younger sister, Lucille, just before Carlyle rang the bell to call the children in. She asked him to phone the Mounted Police detachment in Shelby. She was almost in tears as she told him how she had been – as usual – the first in the family to stir that morning. Not the first, for she had been wakened by little Lazarus, hungry. She had fed him; she had left the tent to build the fire, to carry up water from Beulah; she had returned to awaken Lucille and Martha for school so they wouldn't break their attendance record, perfect since last September.

Martha was not in the tent. At the far end Matthew was pulling on his moccasins and rubbers. Lucille sat up sleep-eyed in the blankets she shared with Martha, little Lazarus propped against the tent wall in his *yo-kay-bo*. Martha was not there, Martha had not been there all night. Martha had not come down from the dance tent with Matthew when it was over as she'd promised. Matthew went outside. She went over to Sam. She poked him with her toe.

"She's gone."

Sam rolled over onto his back, slid his hands under his head with his elbows out, looked up blinking.

"Martha's gone with him just like I said."

Sam hawked in his throat.

"She's gone."

Sam felt for his jacket under his head. "Now she won't go to school this morning."

In his stocking feet Sam went to the tent flap. Called to Matthew squatted before the fire. "You know this happened?"

"What?" Matthew blew on the tea he held up to his mouth.

"Martha gone."

"Hey-uh."

"Who?"

"Wilfrid Tail-feather."

"You taking them grub – where they went to?"

"No."

"All right." Sam let the flap fall, turned back, passed Mrs. Bear helping Lucille dress. He lay down in his blankets.

"Aren't you going after them?"

He stared up at the ridge-pole.

"You go after them."

"She's fifteen."

"She's got to go to school. She's smart there. You got to go after them. I need her around here."

"She's fifteen. I guess she wanted him."

"He took her. He'll rope her to a tree. He'll starve her."

"Not these days," Sam said. "They don't do that." He rolled over. "She's fifteen."

"Everybody knows now," said Mrs. Bear bitterly; she tugged at the belt of Lucille's dress. "Roll out of there. You and Matthew. Go get her!"

Sam shifted his left hip to greater comfort.

"Go get her!"

"She wanted him." Sam said it to the tent wall. "She's fifteen."

"You and Matthew track them!"

Sam closed his eyes.

"You got to go get her! She's got to go to school some more! You got to go get her!"

"Shut up."

"You and Matthew saddle up now and go get her!"

"Shut up."

"Go after her!"

Sam rolled over to his back again. "Hand me that tin fine-cut."

"Get it yourself. Go get Martha!" She slipped Lucille's knotted kerchief under her chin, adjusted the peak. "To the school now. Don't be late. If you don't eat it – bring home the cooky for Lazarus." She turned back to Sam. "You can't lie there like that! Go get them!"

"Hand me that tin fine-cut, I said."

"I said get it yourself! Get her! You want me to hand you that fine-cut! You want me to get her too!"

"I didn't eat yet. Get me grub."

"You get your own grub! You get your own fine-cut! You be what you are! Old woman! I'll go get her! I am the man!"

Brightness blazed, was blotted, as Matthew came in.

"Matthew!" His mother turned to him. "You got to track them!"

"Hand me that tin fine-cut, Matthew."

Matthew handed his father the tin of tobacco.

"I married a woman!" shrilled Mrs. Bear. "I married an ugly woman! Now, Matthew," she turned on him, "you get her! You track them! You!"

"Wilfrid took his rifle," explained Matthew.

"I don't care!"

"I do. Me. He can shoot good."

"She's your sister! Martha! You can't let him do that to her! Rod wouldn't! Archie wouldn't! Moses wouldn't let him . . ."

"Shut up," said Sam.

"No, I won't! I say what I like! I say it! I say anything I want! You don't tell me!" She spit at Sam. "Any man go get her – but you – look at you – look at you there – Matthew you go now – right now! Before it's too late!"

"Too late now," Sam said. He wiped the spit off his forehead. "You go, Matthew!"

"Wilfrid's got his gun."

"Maybe some day some man grab hold of Matthew too!"

"Shut up," Sam said. It was muffled this time, as he licked his cigarette.

"Women – women! Old woman – young woman – all I got women out of me! Matthew, you think you're fine in the Chicken Dance – oh, brave for the Chicken Dance – scared of Wilfrid's gun – took your sister and tied her, and starving her and humping her now!"

"Hump you," Sam said.

"Two women can't do that! Ugly woman – you – face like a hawk's ass!"

"Give me a match, Matthew."

"Don't you do it – don't you do it! Lucille – you'll be late! You don't bring her back – Mounties do it! I'm going to Sinclair, phone Mounties – me! Come on, Lucille!"

Carlyle did not phone the detachment in Shelby for her. He told her the line was down, set the children to desk work, walked back to the Bear camp with her. As they went up over the first bench, Ezra Powderface joined them. Sam was still in his blankets.

"What you goin' to do now, Sam?" Ezra said.

"Nothing!" Mrs. Bear said. "I married a woman."

"You aren't married," Ezra corrected her. "God punished you now. Blanket marriage for Martha too. Sins the fathers and mothers upon their kids." He turned to Sam. "No more of these. You get up."

Sam did get up.

"You go bring them back," Ezra said.

"She's fifteen," Sam said.

"I know. I baptized her. Rollin' in the kinick-kinick with Wilfrid Tail-feather gonna unbaptize her. You bring them back – then I'll marry them for you."

"I think you better, Sam," Carlyle said.

"Maybe she doesn't want to come back," Sam said.

"At least you better go for her," Carlyle said. "Find out if she doesn't."

"They come back she's not marryin' him," Mrs. Bear said. "I don't need any Sarcee son-in-law."

"Take what you got," Ezra said. "Eyes of God they are married. Got to make it right quick. These blanket marriages got to quit."

Sam sat down. He crossed his legs.

"Go after her," Carlyle said.

"No."

"I warned you," Ezra said.

"I heard the warnin'. She's fifteen. She's old enough. He wants her. She wants him. All right." He lay back in the blankets.

"God will punish you."

"Hey-uh. Sometime."

"His punishment will be terrible and swift!"

"I take that chance," Sam said. "First He's got to get to Wilfrid and then Martha. I come next."

"He will! He will!" Ezra said.

"Hey-uh – hey-uh." Sam whistled a jet of smoke up.

"You'd better start after them," Carlyle said to Matthew.

"Wilfrid's got his gun."

"Chicken-dancer!" cried Mrs. Bear. "Hah – chicken shit! Get the Mounties!"

"Got to get them anyway," Ezra said. "Need Mounties to recover stolen property."

"Martha isn't stolen property," Sam said from his blankets.

"Just your daughter," Mrs. Bear said.

"Maybe," Sam said.

"I wasn't talkin' about Martha," Ezra said.

"We won't bother Mounties," Sam said.

"I was talkin' about horses."

"What horses?" Sam sat up.

"He took with them. Raymond Ear saw them going," Ezra said. "They will travel fast on that hot-blood gelding and . . ."

"My horses!" Sam had leaped to his feet. "He didn't steal my . . ."

"Raymond said Wilfrid was up on that thoroughbred black – Martha, the sorrel – the pack-horse was his own."

"Matthew!"

"Wilfrid took his rifle."

A wide sweep of Sam's hand sent Matthew sprawling. "Shut up that Wilfrid gun! Go get saddled! Go get Judea's gun!" He turned to Mrs. Bear. "Blanket roll! Put in some grup! Hurry!!" He turned to Carlyle. "Phone Mounties! Tell Fyfe – tell Ottawa!"

"About Martha," Mrs. Bear said.

"No – my horses!"

"God's punishment was terrible and swift," Ezra said with satisfaction.

"God's no horse thief!"

"His awful punishment," Ezra said.

"All right – Him took those horses – He went a thousand miles – with no tracks I'd track Him too. This time Wilfrid Tail-feather! I get my horses back – or Martha's a widow! Blanket widow!"

With reluctant Matthew, Sam trailed Wilfrid and Martha into the Storm and Misty country. The next morning they reached the bridal camp deep in the crease of Storm and Misty canyon where Beulah took its rise. Wilfrid was crouched alone by the fire.

"Matthew's got you covered," Sam warned him.

"Hey-uh," said Sam's son-in-law. "Martha too. She's got you covered."

Behind Wilfrid Sam saw the glint of early-morning sun along the rifle-barrel protruding from a saskatoon clump.

"I'm getting back my horses," Sam said.

"What about Martha?"

"Just the horses."

Wilfrid poked at the fire with a stick.

"And – Ezra marry you."

Wilfrid nodded. "I'll deal." He turned his head. "Martha!"

With the safety still off, she came out of the saskatoons.

They returned, but did not get around to a wedding.

He hadn't been apprehensive about Victoria until Martha's elopement. He hadn't noticed her showing special interest in any particular boy or man. Perhaps he ought to speak to Jonas – or better – to Susan. Hell no! Warning could have no point beyond his own and her embarrassment. Victoria wasn't Martha Bear!

Late in June, Sanders kindled his fear again.

"Season's been open three weeks." Sanders bent over his bag on the kitchen table. "Good month before they're taking a fly."

"Wet or a nymph might work."

"Not really – maybe in the beaver dam. I hate messing around with bait. I don't know why I get excited so early. A little life fighting – I guess that's it." He straightened up. "Martha Bear's knocked up."

"Not surprising."

"Almost three months I'd say. How's our girl?"

God damn him!

"I said how's . . ."

"Yes. Fine."

"Same age as Marth –"

"Year older – August."

Sanders' fair brows lifted. "When's her turn?"

"My God, Peter – you have to take that attitude towards everything?"

"What attitude? Sixteen. She's pretty. I just asked – passed her on my way to Wounded-Persons'."

"How's Jane?"

"I'll be making out a death certificate for her by the end of the week."

"Elsie and Mary?"

"About like Jane last year this time. I can't get any of them into the San. Like their mother – they'll go – oh, they will go!" He sighed. "Murder! Before next spring the whole family will be wiped out. It's murder, Car!"

"We've tried."

"And accomplished nothing – makes us both murderers, doesn't it! They will – they have already – infected God knows how many!"

"You bringing the X-ray unit down?"

"What's the use! They won't co-operate. Nicotine's queered it."

"Archie – how?"

"Nicotine theory to explain TB explosion – X-ray machine gives it to them."

"No!"

"Yep. Son-of-a-bitch has fixed it so I won't get any takers at all!"

"Can't you straighten him out?"

"Nobody straightens Nicotine out. You got any of those little fur nymphs to spare?"

"Yes."

"Black, I think."

"Or – grey – muskrat belly."

"Sixteen."

"Huh?"

"Victoria. Been ready for it at least a year now. I've examined them at eleven – twelve. . . ."

"Not Victoria! Her mother will take care of that! Susan's ambitious for her. She'll get her Grade Nine – easily."

"And then?"

"She can make it to matriculation. I can get her through."

"And then?"

"I don't know."

"Teacher?"

"Maybe. Susan said something the other day – nursing."

"Great – great!"

"She is not going to get . . ."

"Have Fyfe send down a big, vicious dog for Jonas to tie up by the cabin door."

"She is not Martha Bear!"

"No – not yet."

"Please, Peter!"

"All right, Car. Just you stay by Jonas's door."

NINETEEN

OVER THE YEARS HE HAD NOT NOTICED THE CHANGE IN Ezra Powderface. He supposed he had noted vaguely that the dome-toed black boots had been replaced by moccasins encased in rubbers, the white clerical collar had been traded for a red kerchief knotted at the throat. The fall of G. Bob Dingle's retirement, Carlyle saw him for the first time without his black church coat. He wore the silver-buttoned councillor coat of faded blue. Carlyle realized that Ezra was no longer in his sixties – indeed might be in his mid seventies. The change seemed sudden, like the age-lightning that changed a young girl into a fat-faced woman with ballooning breasts and stomach. It seemed quite right now to think of him as Old Ezra.

"He took it over from Old Esau now," Archie said.

"Took what over?"

"Head councillor – he quit wearin' that church coat then."

But as well, there were other changes in Ezra; though his voice still had resonance, it had lost pulpit cadence. Nor was he as communicative as he had been. "That mean he's stopped being – doesn't he conduct services any more?"

"Hey-up. He still does that. Just because he's head councillor don't stop him from marryin' – buryin' – baptizin'."

"I guess not, Archie."

"You were religious man, Sinclair, then you would be at the service regular and you would . . ."

"That's right, Archie. I guess we're all different. You go. I don't."

"I don't go there."

"Oh – what church do you go to – now?"

"Nazarene. Shelby."

"That's nice."

"My family didn't attend the church tent several months."

"Didn't it."

"We looked at that Christian Science over the Odd Fellows' Hall, you understand – before. Ezra Powderface took that anti-Christ trail now."

"Huh? What makes you so sure Old Ezra . . ."

"He uses that drum now, and that isn't civilized, and it is heathen, and that is the whole situation. I'm very sorry he is doin' that and all his flock followin' after him down that false trail."

"For a man who's followed as many dogma trails as you have, Archie . . ."

"You know, Sinclair – you might be right."

"Thanks. How?"

"What you said back there."

"What did I say?"

"Ezra bein' head councillor now and not conducting church service."

"I didn't say that. I simply asked if he was still . . ."

"Head councillor – that's political, you understand."

"I understand."

"So what if they follow him – why do they follow him for – they aren't clear about that."

"Lot of things we do we aren't clear . . ."

"Because he's minister? Because he's head councillor? Makes him pretty big."

"I guess so."

"Don't mix it up."

"Church and State," Carlyle said.

"Hey-up. That medicine didn't do him much good."

"Oh, yes, it did – trachoma . . ."

"He don't see so good now – five years he'll be like Old Esau. Meetin' tonight – you comin'?"

"I think so."

It would be the third meeting in the last year. As soon as Moon had told him he was considering selling out and retiring to Shelby, Carlyle had discussed the possibility of adding the Moon lease to the reserve. Fyfe agreed with him that the Paradise Valley people must have more land, was willing to approach Ottawa right away.

"But – eh – start the fire on the reserve, Carlyle. Get the councillors together – get the band to . . ."

"They've already had a meeting – drawn up a petition."

"Aye-he – we'll just have to see what transpires."

One of the things that had transpired that winter was that Patty Wildman, playing tag with Warren in the cabin, while Earl and Ruth were drinking with the Harold Lefthands and the Archie Nicotines and the Orville Bears, had knocked over the stove – the baby and Elizabeth and Margaret died in the fire that burnt the cabin to the ground.

In June he took Victoria into Shelby to write her senior matriculation examinations.

When the results came out in late July, she had failed her English and her algebra.

"The English is understandable, Susan," he said to Victoria's mother and to Victoria, "but not the algebra. She had no right flunking that."

"We're ashamed," Susan said.

"That's all right. She'll write supplementaries."

"What's that?"

"Special exams. I've got the application forms. She has to make them out herself – in her own handwriting – we'll do it right now – and register the letter."

"Maybe she'll fail again."

"No."

"What's different from before?"

"Between now and the exam she's going to work. I'm going to cram her as no student has ever been crammed before. She's going to move in here and we're going to work from morning to night – every day!"

"Hey-uh," Susan said. "When do we move in?"

"We?"

"Jonas and me and Victoria and Barbara and Wesley."

"Ah – tonight."

It was crowded in the kitchen as he and Victoria worked at the table, going through old departmental examination papers for fifteen years back – the rest of the Rider family a silent audience.

The supplementary papers were held for him in Shelby post-office. He drove in for them, unpadlocked the sack in the schoolroom, supervised while Victoria wrote the mathematics in the morning, the English in the afternoon. When she had finished, he drove back into Shelby and mailed her papers.

She passed both.

When he took her into the city to begin training in the hospital, she wore the navy suit with lace at her throat – high heels. Just the eyes now! Not much – just a trace of smoke in the eyes!

On the trip back to Paradise Valley, he threw a stone on Pile of Rocks, his eighth. Oh, what can ail thee, Carlyle Sinclair! God, he was going to miss her. He'd get into the city to see her, but oh, God how he was going to miss her!

From Pile of Rocks to the suspension bridge, he changed every plastic ribbon left by the seismic crew.

Just after the afternoon recess he saw Sanders go by the long schoolroom windows – must have finished his calls. When they'd eaten lunch, Sanders' thin face had looked more drawn than usual; his attention elliptical – distracted inwards. Half an hour before closing he decided against sending the children up to the board to draw, freed them instead. Sanders was at the kitchen table. He looked up from his reports; Carlyle saw that there were two round, red spots on his high cheeks – Raggedy Ann.

"Two TB." He flipped the pencil on the table, leaned back in the kitchen chair. "One new-found – refusing treatment."

"Who?"

"Goddam the complete sovereignty of their ignorance!"

"Who?"

"Poor old man you see – the knee – wheesh – white man let go calf. . . ."

"Oh no! Esau!"

"Hey-uh."

"Refused treatment!"

"You know he did! Mr. Rider, I said to him, you are a very sick man. 'Hey-uh.' It is TB, Mr. Rider. 'Hey-uh.' I'm putting you in San. 'Oh no, you're not.' Oh yes, I am. 'Oh no, you're not,' he said."

"How bad . . ."

"In that San they will feed you a steady diet of pork steak and raisin bread – let you smoke all the Phillip Morris cigarettes you want. 'Not this Stony,' he said. Yes, I said. 'Nothing doing,' he said. They will cure you good there, I said. 'Hell they will,' he said, 'that nurse she'll just stuff Fyfe Minimal Subsistence Biscuits up my red ass you see – three times a day till the Bony-Spectre comes for me.' Well, Mr. Rider, I said, he is on his way after you now. 'But he has got farther to ride to reach me here than he has at the San,' he said, 'so I'll just wait for him right here in my cabin.' Then there isn't anything I can do for you, Mr. Rider, I said, and he said, 'yes, there is.' What?, I said. 'Oh, for a draught of that warm Storm and Misty beaker,' he said. Sorry, I said, we don't prescribe that any more. None left you see – cleaned off the dispensary shelves of all those old Storm and Misty remedies – not a single beaker of it left now – all out of Hippocrene too you see – Pure Food and Drugs people found those beaded bubbles were winking carbon monoxide at the brim."

"How long has he got?"

"Too bad it isn't just gonorrhoea, I said, I could help you there with a fine old-wives' remedy – open your window – put a rock on the sill – won't cure the clap, but it'll sure take down an excruciating hard-on if you just lay that freezing rock against the end of it – only effective in the winter months of course – piece of beaver pelt is very good too. He might last six months."

"Oh, hell!"

"Hey-uh. And how's your own good work going?"

"All right . . ."

"What's the latest Paradise gossip?"

"Raymond Blaspheme grabbed Lucy Bear – into the bush – her father went after them – they're living together now."

"Victoria Rider?"

"In training . . ."

"I know – how is she doing?"

"Fine – matron's pleased with her."

"You keep right on demanding good deeds, don't you?"

"I guess I do."

"You do. But what if you're pointing her the wrong way?"

"What!"

"Backwards."

"Oh, for God's sake, you've just come from Old Esau. . . ."

"What are you pushing her into?"

"I am not pushing her. . . ."

"Hell, you aren't."

"I am not! You are not serious!"

"I don't know."

"Damn you – you never are – you . . ."

"I am the old Colonel in Her Majesty's Punjab Pig-Stickers. . . ."

"Look – Victoria isn't a joking matt –"

". . . Colonel Sanders lying out there – Zulu spear through my brisket – pinning me down for thirty days and thirty nights. . . ."

"That was damn unfair!"

". . . it hurts, but only when I laugh. You do it too, you know, Car."

"Not about Victoria, I don't."

"That's right. There's the difference – when you're really scared – you don't laugh. I do. And I am sorry – forgive me – I – I'm scared right now."

"Old Esau?"

"All of us."

"You said there were two."

"That's right. One new-found and refused treatment – Old Esau – one old-found and not refusing treatment. I'm going into the San myself – beginning of the week."

"Oh – Peter!"

"It's all right – no – hell, it is – but Bony-Spectre isn't getting me – hasn't even looked my way for eighteen years – just recently took a couple of steps in my direction."

"I'm sorry – how long will you be . . ."

"Three months – six – maybe a year."

"Aaaaah!"

"I am sorry – that dig about Victoria – wasn't me – Bony-Spectre – you keep up your good deeds. Look after them while I'm gone."

"I will, Peter."

"Give them their cocoa – make sure they eat their Fyfe Minimal Subsistence Biscuits – keep an eye on Archie Nicotine."

"I do – I have to – you know – that motor's still hanging from the cottonwood there. . . ."

"Mmmh."

"He can't make it to Hercules Salvage for his rings and carburetor."

"They elected him a councillor, didn't they?"

"What's that prove?"

"Something. I'm kind of tired. Going to lie down for a while before I drive back."

"Stay tonight."

"Nope – I got things to straighten out."

"Stay for supper anyway."

"Pork steaks? Raisin bread?"

"Sure."

"Going to be a long time on those Fyfe cookies, you see. Sorry about – what I said about Victoria."

"That's all right."

"Keep right on – encouraging her."

"I will."

"You love her – that's import –"

"Yes – don't keep harping on it."

"Keep a good supply of that on the dispensary shelves."

"Like Dingle."

"No! Not like Dingle! Not good enough for her – any of them."

"I know."

"Sure you do, Car. Sure you do. I'm scared – I just hope we haven't got our directions crossed – one way – Storm and

Misty – Old Esau – harmony with horror. Other way – this mess. No choice – there's the hell of it, Car – no choice at all!"

"I have – Victoria has."

"That's nice. You know – you aren't – really."

"Aren't what?"

"A true Aunt Pearl."

"Thanks."

"I suspect you don't shit white. She did – didn't she?"

"I guess so – one time I saw it she did."

"Opposite."

"Of what?"

"Your Paradise Valley people."

"Huh!"

"Black. You should know that – pay better attention. . . ."

"Look – who's the Aunt Pearl!"

"Serious oversight – all that wild game – blue elk. . ."

"I never did get a professional explanation from you – what about Aunt Pearl?"

"Her white stool? Oh – soppy – sippy – bland diet, I guess. You get it with older – no – more likely mucous colitis."

"Whatever that is."

"Anxiety – not ulcerative but – God, now wouldn't that be funny!"

"What?"

"Your anal erotic Aunt Pearl – responsible for the whole mechanistic mess we're in."

"No. Not very."

"Sent us all to play in the technological toy room – she's still burning her string you know – in that great bathroom in the sky!"

"I agree."

Sanders lifted a cupped hand, the thumb crooked back; he made a broad pass back and forth, depressing his thumb. "Haaaaaaah – haaaaaaaaaah – sssssssssssit – pressurized cans of flora green – oh – oh, if only she'd toilet-train the hydro and pulp and gas and oil and the little automobile boys – before they do it all over the whole wild green broadloom!"

He had looked so tired, and after supper agreed to stay overnight, get an early start in the morning. But they talked a long time, over the partition in the dark, after they'd gone to bed.

"I'll probably cough quite a bit, Car – nothing I can do about it."

"That's all right."

"My mother used to swear by a couple tablespoons of honey in a glass of water by the bed. We don't have that on the dispensary shelves any more either. Lost all happy days now, Car."

"Not for good, Peter."

"Hope not."

"I'm sorry, Peter."

"I know you are."

A few moments later, Sanders said, "Car?"

"Yes?"

"You look after them while I'm gone."

"I will."

"Drop me a note if Nicotine ever gets that truck going."

"Yes."

"Or if he doesn't."

"Yes."

"Or if – Victoria doesn't."

"Yes."

"Miss you."

"Me too. Peter?"

"Yes?"

"*Ish-ny-ish.*"

"Haaaaaah! *No-watch-es-nichuh.*"

PART THREE

TWENTY

"I'D LIKE TO PAY THIS MAN'S FINE," REVEREND HEALLY Richards said to the red-headed corporal with the pale eye. "Nicotine."

The corporal pulled a sheet over to himself. "His name, Mr. Nicotine?"

"*His* name is Nicotine. I am the Reverend Heally Richards."

"Sure." The finger moved slowly down the sheet.

"Archie Nicotine," Archie said.

"Sure – sure – ah – yeah – ten and costs – and the charge was indec –"

"We already know that," Archie said quickly.

The evangelist dropped a twenty-dollar bill on the desk, turned, began to walk towards the outer door.

He was half way there when the corporal called after him, "Hold on – you got change coming."

"How much?" Archie said.

"Two-fifty."

Archie glanced after the broad white back at the door now. "You're new on here. I come frequent. Just put it down for a credit on my account."

"I don't keep any – I can't put . . ."

The door had closed behind the evangelist.

251

"Sometime I might want to."

"Want to what!"

"Fart – when I'm in this civilized city again."

The doorman of the Foothills Carleton Hotel was an impossible cross-fertilization between beefeater and medicine man; he wore a long, scarlet tunic, but the beefeater hat had been replaced by a shaggy, buffalo-horned, medicine-man head-dress. No matter how often he stayed at the hotel, Carlyle was sure he could never get used to it. There was, as well, a gas flare burning to the right of the doors on a high standard that came out of the sidewalk pavement. When the Foothills Carleton had been first built eight years ago – and the flame ignited – Carlyle had decided it was an honouring perpetual flame. Six feet below the concrete lay the remains of some unknown rough-neck, representing all those brave oilmen who had given their lives in the search for gas and oil to warm the homes and run the cars of North America.

He stood by the flare and wondered where to begin now that he had driven into the city and registered. First – he was not looking for her in a city of half a million people, but in that area marked out by the shopping-mall and the Devonian Tower – the railroad tracks and the stockyards – the east end of the downtown section – at the most a population of twenty to thirty thousand. Each day he must check out the bus depot for the south-bound and the west-bound – the Indian Friendship Centre – but that would be better in the evenings. Then all the restaurants where she might have been able to find work, and in between he'd patrol the streets, ask any Indians he saw – oh – and the Salvation Army Hostel for Women too. Not the bars or beer parlours – not for her – yet! Again he wondered if he shouldn't go in and see Sergeant Laidlaw at the police station, and again he decided not to; he'd gone there so often to bail out

Archie and the others, and this was not Archie or the others! This was Victoria! He'd find her himself!

So – leave the car in the underground parking lot of the hotel – walk to the bus depot – then the Salvation Army Hostel – then – some kind of regular check-out of restaurants – but not the bars or police station – not yet.

Heally Richards initiated no conversation as he and Archie rode in the white Cadillac from the police station to the parking space in front of the Liberty Café. The short trip was, therefore, silent. When they were facing each other over the table of their stall, Heally said he considered the Liberty something less than four star, but it was only a block from the Devonian Tower, where he must do some taping in an hour. Archie thanked him again for paying the indecent fine and costs.

"About Esau. I mentioned about it to you before."

"Yes."

"Old Esau. Sick."

"Yes, Brother Nicotine."

"Healin' Old Esau for TB. I been thinkin' about that."

"Ever since you spoke to me at the tent last week, I have too."

"I come to a conclusion about that. Maybe we might bring him in here."

"Yes."

"With Prince Dixon's truck we could fix up a bed for him in the back of it. Bring him to you."

Richards nodded.

"All the way in to you."

Richards nodded again.

"If he can make it all the way in."

"Oh, I'm sure he will."

"I mean alive."

"Praise God, he will be."

"Hey-uh. Tomorrow."

"My final service of the rally here is a Saturday. I think the last Saturday would be . . ."

"Tomorrow would be a good time for Esau."

"I've decided on an afternoon service instead of evening – for the wind-up – what I have in mind is doing the Burning Bush Hour live from the tent with the mobile crew. CSFA-TV people have agreed to it. I want Old Esau for that. I want you to bring him in for that Saturday afternoon."

"Alive."

"Well, of course." Richards looked over his shoulder. "Where's that waitress?"

"If he's still livin' Saturday."

"Of course – praise the Lord he will be."

"That's five days – tomorrow would be a lot better. . . ."

"We'll pray for him – the whole congregation tonight – each service between now and then – with our concerted prayer liftin' . . ."

"He might not last anyway."

"Have faith – he will."

The waitress came up to take their order. Silverware clattered to the table; she put out a quick, defensive hand to keep it from spilling to the floor.

"Hey-uh!" Archie said with surprise. "You work here!"

The young Indian girl in green uniform picked up a fallen spoon, began to lay out the settings.

"New spoon," Richards said. Then, as she placed a menu down before him, "I will not need that, Sister. Just bring me a large glass of milk – four slices of bread – white – butter – and a saucer of peanut butter." He said to Archie, "I can tell you one thing, Brother Nicotine – I do have this one little old vice – peanut butter. I have loved peanut butter all my life. Mine was a poor home, but my mother always had peanut butter on our table. I love it to this day – often eat it for my dessert – sometimes it is my entire meal."

"Hey-uh," Archie said. He looked up to the waitress, who had taken an order pad and pencil from her pocket. "Three pork steaks – french fries – coffee." The girl turned away. "Peanut butter for dessert."

The girl left them.

"When you see those dusty geraniums sprawlin' in the window," Heally said, "you can be safe with peanut butter. The young lady. You know her."

"Hey-uh."

"That Indian with the scar – his sister – I was wondering how I might get in touch with them – where."

"They're wicked people."

"We all are. More or less. Some of our services. I've noticed them in the back – didn't have a chance to speak with them. Felt there might be a native shyness that kep' . . ."

"Those Catfaces aren't shy. He's why I was in that trouble you helped me out. He robbed me my rings and carburetor. Gloria with her heels behind is just as wicked as him now."

"We were all spotless of sin – pretty well put me and the Lord right out of business, wouldn't it? They've come to the rally – if they wish to be saved . . ."

"I know them – they're spotted bad, Rev-rund, but it's not for bein' saved they come to . . ."

"We don't try, we surely won't save anyone, Brother. I am not about to leave them in the pit."

"They're in a sack."

"I'm more interested in talking with them now. Saved or not they can be of help to the Lord – you too – if there's any way you can get me a line on them."

"Mainly they hang around the Empress bar – east end here you can run across her – walkin' – either way from that tower."

"But – you don't know where they stay."

"Hey-uh." Archie shook his head. "I intend to find that out."

"If you do – I want to talk with them."

"If you do – you tell me where he is."

"I will."

"You better find him first," Archie said, "and that is the whole situation."

Richards looked at his watch. "Wish that girl would hurry up."

"About Old Esau," Archie said. "Too bad you couldn't do it tomorrow for him."

"No. We've got that all settled now – the last Saturday of the rally – you can park the truck round behind the tent – carry him in – lay him down and let him rest behind the platform. . . ."

"If he don't die too soon."

"Mr. Hillaker's handling out front – he's the one – don't you worry yourself – we'll work out all the details. I always plan ahead of time. . . ."

"If Old Esau died first, then it might spoil your plans."

"Have faith, Brother Nicotine."

"Hey-uh."

"You catch your bus back to – ah – to . . ."

"Paradise."

"In our service tonight we will pray for Old . . ."

"Maybe I'll take another bus."

The waitress set down Richards' bread and saucer of peanut butter, his glass of milk. "Thank you, Sister."

"Wouldn't hurt," Archie said.

"What's that?" Heally had begun to butter a slice.

"If I took another Greyhound later. Come tonight over to the tent. Wouldn't hurt when they pray for Old Esau."

"Of course – of course." Richards dug into the mound of peanut butter. "Come." Carefully he trowelled it with his knife. "Add your prayers to ours."

"I will. Wouldn't hurt to have one prayin' in Stony for him." Archie watched Richards lift the peanut-buttered slice, lips drawing back before the first bite. Beaver all right. "You didn't say grace yet."

Slice half way up, Heally looked startled. "You're right. Hallelujah. Praise Him – peanut butter – praise His name. Amen!" He took a bite, spoke around it. "Short meal – short blessin'. If there's time tonight – you and I and Brother Hillaker," he swallowed, "can clarify details." He took another quick bite.

He had chewed up everything before Archie was half way through his pork steaks. He blessed Archie, and without being asked, gave him ten dollars for the bus, left a twenty-five-cent tip for the waitress, paid the supper bill to the dark-moustached man at the till, left for his taping.

When the waitress brought his peanut-butter dish, Archie said, "Sit down."

She looked over to the till. "The Greek doesn't like that. English."

"Just stand." She wasn't fat like Maureen or Maxine. "How long you been workin' in here?"

"Two weeks. Archie, my grampa . . ."

"He was alive when I left . . ."

"Has he hem – coughed much blood?"

"Hey-uh – a while back – maybe some more – I just got out the bucket today. I was in there since Saturday. He's still alive. You better come home."

She shook her head.

"TB Bony-Spectre – just about ready to take him away now. Did you fail – at the hospital?"

"No."

"I got enough for you too. Rev-rund Richards gave me enough for the bus for you too."

She shook her head.

"Hey-uh." Archie dug out a spoonful of brown peanut butter. "He heals people, you know. He promised he would heal your grampa. . . ."

"No!"

"Saturday."

"He can't heal him!"

"Maybe – he's goin' to take a run at it."

"No!"

"Well we're bringin' him in to him."

"Don't. He can't stand that now! It won't do him any . . ."

"If we got faith maybe . . ."

"No! Won't work at all! Leave him alone!"

After a struggle Archie had finally got the peanut butter all swallowed down. He dropped the spoon, pushed the saucer away. "Maybe you learned all about how to cure TB in that hospital . . ."

"Archie – don't bring . . ."

". . . so if you would come back on the bus with me . . ."

"No."

"All right. Sinclair's lookin' for you."

"I know. Archie – don't move him. . . ."

"You hidin' from him?"

She nodded.

"Doesn't stop you from comin' back to Paradise. They'll hide you there."

"I can't."

"Old Esau might like to say good-bye – he'd know it was you."

"I can't!"

"I don't care why you don't want to say why."

"I'm ashamed."

"Hey-uh."

"I can't do it – I can't go back to the hospital."

"Hey-uh. Those Catfaces been in here since you started work here?"

"Few times."

"All right – if they come in, you wait on them, but you stay away from them."

"You aren't my father!"

"I'm Stony – stay away from them."

"I would anyway. . . ."

"You don't, you'll be more ashamed. You stay away from them, then I won't say anything to Sinclair I found you." He got up. "I got some time till church to kill. Maybe I can run across Norman somewhere – and kill him too."

"Don't bring in my grampa. . . ."

"Hey-uh. See how Richards heals tonight. If he's very good at it, then Old Esau – Saturday."

"He's my grampa!"

"If he's still livin'. I will consult with Susan. You stay away from those Catfaces." Archie stared down at the saucer still heaped with peanut butter. "Rev-rund Richards' mother always had that squirrel shit on their poor table."

His feet – particularly across the ankles – ached. There hadn't been many of the restaurants in his searching area that he had missed. Tomorrow he would have to include bars and beer parlours – but she didn't have any money so it wasn't likely – Oh, Christ – none of the girls needed it. . . . Tonight he'd try the Friendship Centre – around nine – ten o'clock – when things had got underway there.

He could save time on his bus-depot calls; there were only two likely ones each afternoon: the west-bound, which she might take if she were travelling towards Banff and sanctuary in Hanley reserve, then, half an hour later, the south-bound express leaving at 4:20 p.m. This afternoon she had been there for neither of them, and there would be nothing departing to carry her south or west until late evening. Oh, God, maybe he should check out trains too! Yes!

TWENTY-ONE

BY THE TENT OPENING MR. HILLAKER MET EACH PERSON, told them to sit down close to the platform in front. "Welcome, Brother," he said when he shook Archie's hand. Old mosquito. "Take a seat up near the front praise God."

Archie did that. There weren't many people in the tent – just scattered over the benches before the white pulpit. Heally Richards wasn't anywhere around. First time Archie had ever been in a tent this big – with electric lights in it – strings of them from the poles. After the dark spring night, the inside was lit up bright as a used-car lot.

A woman got up from the side front seat and sat down to the piano; then old mosquito-man got up on the platform and told them the first hymn. Another man, very fat – porcupine – led them, and they sang, "Jesus loves me!" and pointed with both hands at their own chest, then, "Jesus loves you!" and pointed with their arms out from themselves, then, "Jesus loves all of us!" and made big opposite circles with their hands open, as though they were wiping something off the air in front of themselves.

Then he saw Heally Richards, down on one knee beside the pulpit, his white back to all the people and his white head down. When the singing finished, he got up and went behind the pulpit. He said they were all welcome to the tent of Jesus Christ. He said for three weeks they had been having great glory in this tent during the Rally for Jesus, and there would be a lot more glory to come. He said there had been many fine miracles and there would be lots more of them. He said the Lord could do anything so long as they had faith and sent their praise up to Him. So far as Archie could tell, Heally Richards didn't sound so much different from what a continuing Methodist did – or Baptist – or Nazarene – or any of the others he had ever taken a try at.

Fear, Heally Richards said, belonged to the devil – not to the Lord. "Faith is the foundation for all His miracles and the devil's fear rots out that footin' and brings the miracles tumblin' down – let that fear into you – it is just the devil knockin' – that's all. 'Here I am – I'm back again' – you let your faith in the miraculous pahr the Lord decay – let the devil back inside of you and he will undo – that miracle. He truly will. If you are not brimmin' with faith – the Lord cannot even tighten up your dentures for you – and don't you laugh now because sloppy dentures are an abomination, and the Lord has fixed a lot of false teeth in His time – saved a lot of dentist bills – oh yes, He truly has – anything is possible to Him!

"Why – in Mill Valley, California, they brought a little ten-year-old girl to me to be touched – Vicky – ten years old and she did not have a tooth in her head – disease had destroyed all the buds of her teeth – and I touched her – and there come out of her a shrill and piercin' scream and you don't have to believe it – but right there – right then – four teeth sprung through her gum – upper gum – and a month later – Vicky – I saw her again, and the Lord, He had not stopped with the one miracle – He had gone right on settin' them off like fire-crackers, because she had – one month later – every single one of her teeth – full set – uppers and lowers of the most beautiful, pearly-white teeth you ever saw. She was standin' there with her momma in the candy section the Mill Valley Pay an' Save with all her lovely new teeth. They had just purchased – ay full pound of – peanut brittle!

"You don't have to believe it nor you don't have to believe the miracle took place in Ashland, Oregon, when His Healin' Pahr cured a woman stone-deaf for thirty years – yes she was, but He cured her so she threw away her useless, squawkin', old hearin'-aid and with her naked ear she could hear ay whisper! Oh no – you don't have to believe it – pretty hard to believe the Lord could do that, isn't it – to have the faith the Lord could do that.

"Oh, I just wish you could have been with me in the Angeles Temple in L. A. last summer, August eleven – to see that little old woman shakin' an' tremblin' with Parkinson's – she could not – hold in her right hand a teaspoon – let alone ay cup an' saucer – but she got up off of the floor where His glory dropped her down, and that arm which had shivered an' shook for fifteen years was as steady as ay rock and with it she picked ay book up off of – the pulpit! She held it high above her old, grey head – His book – the Bible! You don't have to believe it – how He cured her – of her Parkinson's. Takes a lot of faith to believe that! Maybe you haven't got that much faith, but I am warnin' you, that is how much faith you got to have! If – He's goin' to do one of His miracles on you!

"Oh, I tell you – the Lord – praise His name – hallelujah – He can do anything! Nothing is impossible to the Lord! If – you have faith and send up to Him your praise of Him hallelujah! Oh, I know! He worked a miraculous cure on my own dear mother went crazy – she didn't just have a little bitty modren nervous breakdown you know – she went – stark – ravin' mad – overnight! And He cured her! Yes He did! You believe He cured her? You believe that! Believe it! He did too! Why not! He can cure – He can heal your muscles – your bones – your blood – your veins an art'ries – all – of your organs! You're crazy, then He can heal that too. Why – should He – stop at – the neck!

"If you believe – anything is possible! If you have faith, and it takes a lot of it – anything is possible for the Lord! In Winnipeg, Manitoba, a young woman came to me complainin' of this tooth-ache she had. Now I didn't have to be any dentist to diagnose the cause of – her tooth-ache. There it plainly was – that woman had the biggest cavity you ever saw – right back here – left-hand side – one of those big ones there – lower. She wanted me – to touch her cavity. I did. Oh, how I prayed to the Lord He would heal up her cavity. He didn't. He did not heal up her cavity! Instead – He – filled it! You don't have to believe that. You do not have to believe the Lord did that miraculous thing in the city of Winnipeg, Manitoba, Canada – Sunday night – October nineteen – on the stage of the Labour Temple Gardens. You do not have to believe that He filled her achin' tooth – with – gold. And please do not ask me how He did that miracle. Don't you ask me where He got – that gold – from – to fill her cavity because I simply do not – know! All I know – is – that He has got the whole entire universe to get it – from! All I know – is – He could have found it anywhere – He could have found it – on Saturn or Mars – I do – not – know.

"But now – I do know this though – I do have in – my possession – documents – provin' the Lord done this miraculous thing – signed by witnesses to it – I do have those documents with the signatures of the pastor, the Sunday School superintendent – the organist of that church – not Pentecostal – just Nazarene – I do have those documents, and besides those signatures there are the signatures of scientists and doctors testifyin' to – this!

"No limit! No limit at all to His healin' pahr – oh – one thing about that Winnipeg woman – she went home and she was deathly afraid of her husband, and the next mornin' when she woke up, that fillin' had turned – to brass! You don't have to believe it. And the next day – it had turned to – nothin'! Totally disappeared! Fear – the devil – had cancelled that miracle right out! Didn't have to – could have lasted for the rest of her life! That wonderful miracle the Lord had been chomped up by – the devil's – fear termites!

"You get the devil and his fear out of there – you aim for the stars – maybe your gran'ma stole a mule once long before you were born and you're ashamed and you're afraid – now just you forget all about that – you aim for those stars – you'll make it – but – just as sure – as anything – you're still worried about that mule your little old gran'ma stole – you will end up – on the wood-pile."

They sang some more. Then Heally Richards told them to pray, and they did that, but not for Old Esau. Then they sang some more. Then Heally Richards said how sick Old Esau was and to pray for this noble old chief to hang on till Saturday and make it in to the Mercy Seat and be touched by the Lord's healing power through Heally Richards' hands. Archie prayed in Stony. A lot of them were holding up their arms and shaking red ants off them. It had got pretty noisy in the tent. It got a lot noisier, and they were all shouting, but it didn't sound like English. It didn't even sound like Sarcee.

Beer made him feel the same way. Hallelujah!

It was healing time, and the Reverend Richards, just by touching them, dropped five people to the grass in front of the white pulpit. The fat man put a white cloth over their crotches, and Archie didn't understand why he did that to them. Then he saw a couple of them had pissed themselves. Richards could heal all right, and that was the whole situation. Bring in Old Esau Saturday – if he could just keep living that long. Now he might.

He had to get up and leave early to catch the last Greyhound. As he went out through the tent opening, he couldn't help it; he jerked off a couple Chicken Dance steps.

TWENTY-TWO

HE KNEW NOW THAT HE SHOULD HAVE GONE IN TO SEE
Sergeant Laidlaw first thing – reported her missing. Soon as he'd
come into the city. God knew what irreparable damage could
have been done to her in the three days he'd lost! Just that
much more chance of her being found, with the police as well
looking for her – might have made the difference between
finding her and not finding her. Three days and evenings of wan-
dering and aching with confused helplessness! It was all he could
do – visit and revisit the Indian Friendship Centre, the bus
depot, bars and restaurants – searching among the destroyed, the
homeless young, the limbo-dwellers. The longer he looked for
her, the harder it became to find one shred of optimism. Why
should he!

She was gone for ever! She'd left the city. No! She was still
in the city, and if he kept on searching – sooner or later he
would find her here. But of course he hadn't yet, and the odds
against him were high, and it didn't help him at all to remind
himself that he was not looking for her in a city of a half a
million people, for he was. The odds were a half-a-million to one
against him! And he should have called upon the police!

At night in the hotel room he lay in bed and could not sleep
till dawn, and in the darkness the feeling of hopelessness simply

grew and grew to despair. Oh, God, he would never find her! She was now dead to him! Accept it, Sinclair – accept that now! Go and tell the police tomorrow – give them her description, but realize that it will not make one bit of difference at all – that they will never find her either!

Now, he could not find her even within himself. When he tried to summon her face behind his closed eyelids, he could not manage one cue; her eyes, the way her hair parted over her forehead, a mouth corner – all refused to appear to him. The inner magic lantern would show nothing of her to him any more – her small hands – just one of them – lifted to her hair or – cupped – to her mouth in embarrassment – or holding a piece of coloured chalk. But just when he had given up, he could suddenly see her handwriting – the feminine "m"s and "n"s and "h"s and "o"s, gracefully curved and evenly disciplined. He could see a whole lined page from her exercise book. That was all – not a gesture – not her walk – not her laughter; she had been erased from within himself!

Then the smell stole to him – a subtle musk that he couldn't identify at first – it belonged to August and to elliptic, silver leaves – wolf willow! But that was not the right perfume, for it didn't have the light willow sweetness; this was more like the faintest drift of smoke. In the dark hotel room it had surprised him – the shy smell of her hair and she was not lost for ever and he would find her and first thing tomorrow he would go to the police station and report her missing and he would find her or they would find her for him!

Oh, God, he must find her!

The red-headed corporal with the almost lashless, pale eyes was unfamiliar to him. Carlyle told him he would like to see Sergeant Laidlaw.

"Not here."

"Do you expect him in?"

"Not for another ten days. Holidays. Anything I can help you with?"

"You might. I'm looking for a young girl."

"Uh-huh."

"I would like to report a – girl lost." He'd almost said, "little girl lost."

"Her age?" The corporal had pulled over a sheet to himself, taken up a pencil.

"Nineteen – dark hair – eyes."

"Weight?"

"She's – slight. Hundred – hundred and five."

"Height?"

"Not tall. Five one – two."

"Wearin'?"

"I don't know. She's in – been in training for a nurse."

"So she's wearin' nurse's . . ."

"I don't think so."

"How long?"

"What?"

"She been missin'."

"Two weeks."

"First time?"

"Pardon?"

"Lost her before?"

"No."

"I mean – any idea maybe she might want to be lost? She's . . . ," he looked down to his sheet, ". . . she's nineteen."

"No," Carlyle said, "I haven't any at all."

"Your daughter?"

"No – she isn't."

"You're a relative."

"No."

"Friend the family."

"I'm a teacher – Paradise Valley reserve south of . . ."

"Oh." Brilliant understanding lighted the corporal's face. "Just you hold on now. Indian girl – that's different – maybe we do have something for you. Deal – Constable Deal – he's vice an' drugs – Dan mentioned he give a couple warnin's – uh – Catface – Gloria Catface? Is that your missin' person?"

"No. It isn't. Your vice squad wouldn't be having anything to do with this . . ."

"Sooner or later . . ."

"Not this girl. Her name is Victoria Rider. I don't know why – but, she is missing – has been for over two weeks."

"Matter of time – we'll let you know if we bring her in."

"Thanks. And – beyond bringing her in – will you do something about finding her. Sergeant Laidlaw . . ."

"On his holidays."

"Yes. But I would appreciate – whether or not you – bring her in – anything you can do to find her. She's not – she's different from Gloria Catface."

"Okay. Your name an' address."

"Carlyle Sinclair – Foothills Carleton."

"I thought you said Paradise . . ."

"For the next few days."

"Sure."

Carlyle turned away from the desk.

"Paradise Valley reserve."

"Yes."

"We just had one of your outfit. Nicotine."

God, he'd forgot all about Archie! "Is Archie Nicotine in . . ."

"Nope. Released couple days ago."

"Suspended sentence."

"Ten dollars and costs. Indecent exposure."

"And he's been released? Who paid his fine?"

"Some preacher."

"Oh."

"I'll speak to Constable Deal for you. He's pretty good."

"Thanks."

"It can get pretty rough in here for them."

"I know."

"That Catface girl – Dan didn't have to give her any warnin' at all – she's turnin' tricks all right. He give her two warnin's. You know him."

"No . . ."

"CSFA – he's the one on that Safety Corral show with the kids singin' an' dancin' an' playin' their guitars. Officer Dan?"

"I've seen him then."

"He's had a couple Indian kids on Safety Corral. I'll speak to him for you, Mr. Carlyle."

"Thanks."

"She's still in the city – we'll find her for you. And you can do somethin' for me. You tell that son-of-a-bitch Nicotine, next time he hauls out that smoked John Donacker his in public, it'll be thirty days automatic and no goddam fine option!"

Instead of continuing his search longer, he returned to the hotel, went into the dusk of the Wee-Sack-A-Shack Room. Before he had finished his rye and water, he knew it was going to do nothing for his appetite, even though he had missed lunch after his visit to the police station in the morning. But he did feel quite tired, and if he went up to his room, he just might be able to get some sleep.

He had to wait for a large, tanned man in white to step out of the elevator.

He couldn't sleep.

He got up, switched on the television set, lay down on the bed again; there was always the possibility of being bored into sleep. The image straightened itself out in time for a woman to illustrate that her dentures would now permit her to attack an apple without a feeling of insecurity; another refused to give up her favourite brand of detergent; a professional model confided more than he cared to know about her armpits; a homespun man with a truculent air told him the only place to get his bulk spring fertilizer. There came the sound of gunshots, then Western music for a program called "Safety Corral."

"From CSFA-TV, high atop the Devonian Tower," Officer Dan's Safety Corral broadcast one hour of country Western, rock Western, Knoxville Western, gospel Western, as well as animated cartoons, rope twirling, the bass and falsetto repartee of the hand-puppets Bewly and Pewly, Kowboy Kalendar, birthday announcements, and a final five minutes of lost-and-found items. Officer Dan's Safety Corral was preceded by Ping Pong Bingo and followed by the Burning Bush Hour.

Though in real life he was plain-clothes vice and drugs, Officer Dan wore traffic uniform, studio lights glinting off his Sam Browne belt, the polished holster, his black leather boots. The uniform had been his own before he had left traffic for vice six years ago, but now the jacket was restive at its buttons; the belt was tight; the peaked cap with its silver badge seemed to be sitting a little high on a head that had put on middle-age weight. The kids liked the too-small hat and uniform, possibly because it suggested Officer Dan was almost one of them, playing cops while they played cowboys.

The show opened always with Officer Dan conducting the Buckaroo and Maverick Pledge before a corral pole-fence and beside a cherry-coloured stable, out of which was thrust a stuffed palomino horse's head. Later in the show Bewly and Pewly used the closed lower half of the stable door. Above the opening were branded the letters LBW.

Freddy the floor man, in his ear-phones, lowered and swung his arm towards the camera trained on Officer Dan; this full-on shot was all that Officer Dan would ever proffer, for it was as though he had just apprehended the camera and didn't dare chance the profile that would take his eyes off it. Slightly ahead of him and to either side stood a girl in ruby-velvet, barrel-racing costume and an orange-and-black-embroidered boy. Each held up a traffic sign; the boy's said GO; the girl's said STOP.

"Well – well – now, my wrangler friends – both young an' old," Officer Dan read from the back of the girl's sign, "guess it is about just time again for Officer Dan an' his Safety Corral down here on the LBW ranch. That's our brand up there right enough – and we all know what that stands for – don't we now. LBW stands for Look Both Ways, don't it? Yessireebob! Now – I want you to take the pledge with me – raise your gosh-durn right arm out there – no – no – not that one – that is your shootin' arm – you know that – all right now – ready? Say solemnly after me – solemnly – I do solemnly pledge that – I will – whenever I go . . ."

Officer Dan shifted his eyes to the back of the boy's sign. ". . . to cross a street – I will – LOOK BOTH WAYS – by grannies!" Actually, the Buckaroo and Maverick Pledge was not too great a parody of the city's Western Hospitality Pledge, administered by the head of the Tourist and Convention Bureau to visiting dignitaries and convention delegates when they were presented with white cowboy hats.

"And to wind up this session of Officer Dan's Safety Corral – before you mavericks an' buckaroos head for Mom's chuck-wagon with her old pie-drawer on the back – here's some lost-and-found items."

Officer Dan looked down at the card cupped in his hand just below the frame. "Lost – young – apricot – male poodle – miniature ear tattooed. Meadow Lark Park area. Answers to the name of – uh – Demi-tasse." Officer Dan lifted his eyes to the camera. "Guess that's how you'd say that name." He lowered his eyes. "Oh – reward for return or information to his fate. 287-2348."

Officer Dan shuffled the card to the back of his deck, read from the next one. "Next lost item. Girl's perscription glasses. Round black rims. On Johnston Road bus. 284-5490." He made sure the camera was still there before him. "That is a real important lost item, because this little girl is in hot water with her Mom for leavin' those expensive glasses there on that Johnston Road bus.

"Next lost item – Lost – Red Hustler – girl's bike – missing from S. W. backyard. Reward. 252-0650. And for the last lost item we have this serious announcement to make. We would like any information or help we can get to help – us – locate Victoria Rider – missin' since two weeks – age nineteen – hundred and ten pounds – five two – last seen she may of been wearin' nurse's uniform. Now – anybody havin' any notion at all about the whereabouts of Victoria Rider, please get in touch with the city police department. 798-7715. Victoria is one of our fine young Indian friends. From Paradise Valley reserve."

As Officer Dan finished, the telephone number ran across the bottom of the picture three times.

In Room 517 of the Foothills Carleton the Reverend Healy Richards had finished the last of his peanut butter and bread. He pulled back so that he could open the desk drawer against his stomach and slide into it the plates he had kept from the room-service breakfast on the second day of the Rally For Jesus. The nice, warm satisfaction was still in him – seventeen up to be touched, and he could tell that there had been healings – the two slipped discs – upper and lower – the colitis – forget Hillaker's prostate – the tooth-ache. Back trouble and colitis and teeth – he'd always had pretty good luck with them.

It had been a fine service; it truly had, and that was a good sign – attendance growing after the second-week peak – or – rather – after it had slid down in the third week – which it always did. That was the week when his faith slid too, and he could not be so sure that God wanted to use his hands for healing. Then he must tell himself that perhaps the miraculous cures were not so important as the visitation of glory itself when the Spirit of God dropped them to the grass – even though the flesh might not be healed. What about the healing of the soul itself? What about salvation? To be saved from the pit – there was the true miracle, wasn't it?

Hell was real; he had faith in Hell. He even knew how Hell smelled – french-fries and Milky Way chocolate bars – no – cocoa butter that greased their legs and shoulders and breasts and thighs before they were thrown into the deep fat fry of Hell. Maybe it was sin that smelled so sweetly chocolate – greasy sin – LaPrelle Snell – Blanche Haddad. Yes. There were two distinct stages to Hell – first the carnival one – Blue Eyes – Brown Eyes – pink tits – brown tits – the human pin-cushion pulls a half-ton truck with a steel spear thrust through his skin – runs six meat skewers through his tongue and feels not the slightest tingle of pain or even discomfort. Nerves rotted with tertiary syphilis; Professor Noble Wine-singer had told him that. The geek that bites the heads off live Wyandotte roosters – Lizard Lady, with her snake eyelids and her skin to make a genuine alligator club-bag, with enough left over for shoes and belt – Incaboy Pinhead – fiddle the Arkansas Traveller backwards – Blue Eyes whose beauty drives all men mad. Oh yes, he knew carny Hell and its citizens. And he knew the second stage too. Skid-row Hell. Oh, Brother, I have known the Hell of sin and destruction – poisoned the temple of the soul with booze and sterno juice – sunk as low as a man can sink – rotten miserable, decaying McGoof hound – wrung-out winter Christian till He lifted me from the gutter where I lay sodden and sour! Jerusalem Slim He lifted me right out of the Spy Hill Jail – praise Him – praise His name!

And now of course he wasn't going to be able to sleep all night again. LaPrelle and Blanche's fault – funny how you couldn't keep from going back and back – to the hot box apartment always smelling of roach powder, and her unending whine, and the dark, crescent sweat-stains under her arms – well she was Arab, and they did have the crescent on their flag, didn't they? And she had hooked him. Cass had warned him, and he hadn't listened, and married her anyway, and stood it for a whole two years before he lit out sheet-writing, and from that it had been a step up to books – *Masters and Scholars Encyclopedia*. It took more time to score than a magazine subscription – no – not magazine – never call it magazine – periodical – and he had truly made it in the books. He truly had. Oxford grey suit – double-breasted – dark-blue Homburg hat – Packard car. Wasn't another book man in North America was pumped back in the barber's chair every morning after breakfast – had his face swathed in steaming towels and the mint smell of shaving-cream – got that wrinkle from a Waterman's Fountain Pen traveller in Mobile. Why had preachers and priests been such good taps? "You are one of only ten people in this community, Father, selected by Greystone Press for the writing of a testimonial letter such as this one by Franklin Delano Roosevelt and this one by Jimmy Walker – doesn't have to be as detailed or as long as these – just your own intelligent and honest evaluation of the scholarship of the set and the new cross-reference structuring – perhaps

with your own opinion of its usefulness in sermon preparation."
Well – one thing he'd learned: architecture was "ark . . ." not
like in "arch support."

". . . so that we can use it like these others, Reverend, in all
our promotional literature – for our advertisements in *Atlantic*
and *Saturday Review of Literature* and *Ladies' Home Journal*."
Priests and preachers and grain-elevator operators out West.
Why them – something to do with chop-dust and bran in their
crotch? The books had given him a good run for three – no –
five years – could have made a million if it hadn't been for the
liquor – later and later in the morning on calls – two-week bats
and sobering up and drying out and drying out and then the
Long Beach Pike and Professor Noble Wine-singer. "Always try
for the bowel, Richard."

The Professor said he could have been a dentist or a doctor
– given high school and college years ago, and no booze. What
chance of that? – his old man hadn't let him make it past fresh-
man year. Half-assed mechanic with his jack-knife handle
almost swallowed in his hand, and the great thumb used as a
brace while he scraped and scraped and scraped the face of all
his nails, so that Richard winced against when he must go right
through them to the flesh.

Richard Victor Heally – the Heally had been his mother's
maiden name. Once the Heallys had been truly important in
Pinellas County – but not any more – even before the first boom
bust. If only it hadn't been for his father that was going to make
a fortune out of ginseng roots and didn't – that always had a
motor hoisted and hanging from the mango branch and whipped
him once between motors just for hanging a truck tire to swing
on a rope. His branch. But between beatings there'd been exciting times in the little Victory Born Agains church, even if his
father did hog most of the testifying and then later took up

preaching so he could run the whole show. The deeper he got into preaching, it seemed, the more beatings he gave Richard.

There had been a lot of happy times fishing off nigger pier, with the pelicans riding out there and watching your bobber so you had to hoist the bamboo pole quick to beat them to your fish, even though it was generally a grunt that had soft flesh and tasted muddy and had a million bones. There was always the hope that you might tie into a red snapper or amberjack or sheep's-head, and sometimes there were mackerel runs. Once he landed a sting-a-ray with help from the pinto nigger with pink splotches running up and around one eye and from under his chin and across his ear. They looked painful.

Once, when he hadn't hoed because he'd gone roller skating instead, he had hidden from his father, out in the palmettos and saw-grass, and watched a chameleon and kept tipping the leaf so it had to move and do its magic change from rust to green – to almost yellow – to rust again – and he only wished he could do that too. Once when he was swimming with Cass on the Gulf side, the water had been filled with millions of little mint jelly-fish and they had a jelly-fish fight. When the tide went out, he and Cass often went out on the bay side and looked for the piss squirt of scallops and came home with a pail full of them and opened them and cut out the sweet cubes of muscle.

His ninth birthday his mother had given him a pair of roller skates, and from then on his summer holidays were slick. The ball-bearing days rolled on and on as he flew down the streets of the Elysian-Aire development, outward and backward thrusting, arms full swinging, wheels clicking at the seams of the concrete squares, past armless nudes and leaning-forward Thinker and Pegasus and Mercury with inadequate wings on his heels, busts of Caesar and Socrates, and Aristotle and Plato in purest marble. Like Lot's wife they had all been congealed by God when he had smitten the real-estate development before a single mansion had been built. Now it was grown high with palmetto and saw-grass, its walks had sagged and cracked and crumbled – which only made the skating that much more exciting. What must have been intended as the main boulevard of the development was the most lovely stretch of all, lined with the high feather-dusters of palms, blow-torching with rank poinsettia, rushing past him, the wind of his passage cooling against his sweating cheeks, his neck, his legs, his arms.

Long before the holidays were over, his father had con-fiscated the roller skates. He had also broken one rib on Richard's left side, though it was the concussion that had caused his mother to call in Dr. McNew, after his father had rehearsed him on how he had fallen out of the pecan tree. The loss of the skates had truly hurt him more than the cracked rib or the back of his head.

When they took his mother away to the asylum in Tallahassee, his father had taken him out of school, so he never did get a chance to join the lucky guys in Senior High with their pure white shirt sleeves rolled up tight on their biceps, and their collars open, and the loose ends of their bow-ties hanging free down their shirt fronts. Not a chance in the world he would ever get to Gainesville and take dentistry, the way his mother had wanted him to do.

Cass had got him the job in the Spa, just on week-ends at first, then full time, though mostly in the filter house and grinding locker keys – finally life-guarding. Even if he didn't get to go on in Senior High, there wasn't a one of them to touch him on the three-metre board: cut away one-and-a-half, one-and-a-half-gainer lay-out, forward two-and-a-half in pike. And he did have the best tan on the whole west coast, and the blondest hair. Actually it was white, and so were his eyebrows after he started in running his hands through his hair regularly – dipping them in the lime barrel after it had cleared and then under the tap and then through his hair and a finger along each eyebrow.

"You smell stronger'n a operatin' theatre, boy," Pep had said.

When he would have graduated from Senior High, he did buy the purest white suit, and it set off his white hair and blue eyes just beautiful. Praise God it had been a lovely suit, and he had worn it the first time to the Victory Born Agains church, and when those in the bench before him had turned around and the square wash-tubs had been placed by the deacons, he saw that he was right behind LaPrelle Snell. She washed his feet first, and he had felt the tickle of her hands when she dried them, and he wished Cass hadn't said how he'd banged her under nigger pier. Then he washed hers, and he was Christ and she was the apostle. He'd got a hard on even before he'd started the washing, when his eyes had gone hot right up her calf and inside her thigh; as he lifted her foot to dry behind the heels, he saw she had no pants on at all, and bingo right in the middle of the holy ritual of foot washing. At home he told his father she had slammed her foot down in the wash-tub and splashed water all over the crotch of his new cream pants, but his father said, "Picnic pitch."

He said he had noticed that in all his witnessing, his father had never once confessed beating up his kid all the time and taking away his roller skates and taking him out of school and driving his mother insane. This time Dr. McNew had to come to see his father after it was all over. He moved in with Cass.

The next year he started going with Blanche Haddad, lying beside her on the beach, the sweet, lifting curve of her thighs glistening and smelling chocolate with cocoa butter. He ached and ached for her. On the nights it was his turn for the Model A he and Cass had rebuilt, he took her to the Elysian-Aire Development, and their favourite place was under the pendant trunks of the banyan tree – alone except for Pan, delicate on his hoof-tips, his pot belly thrust forward, the backward joints of his hind legs surprising. His marble eyes were clam-blind to the erotic hopscotch Blanche played with Richard, her legs opening, closing, opening again, but always closing just in time. He never wore his white suit when he took her out.

He was utterly unprepared for her sudden capitulation. She engulfed him without warning, and it hadn't even been as good as in church with LaPrelle Snell – a quick and disappointing whir. He had to take her word for it that he had even been inside her at all. After that first time it was almost every night, and she took over like Pep with a diving class. From the time she steered him into herself she never shut up – advising, ordering, telling, checking, criticizing. She was just like Pep: no height, no hurdle, too far out from the board at entry, knees bent, overcast, toes not pointed, went into your twist too soon – too late – sloppy tuck – arsitis in your swan.

Blanche's father owned the whole arcade on Fifth Avenue in the centre of the city; she ran the souvenir and fruit and nut shop for him. It was there that she told Richard, under the hung baskets woven from turpentine pine needles, the gargoyle faces carved from cocoanut husks. She told him by the bin of papershell pecans.

"I got something to tell you, Rich – important."

"Yeah?"

"Important for both of us."

He waited for her to tell him, but a woman had come up, and it was a few minutes before she had picked out a scallop shell made into an ash-tray, and a sea-shell trinket box and candied orange and grapefruit peel to be sent North for her, and then, when the mailing address had been all filled out, she decided to add a jar of orange-blossom honey. When she had left, Blanche said, "But it isn't so bad. . . ."

"What isn't so bad?"

"Dad says he'll give us the shop."

"What do you mean 'us'?"

"Rich, I missed – three weeks – I'm almost due for the next one."

Cass told him she was hooking him, but there was no way for Cass to know that; he just said it.

But Cass had been right; Cass was right most of the time. They had been married in the Episcopal church and moved right into their apartment, which was above a jewellery store in the building her father also owned. For two years he had stood running the shop, being run by Blanche, and the constant curry smell of roach powder.

As he undressed he supposed that it was just about time for him to have the dream again, the one in which he was being forced higher and higher and more frighteningly higher, the sickening vertigo and the awful anticipation as he fell towards the most terrible impact imaginable. He always awoke in time; if he didn't, he would probably be destroyed in his sleep.

TWENTY-THREE

He knew he had not called in at the liberty café in the first two or three days of his search for her, but now he could not remember whether or not the sign had been in the window when he had made his later visits there. Two – maybe three; it was a likely place for her to have found work, with its scaling paint, dusty and distressed geraniums. Quite possible he hadn't noticed the sign before, or the owner hadn't put it up right away when he'd decided he needed a new waitress.

He sat down on a stool. A man came out of the door at the kitchen end of the counter. Carlyle ordered a coffee. The full-moustached man turned away, reached for a cup, turned again to the coffee urn, then back to Carlyle.

"I see you have a waitress sign up in your window."

The man set down his cup. "You looking for work?"

"No – I'm lookin' for . . ."

"Joke, Jack."

". . . Indian girl."

"Last one I'll hire. Ever again. Over a week now it's been six till two for me." The man's eyes did look tired. There was more than fatigue there – a sort of sleeping hunger. Under the moustache the fleshy lips were quite red. "You try to help them an' then every time they let you down – every time."

"Victoria Rider?"

"I guess."

"You did have an Indian girl named Victoria . . ."

"You get a large turn-over on waitresses – even worse on Indian ones. They just quit without . . ."

"And her name was Victoria?"

"Vicky – generally stands for Victoria, doesn't it? Sometimes they get into the till, so then they don't quit – they get their ass fired out of here."

"Is that why she quit?"

"No."

"Then why?"

"How do I know? Maybe she didn't like being up to her elbows in grease and dish-water. Maybe her feet got tired – maybe she took up a more restful line of endeavour – on her back." The eyes were not quite so tired-looking now; the hunger had wakened up.

Carlyle tightened against the anger that suddenly began to tug within him. "When did she leave?" he managed.

"Week – ten days."

"Have you – seen her since?"

"Yeah – walked by the window a couple times – her an' another girl, and then her and a Indian fellow with a cut face. The man and the girl I seen quite a lot around here. Good-looker – you know – not all boobs and belly an' legs like pipe-cleaners way they get – real built for an Indian girl." Carlyle got up. "She's sellin' her ass."

He dropped a dime on the counter.

"I don't encourage them in my place."

"How in hell would you know!"

"What?"

"What she was doing. The man would be more to your taste, wouldn't he?" He turned away.

"Either way, Jack – either way."

As Carlyle reached the door, the man called to him, "Not like you though – I do draw the line – somewhere – at smoked meat."

On his way back to the hotel, he saw her. Just like that! There she was – on his side of the street, but across the intersection and half way down the block. He was so lifted with his happy luck, he didn't see the "Don't Walk" sign; nearly stepped off into the traffic flow – four deep and in full spate. Just as soon as an opening came, he'd run to her; he felt so light with relief, he must run all the way to her! Over the cars, he held her carefully with his eyes. She wasn't walking, for the distance didn't seem to grow between them. Twice he lost her – first, to a large, slatted stock truck and then to a very long, orchid-coloured furniture van: WOLFGANG SCHLITGER MOBILIA AND INTERIORS – SCANDINAVIAN TEAK. Found her again!

The traffic signal changed.

He ran.

On the other side he came up against a line of cars trapped in the intersection by the light change up ahead. He climbed over bumpers; he jumped down to the curb. He ran towards her. Now he could see that she was talking to a large man in white.

In mid stride he bumped against a very solid woman who had capriciously stopped before the slashed-price, ladies' shoe display in a store window. He banked off her to part two girls coming in the opposite direction. The left one made an instant, upright, thrusting gesture at him with her rigid second finger; her friend shouted something. Victoria turned towards him.

She was a young Indian girl. She was not Victoria!

He stopped running, and, as he walked past the two, he recognized the white-haired person in the pure suit. No mistake about him; the negative-man he'd seen a couple of times in the hotel. The two seemed to have reached some sort of agreement – some sort? No doubt about what sort on a street between a young Indian girl and . . . He felt just sick!

Heally Richards had spoken first to Gloria Catface. She had just looked at him, the large, dark eyes committing her in no way at all – to him, or even to the act of seeing. Finally she had admitted that she was Miss Catface, that she did have a brother, Norman, that they had been to a couple of the earlier Rally For Jesus meetings. If he wanted to talk with her, she had suggested, maybe they could do it over a beer in the White Knight. He had told her that he had already drunk deep of the Fountain of Life, and she had said she didn't know that label, so maybe it was keg draught. He explained that he wanted her and her brother to come to the tent meetings, that he wanted her to play the tambourine – the brother to usher – that from the love-offering funds there would be grateful payment, though their much greater reward would be salvation through Jesus Christ, Who did not dispense either by the bottle or draught.

They heard a woman's shout. A man ran towards them, slowed down to a walk, and passed by.

"How much for doin' that?"

"That can be worked out."

"We got to see what Norman thinks. He – generally takes care of – things like that."

"It will be – generous."

For a moment she considered. "I think Norman might agree to it all right."

"Praise Him!"

"Would I be up there – in front of them?"

"By the piano, with the tambourine – and in your native costume."

"I had to hock it at Ralph's – white doe-skin – it was my Miss Fish and Game outfit."

"We'll get it out for you."

"If you got forty dollars, I can get it out right away."

"We will talk with your brother first, Sister."

"It was in the window still a week ago – somebody might buy it cheap. I better get it right away. You give me the forty. I'll go straight over there. It's near our place – just five blocks – the other side of Pioneer War Surplus."

"We'll talk with your brother."

"I don't know where he is right now. Forty dollars."

"After we talk with . . ."

"It's worth over a hundred – all I need is forty dollars."

"All right, Gloria."

She turned to the tall, solid man who had taken her by the elbow. His dark top-coat was open, a narrow-brimmed hat down over his eyes like a tilted flower pot. "Let's you just come with me now." The spring sunshine was like water glint on his toes.

"I wasn't."

"I heard. Forty dollars."

"I wasn't doin' it."

"Inflation's hit just about everything."

"I haven't been . . ."

"Look – I gave you two warnings – I didn't have to do that – now you blew it."

"But – I quit turnin' any tricks. . . ."

"Not the way you stopped those three guys before this one, you didn't." His hand tightened on her elbow. "Come on."

"So – I just said hello to a couple fellows – why you chargin' me?"

"Because – you got no licence to sell your Girl Guide cookies between here and the Devonian Tower." Still keeping her elbow, he turned to Heally Richards. "Usually her price is ten, and you're going to have to take your pleasure somewhere else. . . ."

"Miss Catface was not soliciting me for immor –"

"Oh? You solicitin' her!"

"Of course not! We have been discussing a – an arrangement with her – and her brother. . . ."

"That was exactly the impression I got – you're going to have to make 'em with some other little red hooker."

"I tell you she wasn't – we weren't . . ."

"She was, an' you were, an' I am probably doin' you a big favour – health-wise. Chances are – nine hunderd an' ninety-nine to one she's got fire burnin' in her prairie wool."

"I am Heally Richards."

"So far – I am only takin' her in – but – if you keep on obstructin' me . . ."

"My name is . . ."

"I have not asked you for your name. I have simply asked you – in a nice way – to fuck off!"

". . . Reverend Heally Richards."

The plain-clothes man's eyes were suddenly a lot like Gloria's. "Oh."

"For the past three weeks an' for the next eight days – I am conductin' a faith-healin' rally – for Jesus, praise His name. I would like to explain to you that I have been arrangin' for Miss Catface – and her brother, Norman – to come to our meetin's. There is a possibility that they might care – to help us – to add a touch of wild colour to our services."

"He's goin' to try to save us," Gloria explained, "from bein' wicked."

The detective released her elbow.

"Praise the Lord! Praise His name!"

"The forty dollars you heard was to get my white doe-skin out of hock at Ralph's Square Deal Shop for me to wear up there when I jingle that – that . . ."

"Tambourine. Her brother will usher for me."

"Sure," Constable Dan said. "Praise the Lord."

TWENTY-FOUR

HE HAD BEEN LUCKY TWO TIMES, AND MAYBE THERE MIGHT be three. The first time had happened when the Greyhound pulled into the depot and he got off it and went through and out and headed for the hotel with the fire burning and the red coat with the buffalo horns on. He decided not to go on over to the big tent first; Mr. Reverend Richards might be at his room. If he wasn't, then just check the tent later and tell him Old Esau was still alive and get the gas and cylinder-oil money from him so he could close the deal for Prince's half-ton to bring in Old Esau to be healed if he kept on living. Thirty dollars.

Just as he got to the hotel he was lucky to see Norman Catface coming out of the door, and Norman saw him and stopped in the middle of the sidewalk and turned to get away and then turned back again, as though he hadn't noticed it was Archie right away, and he walked up and spoke first, like he was glad to see him.

"Hey, I been lookin' all over for you."

"No, you haven't!" Norman had the fire burning right behind him.

"I wanted to see you," Norman said.

"No, you didn't . . ."

"Sure, I did."

"I want it back now," Archie said.

Norman's little oat eyes looked from under the hair, like he didn't understand. His mouth opened lopsided, then closed again. He shrugged.

"You know what I'm talkin' about, all right, Norman."

Norman shook his head.

"Empress bar – you robbed me my rings and rebuilt carburetor!"

Norman's mouth opened crooked again. "No – I didn't. . . ."

"That's insultin'!"

"I didn't rob no . . ."

"Saturday – and you keep insultin' me by sayin' you didn't, then I'm gonna kill you right on this sidewalk . . ."

"But I didn't. . . ."

". . . instead of later. . . ."

"I didn't! I . . ." Norman backed away with one hand up and out. "All right – all right! I told you – I told you we didn't eat three days – I told you our need was great for bread. . . ."

"I want it back now!"

". . . two warnin's from the policeman – I told you that. You didn't listen to me – when I explained we needed something for bread, when I told you that – did you?"

"I want it back right now!" Archie held out his hand. "Now!"

Norman backed away some more. "I didn't use it for myself – you know – her need was great, and then when . . ."

"Now!"

"I ain't got it left!"

"How much you got left?"

"Nothin's left."

Very slowly Archie lowered his hand.

"I'm ashamed." Norman's seed eyes were taking little sideways jerks, but always on Archie's face. "I'm ashamed."

"Your life is in great danger!"

"Not for me – for them – I had to take it. Robin Hood!"

"None of that Robin Hood bull shit on me!"

"No bull . . ." This time Norman had to jump back, but the fire post caught him between the shoulder blades, stopped him there.

"You drunk my rings and carburetor!"

Held against the post now because Archie had a fistful of his shirt front, Norman shook his head. "For bread for them . . ." The back of his head knocked hollow metal sound out of the fire pipe. "I'll pay . . ." *Clang!* ". . . back . . ." *Clang!* ". . . borrowed . . ."

"Stole!" *Clang!*

As Archie released his shirt, Norman dropped into a half-crouch; he remained turned sideways, his eyes still on Archie's face. The medicine-man doorman, who had started over to them, had stopped undecided, then, as he saw a group of men getting out of a Shamrock Taxi that had pulled up, he returned to his door.

"How will you pay it back?"

"Reverend Heally Richards." Norman pointed back to the hotel. "I just been seein' him before I saw you."

"Why would he give you money?"

"He saved us – me and Gloria."

"They don't pay for that."

"Didn't say he did – we're helpin' him."

"How?"

"Usher."

"What's that?"

"I take the people to sit down. Gloria – he got her doe-skin out of hock – she wears it and she jingles with the piano when they sing. Sometimes I can ding somebody now and again. . . ."

"All right then . . ."

"He didn't pay us yet – just last week – we get paid after the week. . . ."

291

"How much?"

"Saturday. Fifty."

"Each one fifty?"

"Both fifty together."

"Hey-up."

"I'll pay."

"We'll go up and see him now – you get it off him, then you pay back . . ."

"I tried that before. He won't pay now. We eat good, but no extra cash. When he pays me Saturday – I pay you – forty."

"Fifty."

"Hell – I just – forty-five was all I took!"

"Hey-up. Fifty now. Intrest. Norman, turn around."

"Huh?"

"Face me!"

"I'm ashamed."

"You are going to be dead too, if you don't turn around! I know why you're standing sideways to me like that."

Norman turned to face Archie. "When he pays us – I pay you."

"Hey-up."

"At the tent – Saturday."

"If you don't, I will kill you," Archie promised.

"Sure."

"I mean it."

"Yeah – yeah."

"I done that before, you know, Norman. Do you know I mean it?"

"Sure."

"Saturday," Archie said.

"Sure – I know."

"If you don't – right away after – then it will be the end of you, and that is the whole situation."

"You'll get it back."

Archie shook his head slowly.

"Sure – you will – mine and the rest from Gloria's . . ."

Archie shook his head again.

"I tell you, you'll get it."

"No, I won't."

"Then just kill me now!"

"I'm still considerin' that."

"You aren't killin' me for fifty dollars!"

Archie nodded his head. "That is the amount I will have to kill you for. . . ."

"You won't . . ."

"See what I mean? You don't know it – yet. You don't even know. You're dead now."

"Hell I am!"

"You got no hope. You got no hope to pay back. You got no hope when you don't keep your promise I won't keep my promise to you. Your promise is hard to you – my promise is easy. . . ."

"I'll keep my prom –"

"No – you won't – you're tied up in a sack. You got no hope to untie that sack and get out of it."

"I'll pay you!"

"Bull shit!"

"No bull –"

"You're insultin' me again, Norman," Archie warned him.

"You're insultin' me! Sayin' I won't pay back when I said I would pay back! Sayin' you'll kill me because I won't keep my promise to pay back – that's insultin', isn't it?"

"Not for you. You don't insult easy."

"And maybe I don't kill so easy either!"

"Maybe not – but you will."

"Maybe not!"

"Hey-up. That fifty dollars is very important to me."

"Well – my life is imp –"

"But your life isn't worth fifty cents to me, Norman, and killing you would be a piss-poor deal for me, and that is the whole situation." He went past Norman to go into the hotel.

"And now I'll tell you somethin'!" Norman called after him. "I been feedin' her!"

Archie stopped. "Who?"

"Victoria Rider."

He walked back to Norman.

"She's camped with us now. She's eatin' our grup."

"Hey-uh."

"We been sharin' with her, an' I'll just keep track of her part of it, an' then I'll take it out of what I pay you Sat –"

"How long she been with you?"

"When she quit workin' for the Greek at the Liberty. We befriended her."

"Where's your place?"

"Over there."

"I said, where?"

Norman jumped back as Archie grabbed him by the throat. He did not squeeze very much, just held him. "Norman, you are in very great danger now!"

Norman tried to speak. Archie loosened up a little. "All right – all right," Norman got out, "I don't mind givin' a Stony girl welfare – I'll keep on feedin' her – I won't take it out of the fifty. . . ."

"Don't you sell her, Norman!"

"I won't!"

"Did you yet?"

"No – no I didn't!"

"If you did – I'll kill you – hard!"

"I didn't do that!"

"I'll see. Where is it?"

"Nobody there now."

"Where!"

"Next the Liberty – the corner."

"Nothin' on that corner."

"We are on that corner – in behind the Blackfoot sign – we made a place in behind there. I didn't have to sell her or Gloria – Reverend Richards bought us grup for all last week. I didn't have to!"

Archie let go of him. "Just your sister, Norman!"

"Sure," Norman agreed. "Just her."

He had to wait in the hall for a while before the Mr. Reverend Richards opened the door and told him to sit down and wait for a minute. The Mr. Reverend Richards went to the desk and he did some writing and then he got up and sat down in the red chair by the window.

"He's still alive," Archie said.

"Praise God!"

"Hey-uh. But we better get him in here so you can heal him quick."

"We will – we will – Saturday."

"That's tomorrow."

"There are a lot of necessary arrangements to be made. . . ."

"Not at the Paradise end of it," Archie said. "I already made some. I started a deal with Prince Dixon to use his half-ton to bring him in here to you."

"Fine, Brother Nicotine."

"So you can heal him tomorrow."

"No. The Saturday after tomorrow was what I had in mind."

"Way too late . . ."

"Which is – the wind-up for the entire Rally For Jesus – so you will bring him in then. . . ."

"If he's still alive then."

"Yes – three o'clock – afternoon, a week tomorrow – Saturday – you will bring him in the truck to the back of the tent – and then – inside the tent to wait behind the platform till you receive the signal from Brother Hillaker that it is time to come out – to the front and before the congregation – in front of – the Mercy Seat – for the healin'."

"Mr. Reverend Richards, you do not understand Old Esau's blood situation. I don't think there is enough left inside there to last him another week."

"One week from tomorrow we will be doin' – the last of the service – we will be doin' the Burnin' Bush Hour – live over CSFA-TV – the grand climax of the total Rally For Jesus, and Brother Esau will be the climax of that total grand climax."

"If he's still alive."

"Last week you said that, and you keep right on sayin' it, and it is – a faith-negative statement. You must have faith – the Lord requires your faith."

"Hey-uh."

"You may not realize it, Brother Nicotine, but you do have faith – the Lord has already given us evidence of your faith – because if you did not have it – do you think that He would have kep' Brother Esau alive as long as He has? You must understand that Brother Esau could be dead now. . . ."

"Maybe he is – I left there early this morn –"

"He is not. He lives. I can truly tell you that. The Lord would not let us down – He will not – if – we have faith – in Him. He has already laid His blessin' upon our plans for the wind-up of His holy rally. He has done that generously – He has moved Brother Norman and Sister Gloria Catface to join us – they have been attending our services faithfully – thrice daily."

"I know that."

"What evidence more do you want then? I tell you, Brother Nicotine, our plans are the Lord's plans, praise His name! And the Lord's plans will always run smooth – always – given one thing – your faith and lots of it. His plans roll right along, but only – if – your faith keeps His Gas Tank – filled."

"Maybe," Archie said, "it might be His plans if I was to bring in Old Esau twice. . . ."

"No."

"Once tomorrow, and then twice – a week tomorrow."

"No."

"I don't see how it would hurt. Twice."

"Indeed it would. It truly would. It would simply and clearly show to Him that our faith – in Him – was runnin' very low." The Reverend Mr. Richards got up. "So – we have it well understood now – week tomorrow – Saturday – three o'clock – in chief's costume – in war bonnet. . . ."

"Hey-uh."

Richards walked across the room. He opened the door. "Was there anything further, Brother Nicotine?"

"Hey-uh."

"What?"

"Somethin' else."

"Yes?"

"Prince Dixon."

"Yes?"

"It's his truck."

"Fine."

"But he has to charge something for that."

"I understand."

"He has to keep his gas tank filled up too, an' I got to pay him for that."

"Yes."

"An' for the truck depreciatin' – the tires depreciatin' an' for the wear on his motor depreciatin'. . . ."

"I understand."

"The gas is for both ways – over hunderd an' fifty miles – an' for the oil – his truck uses a lot of cylinder oil now an' then – an' there'll be some grup to pay for – not breakfast, but dinner an' then after you healed Old Esau it would be a long ride back on an empty stomach – so that's grup twice for three people – Prince an' Rod Wildman an' me. . . ."

"That will all be taken care of, Brother Nicotine."

"Hey-uh." He waited.

"You will be reimbursed from the love offerin'."

"To close the deal with Prince, I better – reimburst – him now. I think we should show our faith in him – now."

"The total?"

"Sixty."

The Reverend Mr. Richards reached into his pocket. Archie wished he had said seventy-five.

Going down in the elevator cage, he thought he could have made it ninety. Snow and peanut butter.

Next to the Liberty Café and behind the big sign with the black foot going up and down, he found the camp Norman and Gloria Catface had made with sleeping-bags and Coleman stove and water cans and all that orange canvas slung over the top – thin canvas. But nobody was there. He went to the end and lay down, and then he sat up. All he had to do was take the stove and the sleeping-bags to Ralph's Square Deal Shop and he'd have back right away the money Norman stole from him last week. Then Norman could do what he wanted: he could steal another stove and sleeping-bags, or he could wait till the Reverend Mr. Richards paid him to get them out of hock at Ralph's.

Victoria Rider was walking towards him now. He got up; then she ran the rest of the way to him.

"Archie – Archie!"

"Hey-uh. I want to talk with you."

"I'm so glad to . . ."

"All right, but I'm sorry you're here with them, and I think you better leave them and leave this city and come back with me to Paradise. I'm goin' there now, and I can stake you to your bus ticket. . . ."

"No."

"Just one way – it's out of the love-offerin' funds from the Reverend Mr. Heally Richards."

"I wish I could, but I can't!"

"You got to. Look how you ended up here with them. I told you before to keep away from them."

"I haven't any place else. . . ."

"Paradise . . ."

"No, I . . ."

". . . you can hide there – long as you need to hide. . . ."

"No – no – I can't. I'm not going back. I won't. I'm through there."

"All right – that don't mean you got to be with these Catfaces, does it!"

"Yes, it does – for now, because the Greek fired me."

"Why did he fire you?"

"Because – part my pay was the room above the Liberty – he figured part my work I might do up there in my room too – with him."

"You figure any better here? You figure Norman's got any different kind work for his sister – for you?"

"He let me sleep here – they share with me what they got."

"Hey-uh."

"Archie – it's all there is – till I can find something. I haven't any money. I can't go back – home – hospital – anywhere but here with them!"

"Hey-uh. You think you can untie that sack?"

"I don't know."

"What you goin' to do if you can't?"

"I don't know."

"You think Norman or her – they'll help you untie it?"

"No – oh God, I don't . . ."

"Did he already sell you?"

"No – he didn't!"

"Did he ask you to do that?"

She looked away from him.

"I said – did he ask you . . ."

"Of course he did!"

"Hey-uh."

"Oh, Archie – I'm ashamed!"

"Hey-uh."

"Help me!"

"Who you ashamed for?"

"Me."

"No – who you ashamed in front of? Susan – Jonas – Old Esau – us Stonys?"

She didn't answer him.

"I'll see what I can do with Norman. I already promised him something – he doesn't pay me back my rings and carburetor. I don't know whether it will do any good, but I'll let him know about it again." He looked at her for a moment, then he said, "How much does she cost?"

"What?"

"Gloria."

"Please, Archie – please don't . . ."

"How much?"

"Ten."

He took out the money from Richards. "Here's twenty – that's for twice you won't have to do that if he asks you. Don't let them know you got it. Here."

"Thanks, Archie."

"Sinclair?"

"What about him?"

"You ashamed in front of him?"

"Yes."

"With white people it's easy for us people to be ashamed in front of them, and that's the whole situation. You don't want me to tell him. . . ."

"No! No! Oh please don't – please . . ."

"Hey-uh. I'm kind of tired now – so I'll sleep – but you wake me up so I won't miss that Greyhound." He lay down. "You know, Victoria – I come to a conclusion – they want it that way."

"Who?"

"Those white people." He turned over. "And another thing – you need a lot of luck around them – you're gonna need a lot more luck in this city than you need in Paradise. I been lucky three times today."

TWENTY-FIVE

He had dropped in at the indian friendship centre before he would make his last call at the bus depot for the departure of the south-bound 11:15. Red, white and blue and yellow, cork-screwing garlands of tissue paper swagged the ceiling and walls for an evening of gala importance. The dimmed hall was smouldering with buckskin, plangent with electronic guitars, the drums seemingly amplified beyond belief; the floor was wall to wall with couples. Dancers and band members were, even in the dusk, obviously Indian and Métis and spastic. "Loose Your Lasso from My Achin' Heart!" the singers on the platform pleaded in earnest falsetto. "Blood, Blood Upon the Saddle of My Love!" they keened. "Sweet Grass, the Sweet Grass Never My Pain Can Ease!" The music was almost white; its beat promised sonic privacy for everyone. It insisted with unchanging cadence, not too far off the Prairie Chicken Dance rhythms Carlyle had heard so often in the Paradise Valley night.

He held himself up against the side wall as couples passed him, touched him, bumped and glanced off him. His searching eyes went from face to sweating face, out over the dancers. None of his Paradise Valley people were here. Down at the far end of the hall, the platform end of it, he saw two girls dancing together. The short, fat one wasn't, but the other just could be!

No way to tell at this distance – in this light. Rather than go all the way around the hall perimeter, he cut straight across the floor, working his way through the dancers to the opposite wall, then right on down towards the platform end.

The girls were gone, but this corner of the hall was much cooler. He saw the open door.

The alleyway was darker even than the hall. He stood uncertain while his eyes adjusted to the night. They must have slipped out here! He heard voices. Beyond the garbage cans to his right he could make out some figures, had taken only a step towards them when he felt himself grabbed from behind, a double grip tight on each arm. A third man came round from behind him.

"Shame on you!" The voice was Indian, possibly Sarcee.

"Goddammit – let go of me!"

"We don't like you white people at our red parties. . . ."

"Let go – I'm looking for a girl. . . ."

"What makes you think all our girls are for sale . . ."

"I don't – I'm not – let . . ."

The punch was a glancing one and high off his left cheek. In spite of the men behind holding him, he managed to pull aside and duck down from the next one, then felt instant and numbing shock high in the gut. But the next was his own, and lovely solid, as he got a full swing with his foot to take the bastard snug in the crotch; with the same convulsive burst of desperate energy, he ripped free of the right-hand grip and, twisting round, got the other in the soft belly. He ran, hearing shouting behind him, then the comic clangour of garbage cans just as he passed the shapes against the wall down the alley. Something went by his head – closely – splashing him. It broke, tinkling on the pavement ahead of him. He thought he heard a woman shout. He kept on running.

They hadn't followed him out to the lighted street. He stopped to get his wind back; each breath hurt. His upper arms ached and his solar plexus was tender to the touch. His nausea was subsiding. He felt the side of his face and brought his hand away – wet. It wasn't blood, unless he had bled fortified Niagara wine. Better get to the hotel and into a hot shower there.

He must stink of the stuff! And he must look just great! He could drop into the bus depot and its washroom – clean himself up a bit before he went on to the hotel. That way he wouldn't miss checking out the south-bound bus.

His left eye was already swelling. Most of the wine had sluiced his face and head; he crouched over the basin and lifted up cold water again and again in his cupped hands. He dried off his hair and face with paper towels. When he was done, he saw that there was over half an hour to wait for the bus.

He'd lost count of the number of times he'd come here to meet one of the band – stranded broke – just released after serving thirty or sixty or ninety days in the Bonneydoon bucket. He sat down on the bench beside a girl who had one knee over the other, head tilted down and slightly to one side as she filed her nails; on the other side of her a woman slouching in her mattress fat, knees spread wide. The girl looked up, sniffed accusingly, put her nail-file into her shoulder purse and left.

He saw a youth headed towards the ticket wicket – blue and faded denim pants punched out at the knees – buckskin, fringed jacket – long, black hair to the shoulder – headband. Carlyle started to get up, then sat back as the boy turned away from the wicket. He was white.

The fat woman gathered up her shopping-bag and left.

Except for the absence of carbolic bitterness, the depot, with its seated and waiting people, reminded him of his father's surgery – the same expectant air – arrested people, each with his own inward and urgent concern. Unlike airports and railroad stations, this was not a place where people met people. The buses unloaded outside; the depot doors opened and the passengers entered, looking slightly dazed, as though they had just stepped bewildered from a car wrecked in a highway accident.

". . . Darryl – my second son – he was different – you wouldn't know they were brothers. . . ."

A man had taken the woman's place – must have been right after she'd left; this elderly, lonely accoster must have launched right into it, and Carlyle had missed the gangplank.

". . . real small – so in basketball he dribbled under those big boys – great kid for stilts – any time you'd see little Darryl he'd be on stilts – stilts pokin' up behind his shoulder-blades – walked stilts to school – recess – walked back home on his stilts after school – of course, all the kids used to go for stilts – but in season you understand – like there's a stilts season after marble season, late spring – maybe another one durin' summer holidays – use to be – you don't see kids walkin' stilts the way they used to do when Darryl an' Wayne was young. Of course, little Darryl, he was always on his stilts – all year except winter – in an' out of season."

The bus had come in. People were rising from the benches, heading for the doors. Carlyle got up.

"I live with Wayne now."

She had not showed up – as he had known she wouldn't – possibly never would.

The hot shower had soaked out most of the aching. The side of his left eye had reached its full swelling, he thought, and it was not going to be so bad – possibly a little discolouration by morning. Actually, he felt surprisingly relaxed – perhaps the most since he'd come into the city to look for her. He turned out the light on the bedside table, lay back. The Indian he'd gotten with his toe would not sleep too well tonight.

Well – tomorrow. Funny – the people in the bus depot; it wasn't his father's surgery they'd reminded him of, but something else from that time of his life. The child on stilts. Some sort of child's game? Statues – oh God, yes – that was it – bodies frozen – he and the bus-depot people and the Stonys – all men – held frozen. They must not move – they could not move – not a muscle – an eyelid. Thrown into positions that were so often ludicrous – a leg back and stilled with the toe just touching the ground – or bent as though to kick an invisible ball – body crouched into the defecating position – another in an aborted turn with a hand at the crotch. The game held delight for the one who was It, a delicious sense of power over others. It must have been a game that Aunt Pearl had loved when she was a little girl.

He had not lived with her more than four months – three before his mother's death – one after. Yet he could see her at will: long and thin as milkweed stalk, leaning on her broom and sighing her intransitive sighs. Her eyes were pale like his father's, but they bulged above the short down-arc of her nose; her cheeks suggested chicken wattle. Under the lace at her throat she had a goitre; he supposed his father had told him that, possibly on the long train trip to the city, had cautioned him not to say anything about it.

In the day-coach, which smelled of oranges and bananas and babies' diapers, his father also told him that his mother was very sick, and this was why he would be staying at Aunt Pearl's, and he had asked for how long, but his father had called the pop-and-candy boy over and bought him a lemon crush. Warm. Then he got train-sick and threw the pop back up.

He liked the city with all its noise, the stopping and starting whine of streetcars, the iron grind from brewery drays, the cupping sound of bakery- and milk-wagon horses. He had never before seen telegraph boys like monkeys clever enough to wear uniforms and ride a bicycle – raddle-faced old men with newspapers under their arms, on corners, cawing something over and over again. Green, red, blue, yellow, white, a lot of city people wore uniforms, and they were wise and they were wicked and they were strange and exciting – but not frightening. How could a fair that went on all the time be frightening?

Aunt Pearl's house was a high, narrow one – three storeys. White. It was the sort of house Aunt Pearl would have been, if she had been a house. She lived alone – until his father left him with her. Uncle Edgar had died; so had little cousin Willis in the flu epidemic of 1918. Carlyle couldn't remember Willis, of course, for he had not even been born in 1918, but he did remember a man with a great front that smelled of cigars and horses and something else. He remembered very large hands, which had once gripped the handles of a fresno scoop. Uncle Edgar had been a contractor, and Aunt Pearl several times pointed out to Carlyle sidewalk squares which had printed into them: E. J. ROONEY – 1910.

There wasn't so much to do at Aunt Pearl's. At first, just after his father had taken the train back home, it had been some fun in the toy room on the third floor. Except for a steamer trunk and a table, there was no furniture in there. It was a room bared for playing in, and the trunk and the closet were full of toys; he could play with all of them, Aunt Pearl said, but when he was finished for the day, he must put them all back into the trunk and neatly on the closet shelves. He played with the sand machine first, filling its yellow hopper with very white sand, which trickled into a little cable dump-car. When it weighed more than the balancing weight, it ran down the slant track. It hit a trip at the bottom. It flipped over. It spilled its sand load. It ran back up the track. It filled from the hopper again. It ran back down the track. It did this over and over until all the sand had been carried down from the hopper to the newspaper spread on the floor. Then it was time to fill the hopper again. He did it a lot of times.

All by himself he was able to figure out how to run the little steam-engine with its brass boiler and lovely fly-wheel that had scarlet enamelled spokes. Aunt Pearl hadn't said he couldn't play with it; he didn't say anything about the five matches he got out of the kitchen. He poured wood alcohol into the flat little tin dish, slid the blue flame under the boiler, and waited. You had to help it by giving the fly-wheel a push with your finger, and the piston couldn't make up its mind, and then all of a sudden it could, and it went so fast it blurred, and never slowed down unless you pushed up the handle so the whistle could squeal. It was ill-tempered; it sputtered when it got really busy, and the hot spit stung the back of your hands. It filled the whole room with the smell of oil and steam and fruity wood alcohol.

There was a tiny pulley-wheel where a person could put a string belt and run something off it. But there was no tinker-toy or erector set or meccano in the trunk or the closet, so he couldn't make anything for the steam-engine to run. The wick kept glowing with a couple of red sparks after the tin dish was empty; then the sparks went out too.

The wooden table held the magic lantern, a box of blued tin with a stubby chimney; when you plugged the cord in, the metal got so hot it smelled. The door swung out at the back and had clips for slipping in photographs and post cards and valentines. The magic lantern threw very large pictures on the plaster wall, blurry till you twisted the tin snout – in or out. He looked at Niagara Falls, the Leaning Tower of Pisa, the Great Pyramids, Eiffel Tower, and photographs of little Willis and his own father and mother.

The only time he got outside was when Aunt Pearl took him to visit Willis, and right in the middle of a city wasn't a proper place for a cemetery; it shouldn't really be where there were cars honking. He could see the dome of the Parliament buildings like half a copper cantaloupe, or like one of the St. Johns boys' black-and-yellow caps with their quartering creases running down from the button on top. There was the stamping impatience of a streetcar bell, and then the electric crackle, and he was a little ashamed that his attention had been called away from Uncle Edgar's tombstone and the white marble lamb with its front feet folded under it. "WILLIS SINCLAIR ROONEY b. Jan. 16, 1914 – d. Feb. 10, 1918." Little Willis was under the lamb frozen on its slant slab of marble, but his mind wouldn't stay with Willis because the little lamb sparkled in the sunlight, just like those fat calendars that had a cabin under pines and snow curling down and around the eaves. That snow sparkled. He didn't feel very sad either – thinking "Mary had a . . . ," while up above, Aunt Pearl was crying. She was holding a hand-kerchief over her mouth and nose, and the sound escaping was very regular, like steam hissing from under the train engine.

And now he was thinking about the one lost from the ninety-and-nine and the high stained-glass window in Knox at home and his feet didn't come to the floor when he sat with his mother and father and Christ in His white gown with His Black Beard and Dark, Sad Eyes and the lamb's long legs spilling from under His Elbow and the yellow cart-wheel tipped up at the Back of His Head. He held out three baseballs to Carlyle's father and said to take a try for the little boy and his voice was raw as a scraped knee and his face was sweating in the carnival sun and he had his straw boater pushed back from his forehead. The feathers on the kewpie doll in the crook of his elbow were lovely pink, and there were little roses on the elastic arm-bands above the man's elbows.

Nobody had to tell him he shouldn't be thinking about kewpie dolls and a fair when he was with Aunt Pearl crying over top of dead little Willis and the marble lamb and the glass bell sheltering everlasting flowers. Now Aunt Pearl's head was turned down more and she was tucking the handkerchief into her opened purse. He saw that it was hardly rumpled at all, still in its folded square.

"All right, Willis."

One time when they had come back from visiting Willis he had to go to the toilet, and he didn't know she'd already gone in there and hadn't locked the door. He had opened it on her, quite erect with her dress bunched up in front, her pink bloomers hammocking between her spread knees. It made him think of yarn skein being held out between two hands. Her shanks were long and white. He had shut the door right away, and afterwards, when she came downstairs, it was just as though nothing had happened at all, until she turned away and presented him with her pink, padded bum. She had caught up the whole back of her skirt with the waist elastic. After, when he did go into the bathroom, it smelled charred. She had forgot to flush the toilet too. Little white dumplings.

She was always burning string in the bathroom or in the kitchen. Bad smells bothered her, or any smells that were not perfume smells; yet she was always asking him if he'd gone, the last thing at night when he went to bed under "MACKENZIE FIRST SIGHTING THE PACIFIC" in little Willis's room, first thing in the morning, before he went out into the yard, whenever he came in from the yard. As soon as he had sensed her interest, he was anxious to help her out. Maybe if he ate a lot of apples, or prunes, or rhubarb – drank a lot of water – milk. . . . Instead, he began to make up bowel movements and urinations for her.

"I did a lot this time, Aunt Pearl."

"That's nice, Carlyle."

"A lot."

"Good boy."

"Not just some, you know – a whole lot and it came right up – it nearly came over the top of the . . ."

"All right, Carlyle."

"It wasn't easy – I had to try and try – but when I got the plug out . . ."

"Carlyle!"

And then the telegraph boy had leaned his bike against the fence, and Aunt Pearl told Carlyle his mother had died. They took the train, and the funeral was held in Knox, and people put their arms around him and cried, but it was difficult to know what to do, except to stand still. It was as though his mother had been dead a long time. After his mother's funeral he had cried though, when his father told him he had to go back with Aunt Pearl; it wouldn't be a good thing for him just with his father in the big house. Carlyle said it would be better, though, than being with just Aunt Pearl in her big house, but his father said no. He was back again in little Willis's bedroom with Alexander Mackenzie peering through his spyglass from behind the rock, and beside him, crouching in a breech clout, the Indian with the Buster Brown haircut – quite uninterested in the Pacific, for he was looking down into his lap. The Indian had seen the Pacific before. He had good muscles.

This time he really hated it, and he knew he would hate going to school at St. Johns even though he would have a black-and-yellow cap and sweater and knee-socks and English pants. When school started in three weeks, he was to be a day boy, and that didn't sound like his father meant it when he said it was to be only a temporary arrangement. He wished he were at home with his father's deep voice going evenly on and on through *Wind in the Willows* and *Midshipman Easy* and *Swiss Family Robinson*. When Aunt Pearl said she would read him *Uncle Tom's Cabin* or *Sowing Seeds in Danny* or *Black Beauty*, he said no thanks. He missed even the bitter smell from his father's surgery.

There was really no fun in Aunt Pearl's house, in the living-room with curtains drawn; if he wiped his feet furiously on the rug and then touched the brass plate of the light switch, there was a sound like a tiny whip cracking, and lightning chained from his finger-tip. It showed up well in the darkened room.

But she didn't like him to be there when she wasn't there – or in her bedroom.

Her bedroom was nice, with its great brass bed and the dresser curved in and out and in like a bow, and the colour of pull toffee. There were little eyes all over it. Aunt Pearl said they were birds' eyes. Everything on the dresser was neat; the mirror between the harp arms didn't have a smudge, and the lamp-chimney was beautifully clear, with the curling-irons inside and their handles bent at right angles over the beaded rim. She didn't have to tell him he mustn't come in her bedroom; he knew he'd likely muss it. So – back up to Willis's toy room on the third floor.

But this time the steam-engine wasn't much fun or the hanging clown or the sand machine. The wind-up train just went round and round the track until it ran down and you had to wind up the key again. The magic lantern was still all right, though he had seen Niagara Falls and the Grand Canyon and the Great Pyramids and the Leaning Tower of Pisa a hundred times – and all the valentines.

Generally he did what he was told, so it was hard to explain why he began to go into Aunt Pearl's bedroom. It was just her bedroom; there was nothing for him to do in there. He could scowl and he could snarl and he could blow out his cheeks in front of the dresser mirror. He could push up the outer corners of his eyes so they were Chinese, and hook his little fingers in the corners of his mouth and pull them down, which was funny. For a while.

Everything was laid out neat on the dresser top, the silver brush, the comb, the nail file, the fat thing she rubbed her nails with. They were the same distance apart and they were the same distance from the back and they were the same distance from the front. The lamp with the curling-tongs was in one corner and the powder box balanced it in the other corner. The box had sea shells glued to it. The ones all around the edge just under the lid had two tiny teeth each and under them, in what would be the baby's gum, there was a faint, pink stain as though the teeth had bled a little. The oval lid resisted him; he held it against his chest so he could get a better pull at it. It came off with a pop like a cork and he saw that he had been very lucky; if there'd been much powder it would have sprayed all over her dresser top. He was careful to wipe off any spilled powder with his sleeve.

There was still the powder smell – very faint – and for a moment he felt he might cry, but he didn't. It told him he'd better get right out of there, but he took a last look and reversed the nail file so the silver handle pointed away from the mirror. He turned it around again so that it pointed the same way as all the other things. He pushed the end over so that it wasn't even with the nail buffer. He stepped back and you could see it was crooked. He reached out his finger-tip and pushed it a little straighter. Maybe it wasn't crooked enough now. He'd wait and see.

The next day the nail file was precisely in place, parallel to the nail buffer. She'd noticed and she'd straightened it. But maybe she'd filed her nails and put it back even again without noticing it at all. He moved the comb over to the left – quite a bit. At noon the next day when she sent him up to wash his hands it was back even again. He slid both the file and the comb out of position. Every day for five days he moved the stuff about on her dresser, and each time he had a chance to look, he found them all straightened out again. Finally he twisted the hairbrush around upside down. That evening she told him gently that he must not ever touch anything again on her dresser. He'd won!

313

A couple of days after, high up and back in the corner of the shelf closet, he found the box; from the dove-tail design at the corners he recognized it as a chalk box. When he slid back the lid in its tight grooves, he found it filled with marbles and balloons. Red, yellow, blue, green, pink, orange, he dumped the contents out: round bag ones, long cow-tit ones – one blue one collapsed and wrinkled. He was suddenly not so delighted, and for a moment was going to return all the balloons and marbles to the box and close it and put it back up into its corner on the shelf. He didn't. For a whole afternoon he blew up balloons and twisted their necks round and round so they'd pull in and knot themselves. Then he undid them all and put them back into their box. He did it early in the afternoon because he had the feeling she wouldn't have liked it for him to blow them up and spoil their tight, smooth newness – like the wrinkled, blue one.

He'd better be playing with the magic lantern when she called him for supper. He cast pictures on the white plaster wall until he'd come to the photograph of his mother and father beside the waterfall. His father had a high collar with a large, knotted tie, and his mother's dress had puffy sleeves and she had a bird-wing on her hat tilted on her head, and he began to cry and he took the photograph out. That was when he noticed that the lantern threw a hand-shaped shadow on the wall. He twisted the snout in and then out, and suddenly there was a hand up there. His own! Fingers – nails – creases – ten times larger! He tried the other hand. He took off his shoe and stocking, but his foot wouldn't go in there. He got up on his knees on the table. He found he had to take his pants right off and be very careful of the hot metal and it was blurred so he had to reach ahead and fix the snout. It came clear: his pecker on the opposite wall, way larger than his father's. When he moved it . . .

"Carlyle!"

She was in the doorway and she was looking at the wall, but his pecker wasn't there any longer because she'd made him jump and burn the end of it!

The next day his father had come; he got in on the same train that he and Carlyle had taken before his mother died, and again after his mother had died. As soon as his bags were up in the spare room he told Carlyle he wanted to have a talk with him, and they sat down in the living-room by the bookcases with the lion statue prowling across the top of it.

"Now, Son – Aunt Pearl is a little upset." He leaned forward and touched the ash-tray with the end of his cigar. The ash came away, held together as it rolled, and Carlyle was thinking how it was a lot like the stuff wasps made their nests out of.

"Are you listening, Son?"

"Sure I am."

"You know you're – a week or so you'll be seven."

"Week Friday."

"Ah – she is upset – about you."

"Her nail file."

"Her nail file?"

"And her comb and her brush the way I kept moving them on her."

"No."

"I moved the file over a little so it wasn't straight and then she moved it back and I moved it back crooked and she moved it back and I moved her comb and her brush and I put her brush upside down. . . ."

"No – that isn't it. . . ."

"She didn't like it very much."

"I don't think it's a very important . . ."

"She does. It bothers her . . ." The bronze lion had caught his eye and he had made an exciting discovery the way he sat on the couch below it so he was at the rear end.

"She told me about the magic lantern, Son."

He'd always looked at it from the front.

"Son, the magic lantern."

"I didn't hurt it." Now he could see right up under the base of the tail – for the first time.

"What I'd like to understand – at least I'm trying to – with a little attention and help from you I may – what exactly happened with the magic lantern that's got Pearl so upset?"

For a moment he'd thought he'd been seeing wrong, but he wasn't. Tucked high up under its tail, the lion had a cluster of three balls. Not two. Three!

"Carlyle – you aren't listening to me!"

"Sure I am, Dad."

"All right then – what happened with the magic lantern?"

"She came into Willis's playroom when I was working the magic lantern – you know that's a real magic lantern, Dad – it'll show anything on the wall – not just post cards or pictures – anything! Anything you want to stick in there, it'll show it on the wall."

"Yes."

"Stick your hand in the back and it'll show your hand on the wall."

"This doesn't explain why she's so upset. . . ."

"When she came in I'd stuck my pecker in. When she opened the door it was right on the wall there."

"Your – pecker was."

"Yeah – only big – bigger than the Leaning Tower of . . ."

"Whatever made you do that?"

"I don't know. I just did it. Seemed like an idea and I wondered if it would work and it did. You know that lantern magnified about seventeen times!"

"Well, it isn't exactly what it was intended for."

"I know. That bulb gets it hot in there. I burnt it a little."

"All right."

"She doesn't know that. Maybe – is that why she's upset – because I burnt the end of my . . ."

"No. I don't think so."

"Why should she get . . ."

"Son – for Aunt Pearl it was a little shocking. You shouldn't display yourself. . . ."

"I didn't know she was coming in! She's always coming in on a person – in the bathroom . . ."

"All right – all right."

"You want me to tell her I'm sorry I . . ."

"No."

". . . she's the one walked in on me. . . ."

"No – it won't be necessary."

"Oh – Dad – I want to go home with you – why can't I . . ."

"All right – all right."

"Please, Dad!"

"Hold on now. Look – I'm taking you back with me." When his father had calmed him, he realized suddenly that he had forgot about the lion. He pointed out the extra ball.

His father had hired a housekeeper to look after both of them. Her name was Olga, and she made him a birthday cake for his seventh birthday.

His father's present was a magic lantern, but it only worked with glass slides.

TWENTY-SIX

It was not surprising that aunt pearl had stayed so vivid for him, but he had often wondered why – or rather, how – it was that other fragments of past so seemingly trivial, which ought to have settled evenly down into the prairie of past, lifted: a loose-jointed, slipping clown that hung supplicant from thread between two sticks, a night-gown daisy-white, turning to compost in a deserted barn, a poster in the C.P.R. washroom saying: BEWARE OF STRANGE WOMEN. Yet he could not remember clearly at all his father's funeral. Was it because, without knowing it, his mind had sucked secretly at these things, like Billy Blake with his indelible pencil so that he always had a purple rib down the centre of his tongue? Must be some sort of emotional saliva that had stained these things for him. And the time Old Kacky took up the vanishing point in art class!

Right from the time he had entered the boys' door of Sir Walter Raleigh School, he had flinched from his inevitable destination in Old Kacky's room. But five years later June had come, and then the day that he and the others must leave the Three-Four-Five room, delicate with paste perfume and thick with the smell of plasticine, with rabbit and lamb and butterfly cut-outs against its windows. Leave Miss Coldtart. She had been consistently gently and unbelievably stubborn. Their last day, which was really supposed to be a party, she had one last try at Billy Blake, who had successfully frustrated her for three years. He was unable to say a declarative sentence, nor could he manage an exclamatory or an imperative one. Every single school-day through Grades Three, Four, and Five, Miss Coldtart had called on him to read aloud, hoping against hope that one of his sentences would not turn up at the end like the sandal-toes of an Arabian Nights sultan. The very last day of Grade Five, with cooky and cake crumbs still on the desk tops, she had him read "Pippa Passes" line for line after her. He did – interroga-tively – down to the last "God's in His Heaven? – All's right with the world?"

Then September happened. They must enter Old Kacky's room, with its long maps rolled above the blackboards and, between his desk and the window, an iron tripod stand with sickle-shaped external axis holding the world bubble ready to spin at a finger touch. And now he owned a flat, tin geometry box, with its metre ruler, short and metal, a protractor, a compass, and a hard, hard pencil that had to be needle sharp so that length and breadth and loci would be exact. Hygiene wasn't about washing your hands and brushing your teeth any more; it had grown up: all the body's Latin bones, its circulatory and respiratory and alimentary and terminally incomplete urinary systems. The reproductive system not at all; sex surfaced only in grammar, with the personal pronoun possessing the gerund and the chaste union of subject and predicate by non-thrusting copulative verb.

Old Kacky was just as frightening as imagined, especially when he stood behind a person and confused him at per cent on the board; Carlyle could tell without looking around that Old Kacky's scalp had turned scarlet through the fine white hair. When he was angry, his smell grew strong. Little number foot-notes at the bottom of addition columns inflamed him. They hadn't bothered Miss Coldtart, if you rubbed them out when you were all done. Old Kacky said they were a remembering-to-carry crutch; once it was used, a person would need it all his life. It had taken him some time to recognize Old Kacky's anger smell: oatmeal porridge.

Possibly Old Kacky scared Billy Blake the most. Billy's nose bled easily and melodramatically; often it happened in running, shoving, mêlée games: flying red rain spattering all over a person's sleeve or down the front of his blouse. He bled on the kitchen linoleum of other people's houses; there was still a rust trail over the MacGowan living-room carpet from their couch to the hall door. One twenty-fourth of May he bled so badly out at Tourigny's swimming hole, it had showed in the silty water; if it had been the Rio de Paraguay or the Amazon instead of the Little Souris, it would have bannered down stream and alerted millions of deadly piranha. Actually he could make his nose bleed, particularly if it had recently bled, by simply blowing it hard till the clot came free. If that didn't work, he could put his arms on the slope top of his desk, cradle his head there, and bunt his nose surreptitiously till it happened and Miss Coldtart ran to Old Kacky's office for cotton batting and gauze from the first-aid kit. Then, after it was stuffed, she'd tell him he could forget the rest of his after-four detention and go home. Old Kacky let it bleed.

Old Kacky frightened Maitland Dean the least. Mate was the new Anglican parson's son; there were just Mate and his father in the rectory next to the church. Mel said they had come to town so they could be near Mate's mother who was crazy in the mental hospital. Mel went to the Baptist church. Mate could throw himself up onto his hands to walk endlessly, back arched, shirt hanging down his chin, knees kinked and toes tapping the top of his head. Also, through some cruel sort of muscular self-discipline he could pass wind at will. On request he could let off a whole repertoire: whisper, explosion, two-tone, or in a long string skipping like a flat pebble over water, always without the slightest change of facial expression. Never evidence of effort; the fart that concealed art. To Carlyle he had seemed immediately the most sophisticated boy in North America.

To begin with, history in Old Kacky's room seemed interesting enough – when the great maps were pulled down over the board to show the voyages of Columbus and Champlain and Cartier. The Iroquois were quite exciting, especially in their torture methods: having their victims run the gauntlet, making human porcupines of their captives by pricking them all over with pine-needle tufts. When the resin sputtered and flared, the victims took great pride in not showing their agony; the history book said that when they were ignited, Father Brébeuf and his brethren had conducted themselves well. But Canadian history soon became corrupted into an account of the way people governed and made laws and set up constitutions and Confederation.

Art was a half-hour once a week; they spent a long time on trees; for a hundred miles in every direction from their town there grew not a tree unplanted by man. Learning to draw a tree was complicated. First there must be a pencilled skeleton. Even though both were coniferous, pine and fir trees had different skeletons. Fir branches did not meet at the trunk, nor shorten to a point like pine branches; they laddered up and alternated. Poplars and birches kept forking. After the skeleton was drawn, it had to be covered with short hair-strokes – unless it was a deciduous tree, and then it was a matter of shading in puffy clouds of leaves with the side of the soft art pencil.

Next came sunsets, and a chance to use the paints like brilliant toffee squares in their little tin dishes. They had such a shallow, curving smell, and blue was Carlyle's favourite. The proper way to do sunsets, Old Kacky taught them, was to wet the whole sheet of art paper, then brush bands of red and yellow and blue across the top. The wet paper would dilute the colour bars so that they would fog each other and give you a glorious sunset. Carlyle's didn't; either they refused to fog each other, or they cried right to the bottom of the sheet, which, as it dried, shrank and pulled unevenly into a rippled mess.

Early in October they took up the vanishing point.

Mostly it was accomplished with the ruler, and it was a lot like geometry, only fun. Lower on the art paper than a person would think, the horizon had to run clear across. Then the vanishing point must be marked. It didn't have to be exactly at the centre, Old Kacky said, but a little to the left of centre if a person wanted. Perhaps because he hadn't been listening carefully, he got his off to the right, but because it was the very start he was able to correct his mistake. The next step Old Kacky gave them was to rule two lines wide apart at the bottom of the page, squeezing down to the vanishing point on the horizon. They travelled up the sheet, actually. These lines were the edges of the highway; another would determine the tops of the telephone poles, and on the opposite side of the road there was one to limit the height of the fence-post tips. Before the drawing was nearly done, there was a great skein of lines, very faintly traced, funnelling to the vanishing point.

When his drawing was finished, it was shocking; his eye travelled straight and unerring down the great prairie harp of telephone wires strung along tiny glass nipples of insulators on the cross-bars, down the barbed-wire fence lines on the other side of the highway. And as the posts and poles marched to the horizon, they shrank and crowded up to each other, closer and closer together till they all were finally sucked down into the vanishing point.

There wasn't the faintest shadow or smudge from the temporary guiding lines; he'd rubbed them out carefully with the corner of his art eraser. No accidents as the yellow cube rolled off springy crumbs that reminded him of skin from the wrinkled backs of his heels and his knee-caps when he towelled after a hot bath. He could not get over how doing something so crazy should end up looking just right. Things didn't look the way a person thought they did at all.

But very soon – before art period was over – his drawing didn't satisfy him. Empty. It needed something. Maybe a meadowlark on a fence post – a kill-deer near the road – goshawk hung high. A tiger wouldn't do, of course, unless he put in a circus tent for it to have got loose from. Nothing dangerous went slinking along the highway or the C.P.R. tracks over prairie. There were no man-eating plants or quicksand around Sadie Rossdance's three little cottages; nor did lions and leopards prowl down after dark to drink from Tourigny's swimming hole. Deadly five-minute snakes and hooded cobras, walnut-coloured natives with white turbans on their heads, and rocking giraffes with necks like swaying telephone poles lived far away in their native land – or in *Chums* – or on the screen of the Hi-Art Theatre, where Mel's father played the piano and drums for Ken Maynard and Charlie Chase and Harold Lloyd. This, in a way, gave Mel an extra right to them; he also claimed special knowledge of stinging scorpions because his Aunt Vera was in the mission fields of India for the Western Baptists.

The drawing had to have something more – some gophers, like tent pegs – clump of wild roses – buck brush. That was it! A tree! In the front and to the left, as high as the first telephone pole, he put in a poplar the way Old Kacky had showed them to make poplars. And then another – a pine on the other side of the road, almost half way to the horizon. They looked great! Maybe some gophers and the curved Vs of flying . . .

Oatmeal! He looked back and up over his shoulder. Old Kacky in the aisle reached down, took up the drawing. As he looked at it, his scalp turned scarlet.

"My office!"

With the drawing in his hand, he followed Carlyle there. He closed the office door. He went round the desk. He dropped the drawing. He sat down.

"All right. Why did you do that?"

Badly as he wanted to, he could not find the reason that he had put the trees in his drawing. It had been a sort of an accident.

"You knew we were doing the vanishing point and perspective. You were told to do that. Simply."

He nodded.

"But you went ahead – you disobeyed. Put those trees in as well as the fence and the telephone line."

He nodded again.

"Deliberately."

He nodded.

"Haven't you anything to say – any explanation – excuse?"

He did know that Old Kacky was not interested in an excuse, whatever its excellence. "No, sir . . . it . . . just happened."

"It couldn't. The trees had to be outlined. They had to be shaded. Coniferous or deciduous – they can't draw themselves. Can they?"

"No, sir."

"So, you put them in deliberately."

"I guess I did, Mr. Mackey."

"Do you mean you know you did?"

"Yes, I guess . . . yes, sir . . . I knew – know – after they happened – accidentally."

"What?"

"I mean after they – after I happened to think them – doing them – putting them in there – then I – drew them deliberate."

"Deliberately."

"Deliberately."

"What if a boy did this sort of thing in arithmetic? History? Geography? Do you see what I mean?"

"Yes, Mr. Mackey."

"Deliberate disobedience."

"Yes, sir."

"You know I have to strap you."

"Yes, sir."

Five on each hand. Nothing before in his eleven years of life had hurt that much.

After Old Kacky had put the strap back into its drawer, he told Carlyle that he had conducted himself well and in a manly fashion. He said Carlyle could remain in the office for five minutes before returning to the classroom.

As soon as Old Kacky had closed the door behind himself, Carlyle thrust the incredible pain between his legs; with one knee lifted, he squeezed the hurt, then, with wrists loose, tried to shake off stinging drops. He rubbed his hands up and down on the front of his pant legs.

With some surprise he realized that he was not sorry for the trees at all. It wasn't trees he'd thought of putting – first. A tiger – with satisfied jowls and lovely stripes shaded in with his art pencil. But a tiger would have been ridiculous on prairie. So would Old Kacky. He'd be safe enough on prairie unless he broke his leg and lay out there in forty-below; or maybe in spring, when they ganged up for mating, coyotes might catch his smell and ring him and wait for him to die! In the deep rain-forests or the rubber jungles of the Amazon, though, he'd be in trouble. His strong, scared, oatmeal scent would telegraph him to head-hunting Indians and black, man-eating jaguars. Boa constrictors went by smell too. Yes! Behind the flat head – just like a sack of coal struggling in the boa constrictor's neck!

The pain had completely evaporated; his palms were just warm now. Red as sunburn. He could see there was a slight puffing. His hands trembled. He couldn't stop them; it was a little like looking at them through the lifting drift and shimmer of heat waves. They blurred. Then they starred. He looked up and away from them to the picture over the filing cabinet. The soldiers had bloodied bandages round their heads, just like Billy Blake's handkerchieves, or the newspaper wrappings left over from the farm kids' sandwiches' hemorrhaging strawberry jam. Two artillery horses lay in their harness, all tangled up, legs thrust out into the air as though they didn't belong to them. The legs had been stuck onto their bloat bellies. And now he could read the brass plate underneath: SOMEWHERE WITH A VETERINARY UNIT IN FRANCE. Donated to Sir Walter Raleigh School by KITCHENER OF KHARTOUM CHAPTER IODE.

Suddenly he realized how very still it was in Old Kacky's office. And lonely. Here he stood by himself, and outside the office walls were all the others properly together and busy all around his own empty desk. He had vanished from them. Old Kacky had vanished him from them to vanishment. And then the really crazy thought happened. He was being vanished from himself . . . stepping outside and apart and walking away farther and farther from himself, getting smaller and smaller and smaller . . . dwindling right down to a point. That was crazy and enough to scare the shit out of a person!

Literally.

His stomach had cramped sharply. His five minutes were up! There wasn't nearly time to go to the boys' basement. He'd fill his pants! If he used the waste basket, Old Kacky would see it right away. He could spread some paper on the floor and then gather it up and . . . This time it came lower and worse! He looked at Old Kacky's desk.

The bottom drawer on the left-hand side, brimmed with cardboard folders lying flat. He lifted them out carefully and quickly. He set them down on the desk top.

Just in time!

He replaced all the folders – tenderly. Then he closed the drawer.

It had taken Old Kacky a whole week to find it.

TWENTY-SEVEN

THE LOSS OF VICTORIA HAD SHATTERED SOMETHING INSIDE him. He knew that now. He knew he was not trying simply to find her. He knew that he must put back together something he had been trying all his life to keep from being splintered – broken beyond repair. It was something mortally important to him, and it had never – ever – been whole for him really; Aunt Pearl and Old Kacky had seen to that. And his father.

Victoria Rider had grown essential; he must find her and he must do it to save himself as well. He could not tell which drove him more, his own need or hers. If he were honest with himself – probably his own. It did frighten; it was so goddam ridiculous and unheard of: that Carlyle Sinclair wasn't. You couldn't, for God's sake, deny your own existence. I deny, therefore I exist. Sinclair's Law of Inner Being: No existing self can successfully deny that denying self. No exceptions to Sinclair's Law, except of course the inhabitants of Bedlam.

Two searches now; he'd found Aunt Pearl again – indeed had never lost her – or Old Kacky. How about his father? Why should he be able to recall the curtained pallor of Aunt Pearl's face but not his own father's features? Perhaps it was because his father's had been such a civilized face, with nothing unique about it to catch and to hang in the memory – no ears that called attention to themselves – no eyes that committed in any way; forehead, chin, nose making no statement of their own. Plato's pattern of a face.

But look at Olga's bunty nose, her fleshy lips, high red cheeks, and those startling blue eyes. Feel the soft pressure against an ear, the side of a cheek, the strength of that hand cupping and holding firmly the back of his head – smell her lye ghost bouquet and her edgeless smell of warmth that reminded you of a wax candle or a coal-oil lamp. She had kissed him only once, when she had taken him in her arms after he had been strapped by Old Kacky. She had helped him in the Ten Thousand Dollar Contest.

And there had been Mate. When Old Kacky had found it in his desk drawer, he had lined them all up in the hall and asked for the young savage who had done that despicable thing – to step forward like a man and take his punishment. Carlyle had been unable to do the manly thing. Old Kacky had released them, said he'd be in his office waiting to hear from that boy, or anyone who knew the boy who had done it and realized where his true loyalty must lie. If no one co-operated, then he must whip them all. It had taken him an entire day to do it and then he had lined them up again and said he would whip every male child each day until the mystery was solved. Mate had stepped forward out of the line to take the blame. Carlyle had never been able to tell Mate that he had done it. Once he had almost managed it, when he and Mate were coming back from Tourigny's swimming hole with its hiccuping spring-board where Mate had made everybody laugh by tucking his privates back between his legs and mincing out to the end of the board in a parody of femininity. As they walked the railroad tracks squeezing down to the far line of the prairie horizon, he took a try at telling Mate, by bringing up the art class and the vanishing point.

"Isn't any vanishing point," Mate said.

"Sure – sure there is – in art class."

"Uh-uh – look – they don't meet – the rails don't meet."

"But they look like they come together. . . ."

"Nope. C. P. R. couldn't run their engines if they did – not ten foot if the rails were coming together."

"Not really – I mean they look as though they're coming together, so if you draw them then you got to have them come together in a vanishing point. Mate, you remember the day Old Kacky took me out of art class into his office?"

"Look up the tracks – stays open – same on the highway – stays open – even the way it looks – there isn't any vanishing point. It doesn't come to a point – it only comes almost to a vanishing point. . . ."

"All right – but the art class when we took up the vanishing point and I got the strap for putting in trees and Old Kacky left me in his office, and I got cramps. . . ."

"It's just something Old Kacky told us to do. Walk your ass off and you aren't going to come to it."

"Sure works in art though. It looks right."

"So does a mirror."

"Huh?"

"But when you look in a mirror everything's backwards."

"Anybody knows that."

"But anybody doesn't know it's a third smaller."

"What?"

"You – your face – what reflects is always a third smaller than it is."

"Is it?"

"Always. No – that's not right. Depends on where you stand – less if you're close – smaller if you're farther away – and it's always about a third smaller, but you aren't really smaller – it just looks like that."

"How do you know?"

"I measured."

"Oh. Well – in art class that day . . ."

"I do a lot of crazy things."

"Yeah – like when you walked out on the diving board with your . . ."

"I inherit it."

"How come?"

"My mother's crazy."

"Oh." He'd known it, but he wished Mate hadn't said that. It made him feel a little sick.

"I'll go crazy too."

"Oh no . . ."

"I hope it doesn't happen too soon."

"It won't. I do crazy things too."

"I hope it doesn't happen before I become a famous acrobat."

"I do a lot of crazy things too, but I'm not going to go crazy."

"I will. Actually I intend to be a clown acrobat – that's why I don't keep my knees tight and my feet together and my toes pointed when I walk on my hands – clown acrobat – before I go crazy."

"Once I stuck my prick in a magic lantern."

"Huh!"

"At Aunt Pearl's in Winnipeg. Up in Willis's toy room. Blurred at first, and then I focussed it, and there it was on the plaster wall."

"Hey!"

"It was twenty-nine times bigger."

"Great!"

"I was only six when I did it, and I don't figure I'm going to go crazy."

"You would if your mother did."

"My mother's dead. She died when I was with Aunt Pearl."

331

"Okay – she's just dead. And when you're little you do a lot of crazy things. They don't count then."

"I burnt the end of it." He was not going to tell him now about who really did it in Old Kacky's desk drawer. If Mate wanted to keep on taking the credit for it, then he was welcome to it.

"There's nothing you can do about it – if you inherit it," Mate was saying.

"Maybe you didn't."

"I did."

"How can you tell?"

"Way I do crazy things all the time."

"Not that crazy."

"I'll get sadder and sadder even though I'm making everybody laugh – and sadder and sadder – and then I'll try to cut my throat. . . ."

"No you won't."

"I will. That's how it will happen – and then they'll put me in an insane asylum with a scar around my throat."

He wondered if that was how it had happened to Mate's mother, but he didn't ask.

Before they reached town they came to a shed garter-snake's skin, and they stood together and they looked at it for a long time, and as they stood he realized that he was never going to tell Mate that he knew it wasn't him did it in Old Kacky's drawer. He felt good after he thought that; it was as though he had given Mate something.

The tracks had taken them straight to the C. P. R. station, and when they went into the washroom to take a leak, they found Mel and Peanuts and Billy Blake there.

Even when they hadn't walked the rails back from Tourigny's swimming hole, they often went into the C.P.R. station. Over the urinals there was the big poster that said: BEWARE OF

STRANGE WOMEN. It had a whole list of what these strange women could give to men. Until the first time he'd read the poster, Carlyle hadn't known it was "buboes"; he'd thought it was "blue balls." He'd heard the older boys talk about "clap," which had a nice happy sound about it like "Farmer in the Dell." One time in the fall dusk at McGoogan's corner, he had told Mel that he had a cousin who had died of clap – little Willis. And Mel had been very interested and asked him where had his cousin got it. So he said Willis got it from a railway toilet seat in Winnipeg, where returning soldiers left it after they got it off of strange women in France and it wasn't little Willis's fault. Willis's balls had turned blue, and Mel wanted to know what kind of blue, and he told Mel it wasn't robin's-egg blue – more like indelible-pencil blue, and Aunt Pearl was ashamed of it, so she claimed little Willis had died in the flu epidemic, but that wasn't true. Clap and blue balls had killed him. Aunt Pearl had caught it off Willis too.

In a few days he found out from Billy Blake that the kids were saying he had the clap, which he got from his cousin Willis in Winnipeg who died out of it. Billy said he didn't believe it – or that Carlyle had gleet too. It was then that he realized the wickedness of what he had done to Aunt Pearl – and Willis. The more he thought of it, the worse it seemed that he had said Willis and Aunt Pearl had something terrible and unclean that would make people stay away from them for fear of catching it from them like lepers with their leprosy. The least he could have done was to give little Willis sky-blue balls or iris-blue balls or forget-me-not-blue balls.

Mel was always coming over to his house, and when they played cards together it had to be Snap or Old Maid with the deck he brought with him to use instead of ordinary cards. When they were ten, Carlyle had showed him his father's medical books with the marbled covers that had maroon corners and raised welts on their spines. There was a set of four, and, in the front, the first one had the man with his arms straight down at his sides and the opened palms held outwards. "See, I have nothing on – not even my skin." It was rather sad-looking, and you could peel back the pages like onion layers so you could see the pleated muscles criss-crossing like cartridge belts and the balled eyes staring out blue. It didn't interest Mel at all; he always wanted to turn right to the page with all the female parts – rows of them – sort of like a graduation picture or a stamp-album page. Mel stared at them on and on, and said Joe Bowery had done it to Harriet Winters and then to Sadie Tregillis. He also liked the strawberry-red chancre and always wanted to go into the surgery if Carlyle's father wasn't there, so he could see the little foetus that rocked in its bottle.

On one of his visits, Mel had said that at night Carlyle's father's car was always standing outside of Sadie Rossdance's three little houses. Carlyle didn't see what was wrong with that, but Mel seemed to think there was something wrong with it, though he wouldn't say what. Miss Rossdance was a milliner and lived in three little cottages with bonnet roofs. They were on the other side of the fairgrounds and were separated from the town by a stretch of prairie that was exciting, for here camels and elephants were staked and circus tents pitched when they came to town. This was the campground for gipsies too. These short-lived and seasonal gaieties somehow seemed to have infected the Sadie Rossdance houses with carnival spirit. Each one had a piano and someone to play it. From opened windows came "Roses of Picardy," "Barney Google," "Marquita," "Let Me Call You Sweetheart," and "Yes, We Have No Bananas."

He could not remember the day he had first visited Miss Rossdance's, probably a Saturday afternoon or morning on a return from a gopher hunt on the prairie beyond. After that it had been a regular port of call, because Miss Rossdance always gave him a glass of milk and cookies. She was a slender woman with very blonde hair and pale eyes. She had tight energy that made her talk quickly; she laughed a great deal and had a way of cocking her head as though she were listening with comradely amusement. You could tell she liked children. She had really helped him in the Ten Thousand Dollar Contest he got into when he was ten.

Olga got him into the contest, actually; she had showed him the announcement in the back of her *Ranch Romances Magazine*. The contest was illustrated with the picture of a lovely woman who had just been splashed with mud from a passing Stutz Bearcat; the balloon issuing from her mouth contained a lot of jumbled-up numbers. By the substitution of "a" for "1," "b" for "2" and so on, you were to decipher what she said. The result was puzzling: "Oh my, now you will have to buy me new hose. The best is none too good for me. It will have to be Tite-Wove Lingerie for real value, style and freedom of action!" He told Olga it seemed a funny thing to have in a Ten Thousand Dollar Contest, but she said it was their ten thousand dollars, that they probably put it in to make the deciphering that much harder.

He had mailed his solution, and when the answer finally came it was a large carton containing, among other things, a letter:

Dear Miss Sinclair:

You have perfectly unscrambled the numbers in our Grand Ten Thousand Dollar Contest, which has placed you in the semi-finals along with nineteen other contestants. The next step in order to determine the winner of our first prize of three thousand dollars cash explains to you our shipment of a consignment of Wear-Rite Beauty Garments and Tite-Wove Lingerie. All you have to do is sell these lovely, waffle-knit, misty, sheer garments in plum, puce, magenta,

coral and petal-pink to your friends. See how delighted they
will be. Points will be awarded you per unit sale and so the
deadlock will be broken. Good luck, contestant!

According to the price list enclosed, there was fifty dollars'
worth of lingerie; his friends were: Mate and Fin and Hodder
and Billy Blake and Mel, and he could tell right away how
delighted they would be. He pulled the carton down the streets
in his wagon, into each front walk, trying to sell the stuff to
ladies he didn't know. It was like trying to commit an inept
crime over and over again. He must twist doorbells and interrupt
ladies at their baking or ironing or afternoon napping. It was
wrong to enter strange homes uninvited, and he was quite
unsuccessful. After his tenth attempt without selling a single
article, he said to Olga it looked as though the ladies in their
town didn't go in much for underwear.

He did not know what he could do with the stuff; the
contest people had sent it to him in good faith, and it would be
cheating of some sort to return it unsold; quite possibly it would
be breaking some sort of serious law.

Then, on Government Road, by the fairgrounds, he remembered Miss Rossdance and all her friends, and he began to pull
his wagon filled with contest-breaking chemises and slips and
nightgowns over the virgin prairie wool towards the three little
cottages. The bright song of a meadowlark dropped again and
again, then, carried to him on the prairie wind, a piano:

Doodle dee doo, doodle dee doo.
I like the rest, but what I like best is
Doodle dee doo, doodle dee doo!

He came to the edge of Vandendreisches' barley field with
the moist, early May wind rolling waves through the shrill

green. He saw a gopher sitting up by her hole, paws held up before her fawn belly swollen with spring and young. Woman voices and laughter drifted to him as he came up to the back of the three beehive houses.

They were all on the porch of the first house, in kimonos or wrappers, some sitting on the porch rail, three of them on kitchen chairs; the others were drying their hair; they were leaning forward so it curtained their faces, and they were all laughing and laughing all the while the piano played in the house. It wasn't so much as though they were sisters in the same family but as though they all belonged on the same girls' volleyball team.

Miss Rossdance gave him ginger-snaps and milk. He finished them and sat on the edge of the porch, not knowing how to begin. Then, finally, he told about the Ten Thousand Dollar Contest tie-breaking points. Miss Rossdance got him to bring the carton up on the porch. He didn't have to do any selling at all. The dark lady with thick hair and full cheeks, the one with the thin face and wide forehead with fair hair that seemed to spring up and out like the wings that went with the bald professor clown, Miss Rossdance herself – bought "budburst brassieres with elastic inserts for full control with floating action, circular bust cups," "petti-panties cut in one piece for extra comfort and long wear, with opaque silk tricot and non-chafing double crotch."

The girl with the dark eyes and cream skin, the very lovely one, bought his last nightgown with "eyelet-embroidered bodice with overlays of lace – daisy-white."

He sent all the money away and waited for the contest results. Three weeks later there came another carton with an enclosed note telling him that the deadlocked contestants had been thinned down to nine. This carton contained a gross of bottles of perfume. His father told him he must send them back.

When Carlyle had objected and said he could sell them all inside five minutes out at Sadie Rossdance's, his father became very upset – almost angry.

That was the thing about his father; he could not recall any other occasion when his father had lost his temper with him for anything he had done or had failed to do. Nor could he remember when he had been angry with his father – truly angry. They had been so terribly efficient with each other. It had been as though his father had decided that emotion was waste. It left Carlyle with a feeling of loss; it made him deliberately perform for his father, wanting to do things that would please him. But his father had never really let him know that he had, beyond a few times when there had come an expression of intensity on his face. Actually, after he'd sold the stuff out at Sadie Rossdance's, he saw very little of his father, who went more and more into the den with its leather chairs and pictures of well-bred dogs playing poker. It had been about then that Sadie Rossdance and all her friends left town. No one ever moved into the three little houses after they left.

Carlyle could remember that it had also been about this time of his life that he had begun to have the dream in which he was approached by a flayed brigand with his arms down at his sides and his hands turned out.

The last year that Mate was his closest friend, when they were thirteen, they had played their game.

"I have a word."

"Yeah?"

"You want a word?"

"Maybe I got it."

"Maybe not."

"How much?"

Then you'd tell him what the word was worth: one agate –
two – licorice whip or fried-egg candy or jelly beans. Then he
said yes, and then you told him the word, and if he didn't know
it, then he had to pay for it, but if he did know, then you had to
pay him. For a long time Mate always won, because his strength
was in Latin and he could make shrewd guesses. By using his
father's medical books Carlyle overtook him, until Mate complained it wasn't fair, and Carlyle had to agree with him. But
then Carlyle began to sense a religious taint to Mate's words:
eucharist – apocryphal – transubstantiation – apostolic –
Armageddon.

That fall Mate had left town, sent to St. Johns with help
from some wealthy Anglican who felt it was the right of every
Anglican cleric's son to attend St. Johns. He had said good-bye
to Mate at the railroad station. Just before Mate would board,
Carlyle had leaned forward and whispered to him, "Beware of
strange women, Mate – on the day coach."

Mate's narrow white face with its unflawed innocence had
not changed as he lifted both hands and brought them together
in one flat, rapping clap.

The train pulled away from the platform. He watched it till
it had disappeared into the vanishing point Mate claimed
didn't exist.

They wrote to each other until Carlyle came down with
diphtheria just before Christmas. He was almost a month in the
small isolation building with its coning roof, a lot like the three
Sadie Rossdance cottages. It was set off from the main hospital,
and most people called it the pest house. Nobody could visit
anybody in there, but in the middle of the worst of it, Mate had
come to the window and had raised the window and climbed in
the room with him and then got out again. He had asked Miss
McGeachy later and she had said don't be silly. She reminded
him a great deal of Aunt Pearl, which was too bad, because,

except for his father's visits, she was the only person he saw in all the time he was getting over his diphtheria. She put on and took off a white smock whenever she came in to him; between times it hung on a wooden tree by the door, and he was fascinated by the way she put it on herself and took it off herself; she was meticulously aware of the *out*side of it and the *in*side of it. She explained to him that there was no excuse for anyone getting any disease at all, because germs moved only on surfaces, and if a person didn't touch surfaces, or, if it was absolutely necessary to touch the surface of another person, say by shaking hands, then you must wash your hands right away. People were always unconsciously touching their faces – most likely their mouths and that gave the germs a chance to enter the orifice of the mouth. She said that people should be ashamed, really, of catching diseases.

When he mentioned to his father what she had said about being careful of germs entering the body through the orifice of the mouth, his father had said, "She's right."

"Then a person should be careful – the way she's careful?"

"Crystal McGeachy is extremely careful, Son – of all her orifices."

It was his second day out of the hospital that his father told him Maitland Dean had come home for Christmas from St. Johns, that he had also contracted diphtheria, that he had died. The funeral had been held a week before.

In later years he had wondered why his father and he had not quite been able to touch, for his father was not really so much like Aunt Pearl. Young as he had been when his mother had died, Carlyle suspected his parents had loved each other. Possibly his father had put all his love in one basket. He guessed he had come to that conclusion the spring he'd come home from university for his father's funeral, after the old Buick had run off the bridge down stream from Tourigny's swimming hole. Mel told him his father had been drinking heavy. With the house mortgaged, taxes, electric, water bills piled high, Carlyle had switched from first-year medicine to faculty of education.

Before he had returned to the city after his father's funeral, he had walked out past the fairgrounds to the three little cottages. The porch of the first one where he had sold the lingerie, the floor of all the rooms inside, were littered with the brilliant raisins of flies' bodies. Bare walls, floors, windows staring, it was as though the house's forming soul had fled. In the corner of one of the back bedrooms he saw a woman's high-heeled shoe, and idiotically he was thinking of the Sunday School basement hymn they'd sung in Knox:

> *Jesus bids us shine with a clear pure light*
> *Like a little candle burning in the night . . .*

He guessed that was the way it had been with him and his father: "you in your small corner and I in mine."

He had gone out to the back of the houses to the old barn still there, entered to the unexpected explosion of starring light through knot-holes and cracks between boards shrunk under the years of drying prairie sun. Very faintly the smell of manure lingered, and of vanilla. In the corner where the manger met a stall wall he saw something white almost swallowed in the compost of manure and straw. It resisted him as though it were tethered, then came ripping free. He stared down at it – yellowed with age and rotten with mould. Just below his hand there was a great spreading rust stain, which must have once been blood.

". . . eyelet embroidered bodice with overlays of lace – daisy-white."

TWENTY-EIGHT

HIS HEAD WAS HUNG WITH ICICLES OF PAIN; HIS STOMACH was unbelievable. He had no idea where he lay – in place – or in time. This was not his bed. He was dressed. He was – just. And one other thing – it was night. And this wasn't his own bed, and he was still dressed, and either nausea or head-ache must have wakened him – somewhere – sometime.

In spite of his head he made it out of the bed, took a few steps, was caught just below the knees by the sharp edge of some piece of furniture, turned away and vomited – again and again and again. In the strange darkness he had difficulty finding the bed to fall down upon.

Now his head was definitely worse than his stomach – breakers of pain again and again. He lifted his arm and the green glow of his watch-dial faintly told him it was either twenty after one or five after four. And he was dressed still, and he was not in the fraternity house at all, but in some strange room, and he was going to vomit again. He managed to roll over and hang out from the bed.

It was still dark when he regained consciousness the second time. He was able to undress and roll back on the bed and pray that he would pass out again. Now – unfortunately – he knew where he was and why he was here – that he had just spent a great and successful day along his slum and skid-row trapline where nothing had got caught. His marvellous idea of calling in at the Employment Commission had simply proved there was no record of her seeking employment. He hadn't found her in any restaurant, though he had discovered two new ones he'd missed before; one by the stockyards, another which had looked at first like an antique shop. After lunch he had visited bars and ordered a beer to be barely sipped before he set out for the next place. At the base of the Devonian Tower he had seen the Indian girl he had mistaken for Victoria. He had stopped his search early and ended up in the hotel's Wee-Sack-A-Shack Room, where he ordered rye and water – to be drunk. He had been successful, for some hours later he had left, unsteady but mercifully numb, heading across the lobby towards the coffee shop. He guessed he had never made it.

Somebody's supporting arm had held him, had guided him into the elevator; whoever it had been had unlocked his door for him and assisted him over and on to the bed. The man had seemed vaguely familiar, spoke of Jesus Christ and – now he thought of it – Indians. He had also recommended peanut butter for its protein value on prolonged bats.

Why had he ever thought of himself as a night creature. He might once have been – not now. The darkness was not merciful – sleep, yes – but not darkness without sleep – darkness that would not forgive the light – that was without mercy. This was the darkness he could remember from his prairie childhood, when the whole house hummed and thrummed with the winter wind dirging at the brass weather-stripping.

He fell asleep, and when he woke, it was full daylight. He looked at his watch – three o'clock. The whole room was sour.

When the elevator door opened on the lobby, he saw the man in white. The man turned from the desk and, as soon as he had, Carlyle saw the white eyebrows rise with recognition.

"Brother," he said in his carrying voice. "Praise God you made it through the night."

"You're the one who . . ."

"Indeed I was."

"Thank you – ah – ah . . ."

"Reverend Heally Richards."

"Thank you, Reverend. . . ."

"Thank Him. It was He who placed me in your path – after you'd staggered out of the rum room – He placed me there. I trust you're feelin' much better today."

"Not much."

"That will pass, Brother, praise His name. I know, for I have been there too – I truly have – years ago before He lifted me. But you must ask Him first."

"I don't have any drinking prob –"

"We never do – until it is too late – but just you remember it's never too late – for Him."

"I'll remember – and again – thanks."

"I believe you work with our red brothers – so I gathered last night."

"Yes."

"I have had – I now have – the pleasure of workin' with them too. They are assistin' me with my Rally For Jesus – you may have seen our tent. . . ."

"Yes."

"You work with them upon the reservation?"

"Yes."

"Rewardin' work, I'm sure, ministerin' to their needs. Good Samaritan work must surely please the Lord. All the more reason you must set them a fine example. I find the same thing in my own ministry."

"I'm not a cleric. I teach."

"Oh – you were not speakin' too clearly last night. You are with them on the reservation."

"Yes. Paradise Valley."

"Well praise Him – praise His name! Brother Nicotine – Brother Esau . . ."

"What!"

"These are the very people who have been assisting me. . . ."

"Esau Rider! He's dying. . . ."

"Brother Nicotine and another – Prince Dixon, who has a half-ton truck – are bringin' him in to me. . . ."

"They aren't!"

"They are – tomorrow afternoon – our last service in the Rally For Jesus – they will carry him up to be touched and to be healed."

"You – they can't. . . ."

"I could not deny them the healin' power of God – Brother Nicotine insisted – and pray God we may have a true healin' for Brother Esau."

"Reverend Richards, it will have to be more than a healing. It'll have to be a miracle."

"Which is not impossible to the Lord – or His Son, Jeesuss Hallelujah!"

"Look – this isn't right – Esau Rider deserves . . ."

"Let Him judge that, Brother; join us – tomorrow – three o'clock in the tent of Jeesuss Christ – and you may see that miracle performed upon one of His red children. Right now – I'm overdue at CSFA-TV – for my last tapin'."

Coffee and toast and a boiled egg settled his stomach some; he'd have to find a drugstore for 222s for the head-ache. Jesus, whether he wanted to or not, he'd have to attend the tent service tomorrow. Esau was her grandfather! She'd be there! She'd be there!

While he waited to be served in the drugstore, yet another of the lonely accosters:

". . . not all cash – I hold the mortgage an' that ten per cent is pretty nice comin' in. I bought a four-suiter – rent out three and me in one the ground suites. Keeps me busy lookin' after the other suites. I miss the land too, but you can't get a hired man any more, an' the price of farm property now-a-days, a man has to make up his mind and we did. First we thought we'd get a small acreage on the edge of the city – maybe get into turkeys because Loretta – that's my wife – she always had a good success with turkeys – they're the touchiest of the works you know. Every spring she'd hatch a couple dozen eggs – turkeys just get everything – not like chickens – there's nothin' to chickens. Loretta had a way with turkeys, an' if she hadn't passed on in the middle of everything I would of got a small acreage on the edge the city where she could of raised a few turkeys every year – she hadn't passed on. Ever seen the way those big turkey outfits operate these days? Egg to the oven those turkeys never touch the ground – more like a turkey fact'ry with eggs in the one end an' turkeys out the other – never set foot on the ground – all their life on wire floors so's the droppin's fall right through an' you got to step through this tray of disinfectant to go in – come out again. You know, they put a bit in their beak an' a saddle on their back – not that John Wayne's ever gonna ride a turkey hen – nope – turkey gobbler – that's who."

She'd be there! Oh, pray God, she would be there tomorrow!

Prince Dixon's half-ton had run well almost to the city. Earlier, when they had carried Old Esau across the suspension bridge, loaded him into the back of the truck, their breath had steamed ahead of them, but they had made him comfortable in a nest of straw with two stones that Archie had left in the oven all night.

He had wrapped them thick with newspaper, put one on each side of Old Esau, then blankets, then the red cow-hide, then a tarp. The heater in the cab wasn't working, so it was chilly until they got down onto the flats; after that it wasn't so bad, and by the time they were half way, it was actually hot in there with the three of them. Rod Wildman and Archie took off their jackets, but Prince wouldn't stop to do his for fear he couldn't get the motor going again. They had almost reached the city when the truck did stop. Prince had managed to get it off to the side of the highway. It surprised Archie when he said the gas had run out. Prince told Rod to get the can out of the back of the truck and go up ahead for a gallon, and also for a quart of cylinder oil, but Archie didn't say anything then.

"I need something for the gas." Rod Wildman had the can at the cab window.

"Give him some money for the gallon of gas and for the cylinder oil," Archie said to Prince.

"You."

"You – I gave it to you before – that was our deal."

"I know," Prince said. He had his hands on the top of the wheel and was looking ahead out the window.

"I gave it to you before – for the gas and oil," Archie said again. "Give it to him."

"I haven't got it any more."

"What did you do with it?"

"It bled away on me."

"Last night you said the tank was full."

"I didn't notice it."

"Last night you said it was full and it didn't need any cylinder oil."

"I know that."

"Tank's empty now."

"Hey-uh."

"Pistons need cylinder oil." Archie waited. "Last night the tank was full and the pistons didn't need cylinder oil." He waited again. "How?"

"I guess it happened when we drove to Shelby and back again."

"Last night," Archie said.

"Hey-uh."

"King George beer parlour."

"Hey-uh."

"All the twenty."

"Hey-uh."

Archie leaned against the door to get at his side pocket. As he handed out the two-dollar bill to Rod, he said, "Keep going about three miles and then you'll see a lot of brown bear cubs an' ducks an' geese – tame – look for some pink sand-hill cranes."

Rod started walking.

"You're not dependable," Archie said to Prince, "and that is the whole situation."

"Hey-uh," Prince said. He began to roll a cigarette.

When he had lit it, he said, "I kept up the payments on this truck most the time."

Later he said, "But you didn't get yours runnin' yet."

When he threw the butt out the window, he said, "You didn't get the rings and carburetor for yours yet, did you?"

Archie said, "You want to bleed away something else besides all that twenty I gave you?"

"Maybe you better check Old Esau back there," Prince said.

"Maybe you better."

Prince began to roll another cigarette.

Even though it had taken a long time for Rod Wildman to make the trip to the filling-station and back again on foot because the filling-station owner couldn't leave the pumps which were busy that late in the afternoon, there was still plenty of time to pull into the shopping centre and go inside the Flying Saucer for cheeseburgers and coffee and soft ice cream. When they came out, the truck would not start up.

"It's the battery weak," Prince said. "Redhead gas station's just two blocks over. Go get the booster battery and jumper cables."

"You go this time," Rod said. "My feet hurt."

"It's my truck," Prince said.

"Then you go, Archie."

"I'm payin' for it," Archie said.

Rod went.

The truck started all right. They returned the battery and booster cables.

At each stop light, Prince gunned the motor so it wouldn't die again. They made it over the railroad tracks to the big tent, then around behind it where Reverend Richards had told Archie to go. They were in plenty of time.

As they stopped, Archie said "You an' Rod go climb up back. Start gettin' Old Esau ready."

"It's too soon for that now," Prince said.

"Open up that stretcher we made him an' slide Old Esau over on it." Archie had pulled down a long, buckskin-covered cylinder from behind himself on the top of the seat.

"Over an hour yet," Prince said.

Archie took the lid off the cylinder.

"Maybe he'll get cold waitin' till it's time," Prince said.

"Lay the warm rocks in against him an' wrap the blankets over him an' the cow-hide again."

Inside the tent, the piano began to play.

"See," Archie said. "Pretty soon Old Mosquito Man will give us the signal an' we won't have him inside there behind the platform."

Rod and Prince got out as Archie began carefully to slide the eagle-feather war bonnet out of its case. He was still fixing the feathers when Rod and Prince came back again.

"I slipped on the floor the box where he bled," Rod said.

"Lot of blood all over it," Prince said. "Maybe he's dead."

"Couple times before we thought he was dead but he wasn't," Archie said.

"Now he is," Prince said.

"Let's see," Archie said.

When he had climbed into the back and looked and listened, Archie climbed back down to Rod and Prince.

"Is he dead yet?" Rod said.

"Hey-up," Prince said.

"It's hard to tell with Esau," Archie said, "whether he's dead or he isn't dead."

"I don't think there's very much blood left in him," Rod said.

"He's dead," Prince said.

"I think he's just almost dead," Archie said, "an' that's the whole situation."

"He's dead," Prince said.

"So we will carry him in there an' wait for the signal. If he isn't dead, Mr. Reverund Richards might heal him. If he is dead – it won't make any difference anyway if we carried him in there."

TWENTY-NINE

BEHIND THE PURE PULPIT IN THE CENTRE OF THE PLATFORM
he sat with elbow on one knee, bowed forehead cupped in his
hand. He must be invisible to most of them, for they were to
him. All the same he could estimate that the tent was nearly
filled, slopping with their restlessness – razor-backs rooting and
grunting through palmetto under turpentine pine. These elastic
moments excited him as they always had; he could smell the old
carnival and revival salad of crushed grass and sun-warmed
canvas stung with the vinegar of sweat. There was a slight bitterness too, for Hillaker's bench planks had been delivered
green, still wept slow and amber tears of spruce sap. Several
people had complained through the rally – pitch stains. Now
then – just might be something there! Tell them to just forget
about those pitch stains there – tell them they didn't worry the
Lord any. Those sin stains – great – black – pitch – sin stains all
over your soul! Hallelujah! That is what worries Him and His
own livin' Son, Jeesuss!

Thanks for that one, Lord! I'll just use that today, praise
Your name and keep it coming! Let it work for you today! Oh,
let Your own great glory enter this tent and be witnessed by
them all – by the young lady reporter sent from the religious
page of the morning newspaper! Let it go through that camera

and travel to hundreds of thousands of television screens for fifty miles in every direction from this glory tent! Hear me, Lord – oh hear me now – hear Heally Richards!

It would go well! He'd bring it off! CSFA-TV had finished setting up in the centre aisle. If only they could have managed colour for the scarlet and yellow of old Esau's beadwork and eagle-feather war bonnet. But it couldn't be helped; colour mobile unit took double the crew and four times the cost of black and white. What a shame though – to lose Gloria Catface in colour – the yoke of crocus blue over her breast – the head-band bugle-beaded with gold crosses, circling her hair falling black and free to her hips and the small of her back. Sixty-two dollars. In the clean snow of her doe-skin with its fringed skirt, she was worth it! For forty dollars he'd redeemed her Miss North-west Fish and Game outfit from the window of Ralph's Square Deal Shop, then another twenty-two dollars to Sunset Dry Cleaners. Princess! Probably was one anyway. She'd been redeemed, and now she was one of His royal ones. That made her Princess Gloria and that was how he'd introduce her. Princess Gloria!

Her brother would still be ushering people to their benches; Hillaker would give her the signal when they'd stopped entering; then she'd take her place by the piano, pick up the tambourine. She was a natural with it; he'd showed her how to work it from wrist to elbow and back again. She'd picked it up right away, the gay, shallow clink right on beat. Her brother had suggested a Chicken Dance drum to be used just as Old Esau was touched. Almost – he almost wished now that he'd gone along with it. No! Not really; it was pagan! Oh Lord, make there be a miraculous cure this afternoon! Old Esau's!

There would be – there would be! Many of them! He'd touch three times, the first time after the singing warm-up: do Hillaker and his prostate – the shoulder bursitis – the cataracts.

No – not the cataracts – save them for the second or maybe the third batch – eyes of the blind shall see. Replace the cataracts with touching the constipation and there might possibly be three more from the raised hands out there. The second bunch would come after the praise is mist from Genesis and before Ezekiel and the valley of dry bones. Oh Lord, make sure there's glory by then and talking in tongues and as many as wanted to could crowd up – but in the last ones – for climactic effect – the tick dollar, the breast cancer, the cataracts – yes – and the cook who had lost her sense of taste and smell – in that order. Smell and taste right after the cataracts. She had spring flu and he'd be able to handle her pretty dramatically – cup her nose and mouth. Maybe he should have arranged for someone to be ready with perfume. No – there was sure to be one woman in the front row with a vial in her purse. He'd simply ask for it – hold the bottle close under her nose with the cork out. Then let the glory build and build till they carried Old Esau out from behind the platform and round in front of the pulpit.

He'd set up everything; the crew would start rolling right after the second touching, run live from there to the end of the hour. There was nothing he'd missed. But had he warned Nicotine to be very careful, carrying that stretcher! Could be twenty brothers and sisters lying all over that grass before the pulpit. Of course, he'd cautioned them twenty times. Oh, Lord, watch over where those Indians lay down their clumsy feet! Oh God, please – please choose – through Heally Richards – to lift up that old Indian from that stretcher before the Mercy Seat! Raise up that feathered, buckskin Lazarus with Your revivin' pahr! "Esau – Esau – take up thy stretcher and walk!" Walk right up that aisle towards the camera dollying back – then holding and zooming till that skull face haloed with blood and gold fills the frame on every turned-on set from the flats to the Rockies to the Montana border! Rise up, Esau! And Heally Richards too! Right up out of the evangelic bush-league – clear to Billy and Gipsy and Aimee and Oral! Hallelujah!

There she was now – pure white and forget-me-not blue by the piano. Hillaker must have given the signal. The excitement had turned a little sick down there now. Time for Heally Richards to go up there now, Lord. Use me. Lord – oh, use me, this time, please! Show me You intend to use me!

Odd. It had taken exactly nine steps to reach the pulpit. The bench rows came out odd too, and there were three aisles – or five counting the spaces between the row ends and the side-wall canvas. The tent was full right to the back bench, which wasn't completely a good thing; it could mean the congregation was adulterated with the simply curious and the unbelievers. They could be stiff; he wouldn't know until he began to work them.

"Welcome to the tent of our Lord, Jeesuss Christ. Praise Him – Praise His name! I would first like to call your attention to our lovely little girl with the tambourine today – you've seen her – just heard her – Princess Gloria – full-blooded plains Indian girl – left the pagan faith of her wild forefathers – the heathen witch-doctors – accepted Jeeesuss into her soul, hallelujah – Praise His name – Praise Him! Thank you, Sister Gloria – the Lord loves music too – He truly does."

So – if the bench rows were odd – the aisles were odd – odd number of steps to the pulpit – make sure of an odd number for each touching. . . .

". . . thanks to Brother Hillaker we have received two-by-twelves which are not fully seasoned. Brother Hillaker keeps on telling me that this is not unusual in most lumber today. It is green lumber. I mention it because several of you have complained to me through the week – resin stains you have received on your clo'es. Well, I am sorry about that – those stains worry you, but somehow I don't think they are worryin' the Lord a very great deal – or His own livin' Son, Jeeesuss. Jeeesuss is not worrid about those little bitty pitch stains on the seat of your skirt, Sister – seat of your pants, Brother. Not Him! I can tell you what He is worrid about – if you'd like me to – and I'm not so sure you'd like me to. Just you let me tell you what Jeesuss is worrid about – those sin stains there – those great, black, pitch sin stains you got all over your immortal soul! I know – I know – you are worrid whether the dry-cleaner will be able to clean your clo'es. My suggestion to you – this afternoon – you are dealin' – with the wrong – dry-cleaner! Take your soul over – to Jeeesuss Christ and let Him dry-clean it for you! Tell Him that Heally Richards has recommended Him – He is very good at it! He doesn't advertise, but He has been in the dry-cleanin' business for nearly two thousand years, and He can clean a sin-stained soul till it is white as virgin snow! His cleanin' fluid is His – and His alone! He uses – His own – blood! Number 259 in your hymn books – but you won't need them – you all know it – 'Washed in the Blood of – the Lamb!'"

And the hymns would be all odd-numbered too – oh, how the glory would come down today! He could tell already – good – they felt very good – all of them leaning up to him – solid – willing solid! Oh, thank You, God – praise Your name! With Old Esau it will work today, and Heally Richards is on his way! With Gloria and her brother and his half-cat face out in the back row there – over to the right. No – not the brother! He wouldn't do at all! Might take Nicotine to Santa Barbara maybe – arms folded, staring out over the congregation – wearing one of those buffalo-horn medicine hats so he was actually the heathen priest – have him witness – he could describe the horrors of his pagan past, then rip off the hairy head-dress as though he were shucking his cruel and heathen husk. Nothing wrong with that – Lord didn't object to a good show – look at the Passion play – Easter services with candles twinkling up the whole mountain-side – Gloria and Norman Catface – no – not her brother or even Nicotine – pick up one in California – glossy photographs for the religious pages – advance notices – terrific – terrific!

Empty space now beside Hillaker back there! Where was Norman anyway! Been told to sit by Hillaker, ready in case of late-comers. Why couldn't he do as he was told! Why couldn't Hillaker make sure he did! There he was – still in the back row, but over next to the aisle now.

"Now – we do want glory here, don't we – you want the Lord's blessin' here – don't you? Well – wantin' it and gettin' it are two different things. It is not going to come down just by its own accord. I can tell you that. His blessin' just doesn't happen. I can truly tell you that. Look in your Bibles – you look in there now – you look in Genesis – '. . . for the Lord God had not caused it to rain upon the earth!' Why not? What – why had He not – caused it – to rain upon – the earth?"

First the pitch-sticky bench planks and now Norman Catface! He'd warned Hillaker to keep an eye on Norman, so right at the start Hillaker has to let him loose – let him leave his seat – and now the Indian wasn't even next to the aisle. Oh – there he was – skipped across the aisle and a whole section of benches so now he was in the centre. How had he managed that – there'd been no movement – or rather – why had he moved his seat twice? What was he up to anyway!

". . . I'll tell you why He had not caused it to rain upon the earth. The answer is very simple. He couldn't. That's right. He couldn't. Surprises you – doesn't it – that the all-powerful Lord God Almighty – could not – rain – upon the earth – at that – given time. I will tell you why he could not. . . ."

Gone from that spot – empty space where the scarred cat-face had been! Vanished!

". . . there can be no rain – if there has not been – vapour." They didn't feel so good now. "Has to be vapour go up from the earth first to form a cloud and then – not until then – can rain come down from that heavenly cloud . . ." They didn't feel good at all. ". . . to water the whole face of this earth."

Appearing – disappearing all along the back bench – slashed – impudent demon face – putting him right off his pace!

"We do want God's glory, don't we – we want it to rain down on us today – don't we! But how! How can His glory and His blessin's rain down on us without any steam or vapour goin' up to Him in the first place! Your praise is what He needs to prime Him to let loose of his blessin's! How can He – possibly – rain down His blessin's on us when not one wisp of the mist of your praise has ascended up to prime Him!"

Clear over against the other side of the tent now! No matter how hard he tried he couldn't catch that Indian moving. He must be crouching and using the bodies of those in the back bench for a screen – slipping deftly and quickly from person to person till he could slide into a new open space on the planks! But why? Why!

"I have not heard – so far – very much praise going up out there. I don't think you truly know what praise is – oh yes – a mean little amen or hallelujah over here – a weak little praise the Lord over there. I am talkin' about shoutin' praise – chorus praise – tenor and bass and soprano and alto praise – Gregorian – Pentatonic – which is just the five notes – I am talkin' about praise in tongues!"

Still in the same place – leaning over to the man he sat beside now – Norman must be saying something to him – to each of them. A few minutes with each one, then snatched from sight to pop up farther down the bench. Get word out to Hillaker during the next singing. Have Hillaker sit next to that Indian and stay next to him. Better still, tell him to get right out of the tent.

"Nobody's raised his arms out there! Maybe somebody has, but I don't see them. I don't see any forest of arms out there!"

Stalking him just as truly as though he were gliding from tree trunk to tree trunk!

"Just what is stopping you – holding you back from liftin' up your arms! A man come down that aisle and he holds up a loaded gun pointed at you and he says, 'Lift 'em up – I'll shoot you dead if you don't' – well then I guess those arms would go up out there quick enough! Oh yes, they would. You wouldn't have to even think about it. What's it mean those arms raised up – it means surrender – I surrender myself to the blessin' and to the glory of the Lord! Hallelujah! Praise Him! Praise His name! I am ready – I am ready, Lord – to receive Your glory and Your blessin'!"

But there wasn't going to be any glory here at all. There were arms raised now – here and there – but they were not truly asking arms – automatic praise that couldn't possibly bring bless-ing down – non-priming praise and from somewhere near the back there was just a skimpy babble of tongues. Norman Catface had ruined it! As long as that Indian was in this tent, there could be no total glory!

Carlyle was almost certain she had not come; ever since the scar-faced Indian had showed him to his bench seat, his eyes had roved the tent without sight of her. It had seemed a good idea – promising – for she had always been the closest of the grand-children to Old Esau, bucking wood for him, hauling water, cutting kinick-kinick. She might still turn up, he told himself, but he knew she wouldn't. He could not help the realization that he would never see her again.

Oh, Victoria – Victoria – dear little lamb, Victoria!

Heally Richards' voice had confident power; he seemed so sure of his sway over the congregation, yet from the time his white figure had risen behind the white pulpit on the platform – the chocolate face under the white, cresting hair – he had been instantly theatrical. In white – he should have suggested something more than he did – medicine – the laboratory. He didn't. Hair-dressing parlour – the barber chair. Why was it that grass under canvas was so impossibly green – between the benches – down the aisles – as though they'd been carpeted with undertaker's grave grass.

Richards was admonishing them now, near-impatience sounding again and again. He wanted something from them that they weren't giving him. Asking them – no – ordering them to prime God with Gregorian and Pentatonic praise. In spite of himself the man was having an effect – as though cloud had slipped over the sun and darkened the landscape below, and God knew, it was dark enough! Aunt Pearl had given him this feeling when he was child. What was it? Not that she had disliked him – hated him – not that clear – as though there'd been a halo round her – or the absence of one. That was it – Heally Richards had no compassion halo. He was ordering them into a moral box to suit himself only – not them.

The man to his left had gone into that box, head back, eyes tightly closed. He was gibbering! The scarred Indian who had done the ushering was on the other side.

"Hallelujah!"

The Indian leaned closer. "Excuse me, Brother."

"Hellalbluh-luh – lalla-lall –"

"Could you have somethin' for a wicked man, Brother?"

"Hellaluhjah-ella-ella-lalla-roonay-horah-arah-aran –"

"We haven't et," Carlyle heard him say. "Princess Gloria and me a long time now."

"Lallalla-sem-tuh-ziddy-ay-ti-lilly-tiddy-lilly-ay-ohhh," the man replied.

"I'm ashamed to ask it now, Brother – here in the Jeses tent. . . ."

"Siddhazzah-lalla-leck-bruh-lep-toray-milknahlallabella-lla –"

"I don't think you understood me clear my question – our need is great for some bread – dollar or two. . . ."

"Gay-vah-gallallalellah-jebuukalla-shytite-shilly-shallall-la-allom-nah-shittom," the man said.

"And on you too, Brother," the Indian said. Carlyle saw him rise up and go forth and depart from the tent.

Not until the end of "Come Just as You Are" did Richards realize that Norman's disappearance was final. He had more than cancelled out his sister, Gloria. Right back to the beginning now, and thanks to Norman Catface, it would be uphill all the way.

"You ever heard of the day the Lord spoke to Ezekiel – right out and spoke to him and said for Ezekiel to go into the valley of dry bones – dry dead bones, 'Zeke,' He said, 'I want you to go – into this valley of dead bones – head for the boneyard, Zeke,' He said. God has a sense of humour. Oh, don't you ever mistake that. He truly has. And Ezekiel did go into this valley of dead bones – a dead, dry desert of dead, dry bones – he walked around a pile of rib bones – that pile of shoulder bones over there – then there was this pile of skulls right here – all skulls all piled together – that's where all your real trouble comes from – doesn't it now – those there head bones – he climbed over them and came to the femur-bone pile. Know what a femur bone is? Any of you know? Well, it's this one right here – your thigh bone – all piled together in that thigh-bone pile – all the bone piles separated and no good to each other at all.

"And then – the Lord said, 'Zeke – can these bones live?' Zeke thought to himself – live? – dry bones live? – dead, dry bones live? – how can they – how can they live? Just you imagine what Ezekiel was thinkin' to himself when the Lord said to him, 'Oh, son of man, can these bones live?'

"Ezekiel said, 'You're the One ought to know.'"

"And the Lord said to him, 'Prophesy to these bones – prophesy and say to them, O dry bones, hear the word of the Lord. Thus says the Lord to these bones: Behold. I will cause breath to enter you, and you shall live. And I will lay sinews upon you and will cause flesh to come upon you, and cover you with skin, and put breath in you, and you shall live; and you shall know that I am the Lord.'"

Now they were coming with him again! Oh, they were coming good now! Just the self-conscious beginning – no moaning yet – the hallelujahs were still deliberate – not bursting from them in spite of themselves – but all the same there was a stockyard restlessness, and he could feel anxiety out there. Strong.

"So – Zeke, he prophesied as the Lord had commanded him. Oh, he prophesied all right; and as he prophesied, there was a noise, and behold, a rattlin'; and the bones came together, bone to its bone. From the pile of ankle bones over there came the ankle bones – the head-bone pile the head bones – femur bones the femur bones – shoulder bones – rib bones – back bones – right! The right bones with the right bones! And he looked and there was sinews upon them and flesh had come down upon them! Flesh – raw flesh! And there is nothin' wrong with that flesh! Sister – don't you be scared of flesh now! Flesh is good!"

It always smelled the same – the rich yet fusty smother of their need – roach powder!

"There is always the skin, Sister, to cover that flesh. You know what skin is? Skin – is just another word – for love! It expands and it stretches like love – and it covers all that raw flesh on your bones! You need skin, Sister – because you'd be a pretty messy thing without that love-skin coverin' that raw flesh – wouldn't you, Sister! Wouldn't you now!"

"Hallelujah – hallelujah – hallelujah!" It fire-crackered all over the tent now!

"I'd ask you to come up here and let me touch your skin –
touch your love-skin!"

"Hallelujah – hallelujah!" Just listen to them lowing there!
And soon they'd gobble – too soon – oh yes, too soon!

"But I can't – you can't walk up here to me, Sister! Oh, no,
you cannot, for there is no breath in you! Yet! Look what the
Lord said to Ezekiel – 'Prophesy to the breath, prophesy, son of
man, and say to the breath, thus says the Lord God: "Come from
the four winds, O Breath, and breathe upon these slain, that
they may live!"' And Ezekiel did! Indeed he did! And the
breath entered them and they lived! And they could walk!
Walk up here to me, Sister – I want to touch you! Oh, I want to
touch you now! And you, Sister, come up here so I can touch
you! And you – and you!"

They came – oh, praise His name they came – praise Him –
praise the shoulder bursitis – praise the constipation – the
arthritis – the mother shoving forward her son with his child
prize-fighter face tilted up – Hillaker and his prostate! Blue and
white and gold caught his eye at the end of the line. Gloria!
Glory had moved her! From the piano where she'd been told to
stand! The glory had entered her and moved her to come to him
to be touched! And she would be touched first – hers would be
the first glory!

"Under the blessed spout where His great glory pours out!"
Never before – he'd never shouted that before! It wasn't his – it
was His!

"The Devil is a liar and my soul's on fire!" His too! Oh,
glory! "Glory-glory – Gloria – Jeeesuss – Jeesuss – praise Him –
praise His name! Hellalujah – hal-ella-ella-fellella-lall-lall-
lully-olla-filla-lillen-lora-allalla-bellen-seesa-blalla-juh-blessah-
balla-bella!"

He could feel her harsh nape-hair, wiry to the palm of his left
hand, the tiny glass seeds of her headband printing themselves

against his other palm cupping her forehead. He tipped up the lovely flower face. He leaned over, his ear to her mouth.

"Your pain and sufferin', Sister Gloria – that you may have it lifted from you now, praise Him!"

"I think it's clap," Gloria said, "again."

He could see that the television crew were filming now, that the services were approaching a climax. Something had gone wrong up on the platform when the evangelist had tipped back the head of the Indian girl. In her white doeskin she was quite lovely.

Oh, Victoria – little lost lamb, Victoria!

But Richards had moved on to the mongoloid child proffered by his mother, and then the old lady holding up the two arthritic bouquets of her fingers. Many in the congregation were lifting their arms with palms up and asking. They wanted the impossible, and he promised to shrive them of their mortality, to lift from them the terrible burden of their humanity, the load of their separateness. Now their bodies lay at his feet with arms and legs twitching. They moaned; they whimpered; they gibbered childhood echolallen.

He'd been here before; the soft explosion of recognition was unmistakable. But it had nothing to do with church – with any religious service he had ever attended. Indeed, the hortatory voice of Heally Richards did not belong to what he was trying to recall. The voice riding high over the congregation chorus kindled only resistance in him – unwillingness to be urged – like a cow turning off, now one way and now another, refusing to be herded by the voice behind. Yet he had heard these same beseeching harmonies that came and were destroyed again and again. He'd heard that lyric ecstacy that decayed to frightening anguish; he'd heard it flow from others no longer able to keep their own plight to themselves – or their own delight at releasing it when the bonds of self had been broken. Oh, God – oh, God – if only his own could be!

The Lord had sent His glory – He had truly sent it down – now it hummed and pulsed all through them – Heally Richards was His rod! Divine and healing lightning – came again and yet again – as he touched them – healed them – dropped them – blessed be the name of God!

"Praise His name I smell again!" The cook, who had recovered her sense of taste and smell, mewed, closed her eyes, slid from his hands to join the body litter on the grass before the pulpit.

This was it – the true glory; now his body was incredibly light and floating free. Hallelujah, how he hung in marine dream glory, the wondrous bubbles rising round him and through him, lifting him softly stubbornly upwards, praise Him, praise His name! Just like the time that he and Cass had pressed their wrists out and up against the casing of the filter-house door – then stepped forward to feel their feather arms rising of their own magic will. With each touching the exquisite anticipation grew – each time he laid his hands on each trembling head – with each convulsive squeeze and twist, the glory strengthened more. Each time he conquered each rigid body – felt it submit – the glory swelled – oh, the flower glory!

"Feeeeeel Him – feeeeeel His healin' pahr – feeeeeeeeel!" Seize and squeeze and heal and drop – seize and squeeze and heal and drop!

High – so high – he was so clear to Jesus high above them now he hardly heard the fumbling crump as their slack bodies hit the grass at his feet. Seize and squeeze and heal and drop – seize and squeeze and heal and drop!

"Heeeeeeeeeealuhbleeeelah – flesssahgubjayzuh – jeeeeee-zuh – sidddah – haaazzahdrupelllllllal-goruhgull-geerellan-oh!"

Seize and squeeze and heal and drop – seize and squeeze and
heal and drop! Hallelujah, he was truly flying now, praise His
name – right through wondrous glory light! Full lay-out – five
six – seven-and-a-half gainer! BUMP. Full twisting two-and-a –
BUMP – half cut-away!

BUMP!

Archie Nicotine's jolly demon face; behind it – Rod
Wildman's thin, dark one!

Both Indians stood erect, with chest and stomach out, their
arms straight down at their sides, between them the stretcher.
Old Esau lay supine, the sharp toes of his riding boots pointing
straight up, his left arm fallen down and slightly back so that it
rested with the palm turned up on the grass. The scarlet and
yellow eagle-feather war bonnet had slipped forward and down
to swallow all his face.

And the glory had been sucked right out of Heally Richards.
With stomach-pit sickness of nightmare falling, his flight was
ended. There had been no lower and lower planing; at first sight
of the Indian cadaver before him, he had been shot – dropped
from dazzling realms of holy light, one wing outstretched, the
other flailing helplessly, falling to dark earth, head over hopeless
tail-feather.

Archie and Wildman now bent evenly and laid Esau tenderly down upon the grass. They stepped back and aside, and as
they did, the round and seeing eye of the camera dollied
forward, stopped, tipped and tilted down upon Old Esau. Off to
the left the sound man, with his pack slung over one shoulder,
took several crab steps, held out the cylinder of his microphone
towards Heally Richards.

Oh, God – Oh God, why hadn't he seen the old man before
this moment! And now – mirrored before the whole world –
with no life-net – impossibility! Oh, why had He done this to
him! Why had he forsaken him! He had never asked Him for so

very much – only to save and to heal now and again – never to raise the dead! Why had He dumped this down in front of him! Why would He ask Heally Richards with old and slack and tired muscles to lift this weight – not ten or twenty or a hundred pounds beyond his strength – but tons! No choice! That was the terrible thing about it! He was lost if he did not accept, yet he would be destroyed if he tried!

He bent over Old Esau. He reached out his hands. There was not the faintest scent of glory now, only the charred bitterness of willow smoke – as though someone had just kicked apart a dead camp-fire.

"HEEEEEEEEEEEEEEEEEEEEEALLLLLLL!

"IN THEEEEEEE NAME OF JEEEEESUSS – HEEEEEEE-AAALLLLLL!

"PLEEEEEASE HEAAAAALLL – THIS BLACK SON OF A BITCH! HEEEEEEEEEEEAALLLL!"

Oh God, Oh God, his arms were rising – just like when he and Cass had pressed their wrists against that door frame! Of their own accord they rose before him. And lifting under them and with them Old Esau floated up! Still faceless under the slipped war bonnet, legs straight out before himself along the stretcher, Old Esau sat upright now. A miracle – a true miracle! Heally Richards had raised the dead! He lived again! Praise Him – praise His living name! Hallelujah – hallel –!

Esau's descent was a blink. From beginning to death, the almost-miracle had lasted for eleven seconds.

Too late – helplessly looking out beyond the television camera and over the congregation, Richard Victor Heally discovered that the tent had four poles.

THIRTY

THE CHARADE PLAYED OUT WITH THE UNDERTAKER IN THE subdued walnut office of the funeral parlour a dozen blocks from the Rally For Jesus tent had been brief. It was solemn and unreal, except for Old Esau, who had left the tent the same way he had come: in the back of Prince Dixon's truck – but with one difference: he *was* dead. He lay now in the basement slumber-room of the funeral parlour, still wearing his chief's dress, eagle-feather war bonnet, his broken riding boots pointing their sharp toes up to the fluorescent lights above. Faced with the task of handling the ugly awkwardness of death, the Indians and the undertaker seemed quite matter-of-fact. Sensibly efficient, the undertaker did not embarrass with ritual sympathy; he asked Archie to sign a release-of-the-remains form, explained that Mr. Rider would be ready by two o'clock the next afternoon. He had Carlyle sign a for-services agreement in the name of the Indian Affairs Branch, in triplicate. No more complicated than a department-store refund, really.

It had been only four-thirty when he had given Prince and Rod and Archie fifteen dollars for their supper and hotel, drove away to check out of his own room. He had left his car in the hotel parkade, walked up to the street and round the corner, when he saw Victoria. She was coming towards him, and the sight of her was as shocking as Esau's incredible return to life had been. The black dress with lace at the cuffs – her throat; she was carrying a shopping-bag. Blessed relief washed through him.

"Victoria – oh, Victoria!"

She had turned away from him; now she walked quickly back down the street. He caught up to her, took her arm.

"Wait – wait – don't – I've been look –"

"Please – Mr. Sinclair . . ."

"Victoria – I only want to help you. . . ."

"I don't want you to."

"Please – let me . . ."

"I don't want you to help me."

"You have to have help – you've got to let me . . ."

"I don't want it! Please, leave me alone! You can't . . ."

"I can – yes, I can! I've always . . ."

"Not now – not any more."

"Please!"

"Not any more."

"I've talked with the hospital – the matron – they understand – they're willing for you to . . ."

"No."

"You don't understand – it's all right for you to go back . . ."

"It isn't all right. I can't go back."

"You mean you won't." With some surprise he realized now that it was not relief he felt, but impatience at the unnecessary anguish she had caused. "You can tell me why not, can't you! You must have some explanation!"

She shook her head. His hand still on her arm, he stopped her. They stood in the middle of the street by the standard with its guttering flare, almost invisible in the bright afternoon. The scarlet doorman with his impossible buffalo head-dress was vivid. Victoria looked down past her grocery bag to the walk.

"Victoria – please."

"I can't go back to the hospital any more."

"Yes you can – I've already straightened it out for you."

"There's nothing to do now. It isn't any use."

"Yes, there is – there is! No different from the other times – at Christmas time when you . . ."

"There isn't anything to do – nothing for you to do – nothing for me to do."

"I don't understand." He waited for her. "You know – we've been through all this before – we worked it out – you made it – you passed . . ."

"It isn't like that. It isn't exams this time."

"Then what is it – tell me – at least tell me!"

"I'm ashamed."

"That doesn't tell me anything."

"I'm ashamed."

"Oh, for God's sakes – stop saying that! It doesn't explain anything!"

"But I am."

"Great. So you're ashamed. Doesn't stop you from going back."

"Yes – it does."

"Look – I am not asking you to do anything impossible! I am not asking you to . . ."

"Yes – you are – asking me to turn the mountains upside down . . ."

"No, I'm not."

"Stop the spring run-off . . ."

"Oh, don't pull that on me! You're Victoria and you are special – to me! You are the whole thing! You have been the whole thing for a long time! Do you understand that? Not just for me – for all of them."

"Please, Mr. Sinclair – don't load me up like that."

"I'm going back to Paradise now – you're coming back with me."

"No."

"Look, Victoria, don't just say no – at least give me some explanation – you owe me that – don't you?"

"I'm ashamed."

"Don't be – there's nothing to be ashamed of."

"Yes – there is – there's a lot now."

"Failure? It isn't something to be ashamed of. Not trying – you can be ashamed of that – but you have tried and you haven't failed. They're very pleased with you – they want you back." He released her arm. "I haven't a daughter of my own – but you are my daughter. I couldn't leave my own daughter – I can't abandon you. I won't!"

"You have to."

"Why?"

"Please, Mr. Sinclair – don't make me tell you."

He took her arm again. "Please – tell me."

She looked away from him. When she spoke, it was just a murmur.

"What did you say?"

"I said – I'm pregnant."

"Oh, God . . ."

"I'm ashamed."

"No!"

"Christmas time."

"All right. All right, Victoria."

She began to walk away from him. He did not try to stop her.

He made it past the scarlet medicine-man doorman, across the lobby desert, then up the elevator. He walked down the tunnel hallway, opened his door and stepped into the cube trap of his room. All his muscles had softly slackened, strengthening stiffness erased from knees, from elbows. He had to sit on the bed. Now he knew. Oh, God, he knew! His hands were trembling, and he was so cold, and he was not one bit different from Heally Richards. Mounte-pulpit Sinclair caught in the end trap – the self trap – suffering superlative pain for which he'd had no training. How had he lived so long without discovering this opposite of ecstasy – virgin Sinclair unprepared for the orgasm of pain.

Meet it – fight it – overcome it. I hurt, therefore I am. Oh, Jesus, he needed help – badly. And there was no one to help him. No one could help him. He had never helped them – really – how could he have – without knowing. Till now. His Samaritan role was nothing. What a fool he'd been just to feed, just to clothe – to keep alive only. They perished and he taught them arithmetic; they thirsted to death on their time desert and he gave them reading and spelling lessons.

He stood up. He'd better check out, get back to Paradise. Why – oh, God, why had he been asked to accomplish impossibility so far beyond his strength – beyond all human strength. Maybe he'd better have a drink before he packed. The worst of it was he hadn't known till now, so that without twinning pain his compassion had been specious. And he hadn't known – oh, Jesus, he hadn't known at all – he hadn't known that it was no use at all – that nothing could be done at all.

He stepped into the empty elevator, pushed the button for the ground floor. The Wee-Sack-A-Shack Room was dim, and now he knew why they kept their bars that way. Rye and water, Mr. Weesackashack. Do your tricks – quick wrist-flip – measure – tip and pour – dab and poke – nothing up your sleeve. How many hours had he and Mate practised before the mirror, coin between the fingers, trying to learn the tucking disappearance magic – oh, for God's sake, Sinclair, pay attention to yourself – the one that's now hurting you! Look – look there beside the bartender's coyote face – mirror me – oh, mirror me – but not too true. That was all he'd done – given her a mirror – showed her for the first time to herself. He'd been her mirror, and for him she'd capered and postured and made faces, done all sorts of tricks he'd asked her for, but she couldn't do them worth a damn if he wasn't there to mirror her.

And now the whisky trick. None of her people could do the mirror trick – or ever would be able to, for the mirror held up to them simply told them they were separate and they were alien and they were opposite people. Be ashamed, the mirror said to them; not more aware – not more conscious – effective – just more ashamed.

The second one helped more. Weesackashack's patrons sat side-saddle on their chrome stools, their eyes turned up to the television screen high on a corner shelf at the end of the bar. Violence and grace growing – decaying – swift, gliding patterns forming – flowing – breaking – re-forming. Pretty smart trick with a whole continent watching in the dimness of their dead little Willis's toy rooms, all together watching the magic-lantern reflections dancing there.

Oh, her terrible weakness, against the inner vision he had tried to keep lighted for her. He had kindled it, encouraged it with his strength, shielded it with his love. She had winced from it, let it gutter low, the hot tears sliding slowly down his heart, to grow cold and harden there. Tonight she had just blown it out. There would never be another Victoria flame.

Little lost lamb soliciting – little lost lamb screeching Stony hate and obscenity on city streets, dark hair curtaining down her convulsing shoulders as she vomited in alleyways – little lost lamb left to freeze alone outside the beer-parlour door – heat-cherried stove-pipe knocked loose and stoves tipped over in gay tag – little lost infant charred in the crib! *Little lost lamb, Victoria!*

They turned back to the bar now. The clever-faced bartender reached up and switched from the station commercial. Limp caramel hands resting on their wrists and turned upwards with a scarlet flower cradled in the opened palms. Long and tendrilled hair – white gown – the syncopated gentleness of the East Indian voice saying that pure self could free itself from impertinent reality – that it could soar and float in rare inner air. And that was Sinclair's heart in those curved fingers closing. He could feel them tighten and it hurt and it would hurt much worse, for she would close them more and more on his carnation heart. I am ashamed – I am ashamed.

The coffee smell had travelled right to him as soon as Archie Nicotine had rounded the big sign-board with the black foot and the moving toe. He was just half way to the end when Norman saw him. "Where'd you go to?" Norman called out. Under the orange parachute Gloria was stretched out, leaning on one elbow on the sleeping-bags. Victoria Rider was slicing bread on a board between two of the war-surplus cans. The gas stove was fizzing, steam breathing off the pot of water there – three cans in it. Norman was squatted by it. "I was lookin' for you – all over the Jeses tent."

"I didn't go any place, Norman. I stayed there with Old Esau."

"I couldn't find you. . . ."

"Maybe you didn't look very hard." He turned to Victoria. "We took your grampa to the funeral parlour. Sinclair and me fixed all that. I figured you would be there."

"No."

"His body is at the Chapel of Silver Bells – Seventeenth – if you want to go see it. You can see it by tomorrow."

She nodded.

"Funeral is at Paradise – Tuesday – two o'clock." Archie turned to Norman. He held out his hand. "Now!"

"Sure – sure." Norman slid his hand into his pocket. "That's what I was lookin' for you for – to pay back."

"Hey-uh."

"With intrest." Norman took out a fistful of bills; he held them out to Archie.

"Half's mine," Gloria said.

Head down, Archie counted the five tens. "Hey-uh." He put them in his pocket.

"Half's mine," Gloria said.

"I heard." To Norman he said, "You're lucky."

Norman snorted. "We're broke. You took it all. We got nothin' to buy bread now."

Archie looked over to the stove – to Victoria with the bread knife. "You got grup."

"That's right," Gloria said. "Tomorrow we won't – it'll run out quick. Half was mine."

"You used mine too when he stole it. How come you got grup if you didn't have anything to buy it . . ."

"Ask her." Gloria jerked her head to Victoria.

"Huh?"

"She isn't tight-ass like most Stonys."

Archie turned to Victoria, who was buttering bread slices now. "You found another job?"

"Ai-yigh!" Norman dropped a hot can he had snatched out of the water. "They're done now – let 'em cool a bit."

"You found a job?" She didn't answer him; he turned back to Gloria. "You got the grup."

"She got it. Tonight we're her guests for a change. Ask her polite, maybe she'll invite you too – beans – coffee . . ."

"Did you buy it?" he asked Victoria. "That grup?"

She nodded.

"But you didn't get a job yet?"

She shook her head.

"He send you out?"

She didn't answer him.

"When?"

Gloria said, "Quick trick – ten bucks – because we had to keep that fifty for payin' you back. Her bread – her beans. You want some?"

"Hey-uh." Archie sat down with his back against the bricks of the Liberty Café wall.

"Why don't you get some beer out that fifty?" Gloria said.

"Hey-uh." Archie rolled over one way so he could get at his side pocket. He unwrapped a ten and handed it up to Gloria. "You go get it."

"Great! Couple cases! I'll bring the change . . ."

"Keep it. I don't want any of it back."

"Hey – what I said – I take it back!" She left.

Victoria wouldn't look at him. Norman was down on one knee with his elbow going up and down high as he jabbed at the top of a bean can with the point of a hunting knife. There were two other cans steaming on the ground beside him. Archie got up. He picked up a can and tossed it back and forth from one hand to the other. Then he stopped that. He held down a hand to Norman, who had laid the knife down on the dirt.

"Let me have it, Norman."

Norman handed the knife up to Archie. He had just picked up a tablespoon and lifted the open bean can to his mouth, when the hunting knife darted out and up. Even as the can dropped and Norman scrabbled to his feet, blood sheeted the lower left side of his face right into his open shirt collar.

"Just sell your sister, Norman."

Norman said a muddy mumble.

Archie wiped the blade off on his pant leg. "Close your mouth, Norman."

Norman tried again.

"I said you got to close your mouth, Norman."

The right side of it was closed, but the left – up to his ear – was still flowered open. "Even with your mouth shut, it stays open, Norman," Archie said. Norman moved back and away from Archie, so that now he crouched in the corner the fence made with the brick wall. "You better hold it together, Norman – and press it so you won't have a great loss of your blood."

Norman's hand flew to his cheek. The blood instantly barber-poled his fingers.

"Come on," Archie said to him.

The hand wore a red glove now.

"Come on." Norman shrank back against the fence, put out his left hand to fend Archie off. "If you could see it like I can – it's cut right through so it spurts, and you got to get to the hospital or you'll die – before Gloria gets back with the beer." Archie took another step towards Norman, trapped in the narrow waist of the sign-board and the wall. "That's all, Norman. See." He held out his empty hands. "I put it in my boot."

Norman froze in his crouch as Archie's hand touched his shoulder. "Holy Cross Emergency is where you got to go." The blood was dripping off Norman's elbow now. Archie slid his arm all the way round Norman's neck. Norman seized up again, then everything seemed to run out of him. "It's the closest, but it's still a hell of a ways. You need me to come with you in case you lose conscienceness, and that's the whole situation. Come on." To Victoria he said, "That was for you, you know. Go ahead of us in case of Gloria. You're coming back to Paradise with me."

As he and Norman came from behind the sign and headed for the railroad tracks and Holy Cross, he said, "Just your sister. Next time it's the nuts, Norman."

THIRTY-ONE

Through csfa-tv, esau rider's death had received
excellent regional coverage and, as well, national, for Canadian
Press had carried the story. His funeral was held in the Paradise
Valley church Tuesday afternoon. Out of the mountains, from as
far away as the Windermere and the Kootenay flats, down from
the hills, in off the plains, from the city itself, the mourners gathered well, Blood, Sarcee, Blackfoot, Cree funeral delegates, legal
counsel for the Indian Brotherhood, provincial Deputy-Minister
of Cultural Affairs, Indian Department officials including Fyfe,
Eastern slope ranchers from as far south as Waterton Lakes, for
whom Esau had once ridden, some of them still grateful for heifers
saved by the small hands so deft at intra-uterine dissection of
unborn calves. Herded on the other side of the suspension bridge,
their cars and trucks gleamed and glittered in the sun, for the day,
which had first threatened rain, had forgiven. One of the cars, a
Cadillac bearing Montana licence plates, had arrived early
Monday evening. It belonged to a man resembling a younger Esau.
He was a veterinarian, a state Senator, and a half-brother of the
deceased, Fyfe had explained to Carlyle, a summer child con-
ceived by the auxiliary Snake wife Esau's father had lived with on
his annual sojourns below the border until the turn of the century.
He sat with the family, and Carlyle knew that under the grey

business suit and white shirt there would be no Sun Dance scars. Jake Rider's tulip-, diamond- and dog-rose-patterned kangaroo-hide riding boots and snowy Stetson must have cost more than his half-brother's funeral.

Church services over, they left the little church, followed the pallbearers up and across the first bench, then through Beulah Creek, a dry, white-pebbled artery, its foot-bridge superfluous now. After Jonas Rider had thrown a handful of dirt down on his father's coffin, the men replaced their hats, the women gathered their children, and they walked back over Beulah Creek to the dance tent, where tea and chocolate-coated marshmallow cookies were served. Pop also was handed out from wooden cases stacked against the shady side of the tent. There would be a dance that night, though none of the immediately related Riders would attend.

Carlyle did not see Victoria at the funeral, nor Healy Richards. He walked back to the agency buildings with Fyfe, then accompanied him to the bridge.

"If I've failed with her – I've failed with all of them."

"You may think so now, Carlyle, but . . ."

"No – no – no – no! This is it – I have no more – nothing left in me!" They had stopped at the gently urging centre of the bridge.

"Yes, you have. . . ."

"It is beyond human capability! Not just mine! Anyone's!"

"That's not right, Carlyle."

"Yes – it is! She was beaten right from the start – I was – we all are."

"You can't give up."

"Hell I can't – oh, the hell I can't! There is no other choice – never has been! Despair like me, Ian!"

"You're wrong. . . ."

"Oh God, be realistic – look around you! Look at the mess it is! Always has been! Victoria is one knocked-up mess! I am!

The Stonys are! Right from the beginning the whole human race has been one God-damned mess!"

"Carlyle – Carlyle – I told you – I warned you. . . ."

"I know – I know – now I know!"

"I've despaired – often – oh yes, I have – when I was working out the Fyfe biscuit – again and again . . ."

"Ohhhh!"

". . . what if I'd given up . . ."

"I am not talking about Band-Aids!"

". . . there would never have been any Minimal Subsistence . . ."

"Ohhhh, Ian – Ian – you were defeated long before I was! Don't you know it – yet!"

"I have not been . . ."

"We have just buried Heally Richards' failure! And your cooky magic doesn't work one bit better either! It won't sustain life! For a very good reason – they won't eat it! Your Holy Sacrament wafer is just oatmeal concrete! It is nothing! Nothing!"

"Now, Carlyle . . ."

"It will not bring them back to life! And Esau's Storm and Misty magic – we buried that too! It died with him! Once it was something, but your cooky – Richards' laying on hands – are less than nothing! I am less than nothing! You know why?"

"I'm not interested. . . ."

"Because we are funny as well! You and I and Heally Richards are so God-damned funny!"

He felt the angry bounce of the suspension bridge as Fyfe turned from him. Fyfe's voice was level and low. "With Victoria – I'll still be interested in hearing what transpires."

The rain had stopped, but a steady drip persisted from eaves and trees. Arms loaded, he stopped half way between the wood-shed and the agency building. Just above the mountain peaks the clouds seemed to hold motionless, but their stillness was illusory, for the whole sky was restless, sifting and drifting endlessly. Ever since Esau's funeral – oh, God, ever since Victoria had told him – time had lost its edges, and his thoughts were formless and aimless as the shredding cloud above. Smoke was lifting from the stove-pipe of Esau's cabin. Once more.

"Do that under the trees, Ezra." Old Ezra in front of the Powderface cabin, his councillor pants streaked a darker blue where he had dribbled, looked at him from under tent lids – eyes smoky with cataract. Just like Old Esau's. "Under the trees, Ezra. Children will be by the school soon. Do it under the trees."

"Hey-uh. Meetin' tonight."

"I know, Ezra."

"You write it for us."

"Yes, Ezra."

"Dance after it."

"I know."

"Wet."

He was right; the saucer of ground between the Powderface door and the trail was brimming. "Big run-off, I guess, Ezra. Be a good grass spring."

"Hey-uh. Beulah."

And a big dispensary spring too; yesterday the children had snowed his desk with notes: aspirins – Mentholatum wanted, cough medicine for the baby, green liniment for the father, ginger to sting the old blood, belladonna plaster for the back, mustard plaster for the chest, great need for bismuth hydrate, epsom salt, please. Coughing and throat-clearing and snuffling had almost drowned out the tree-toad pipings of the little Grade Ones during their reading period. Oh, God, all the measuring, pouring, counting, labelling – murky medicine bottles with their sticky shoulders and sugar-encrusted necks! He was very tired.

He had held himself against the current too long; all he wanted to do now was to give up and be swept away. He had lost all will for living – for self-determination. His life had been a long illness, survived with energy left only to let him breathe and to be. His body must bother him no more with any of its minor or major hungers.

He did make it to recess – or almost – he turned them loose ten minutes early. And just before he returned to the classroom, Madaleine Meadowlark was at the door, a wide strap across her throat and down under the buttocks of her crying baby swathed in brown blanket.

"Something for the burn. The baby burn."

It hadn't been a bad one. He rang the children in, began the Grade Five spelling lesson.

"Now – this word . . .," he tapped the first on the list he'd written on the board, ". . . in the States it's spelled 'c-o-l-o-r' but we spell it 'c-o-l-o-u-r,' and your next word . . ." He lowered the pointer a notch.

Oh, God, it had grabbed him again – the time the whole Rider family had moved in, and he had crammed Victoria for her supplementals. "Porridge . . ." How she had hated it. ". . . you know what porridge is. It's what you eat in the morning for breakfast." What had they eaten? Chunk of boiled elk – tea – frying-pan bannock?

"Ralph – what's porridge?"

He had to wait for Ralph to look up from under his lifeless mop of hair. The boy smiled with embarrassment. "What do you do with porridge, Ralph?"

"Eat it." The words were hardly audible. Ralph lowered his head again.

"That's right. Anyone know what it's made of? It comes in a box – a sack – you buy it at the store."

"Wheat." Someone had whispered over to his left.

"Yes. Cracked wheat and oats. Oatmeal – in Scotland – where Mr. Fyfe comes from – they eat porridge made of oats three times a day. It's good for you." Oats – oats! For horses, not humans! Elk – deer – boiled spring bear – muskrat legs – porcupine. "It fills you!" His voice had tightened as though they had contradicted him. "It has vitamins – it fills!"

He saw Ruby lean across the aisle and whisper to Janey Shotclose. Not innocent at all! He knew – he knew! The whisper was sly – it lisped of and hissed of young bodies epileptic in sweet grass fishy with semen – eager legs in denim – tangle of cotton skirts and underclothes ripped! Grade Three!

"Outdoors! What does this one mean? Where is outdoors?"

No one volunteered.

"Is it here? Where you are now? Inside this place? Is that it? Or is it –," he lifted the pointer towards the window, "– out there? Beyond the door? Outdoors?"

Several heads nodded.

"That's right!" He said it heartily, as though they'd all jumped to their feet and shouted the answer at him. "Now – all of you – write these words down – neatly – carefully."

They opened their scribblers. They picked up their pencils and bent forward.

If only he could have missed the meeting, but they needed him to take down their statements. They would send them with the petition to Ottawa. There would always be petitions with attached individual speeches saying exactly the same things.

The meeting was held in the dance tent; it was still quite light after supper when he walked up over the first bench, crossed Beulah Creek bridge. A few minutes after his arrival, Prince Dixon walked to the centre, stood with thumbs hooked in his belt, his eyes on the circle of attentive people. He explained that they had met to talk to Ottawa, for they were in need. They wanted more land so that they could raise wheat and oats and vegetables and more stock. He sat down, and his place at the centre was taken by Judea Shot-close.

"Since long time ago these Indians are suffering and now he's thinkin' he cannot make a livin' and he knows that. We need more land, and now I talk with government friendly to go along with me in a peace way."

Carlyle took down Judea's words.

"We suffer too much from not havin' enough land for us all. The children are sick. That's all."

Then it was Ezra Powderface's turn. "Thank you, Mr. Sinclair, for writin' our meetin'. I would like to say a few words. I want to say the first time – we lost the good life of the Indian. We lost all that now. Before white people come to this country Indian had a good livin' – never hungry for himself – for his horse. Been huntin' in the fall – put up for dry meat and put up for dry berries too. We lost all that now; we lost the Indian good life. Those days we had buffalo-hide wigwam that was wind-proof – cold-proof. Now we haven't. The Indian child get sick out of it. There is why my people suffer in their heart. We like to put that sufferin' out of our soul." He paused. "In the name of Jesus Christ, who died for all of us amen. That's all."

Archie Nicotine stood up. "I am duly elected councillor. My grandfather was a chief. God made this land and the mountains too, and that's why I think we are born red and why we belong here. Our blood is in that ground and hills. Our great fathers were buried there, and we want to live here with them. We can't leave these hills, but now without enough land we need we are just like in a sack. We got to untie that sack. My grandfather told me when the first Peace Treaty Number Seven was made under the red flag and the Majesty of the Queen, she promised this: she would help us Indians when they were up against it. All right. We're up against it now. I want to hear from Ottawa let us have more land before long. Whenever the government tells me to do things, I got to do. I obey what government says. Now the government better obey me, and that is the whole situation."

The meeting, as always, closed with a hymn and a prayer.

As he walked away from the tent, Archie Nicotine joined him.

"I brought her back."

Rod Wildman caught up on the other side. "I got the team," he said.

"Hey-uh, in the mornin'," Archie said. "She's not livin' with Susan and Jonas."

They had reached Beulah Creek bridge.

"In the city – I found her campin' with those Catfaces."

Their footsteps clocked unevenly over the planks of the bridge.

"Dance tonight," Archie said.

"Tom MacLeod," Rod Wildman said. "His harness too. But one trace missin' from it."

"I'll get it."

"In the mornin'," Rod said.

"Hey-uh."

Rod turned off towards his cabin.

"She's alone now – that bull-pasture shed."

They were walking down the first bench.

"There's some wicked ones around here too," Archie said. Just before the Powderface cabin, Archie stopped. Carlyle walked on.

"It comes free in Paradise, you know," Archie called after him.

He did not bother to light the lamp, though the sun had left the kitchen windows. He tucked kindling into the stove that had died in his absence, waited till the untidy crackle of resin told him to add birch chunks. He put on the kettle. He set out his dishes on the oilcloth. He turned on the radio, got only a dim twitter. Batteries gone.

As he smoked in the deepening darkness, he heard the sound of hoof against stone, the chink of halter shanks, voices riding by the house. The room became refined by the miller light of the full moon rising. Several times there came a tapping at the door, but he did not stir. Finally there were no more tap-pings. He would not be bothered for the rest of the night – by Indian callers. For a moment there came back to him the profile of a woman seated in a window bench, her knees drawn up and arms clasped around them – and oh, the sad and shallow curve of her neck with head tilted down. So still – so still for hours! Once more, on an institutional counter, he signed away all happy days; he accepted a big Manilla envelope with its tiny silver wrist-watch, engagement ring, wedding band. Then a train was being sucked into the prairie vanishing point. He stood alone on a platform on a friendless planet.

In the swarm of a city street, he felt again the warmth of a child's hand seeking his own, and, oh God, he must aim his attention so very carefully now! Focus – focus the delicate shutter slices of recall – curving – closing right down to whistle aperture. Snick it shut. No more. Admit not one hurtful memory ray of feeling!

Soft – distant – the dim pulse came to him. He listened, then clearly recognized the bump of the dance drum. He got up and went to the kitchen door – opened it. Spring's cool breath carried to him the wild drift of the Owl Song pure upon the night.

Before he had reached the bridge over Beulah Creek, he could see the long glow of the dance tent through the trees; magic-lantern shadows were thrown against the walls and slope roof, swelled, contracted, vanished, reappeared gigantically. Just before the tent flap, he tripped at a guy rope, caught himself, stooped to enter.

His way was blocked by Tom Snow, who stepped aside with a sort of relaxed arrogance, his cigar at a steep angle, his Stetson white, his denim smock piped with sheep's wool. As he turned his head, there came a stabbing flash of the eye – the sweet bouquet of Catawba wine. There were a number of Hanley boys about the tent; likely that all of them had been drinking on their way down to Paradise.

At the far end of the tent, a hoarse command from Louis Chinook touched off the six drumsticks in the tulip-tump-tip beat of the Rabbit Dance. Head back, cords pulled out on his neck, eyes closed, Wayne Lefthand started the song with a ventriloquial glitter of sound; before he had fainted altogether from hearing, the other singers came in with deep ah-hai-ah-hai rising and falling in their throats like moths over lamp-chimneys. And now, one slowly coiling creature on many tan, bound feet, the dancers shuffled past Carlyle. The tail drew opposite him, and he caught swift sight of her on the opposite side of the tent. It took a moment for the contraction at his heart to ease off.

She sat alone – like deaf-and-dumb Sally Ear. How in hell was she living? With her family? No – alone, Archie Nicotine had said. Band rations only? Cutting her own wood – hauling her own water? Fair game for any of them now – one night one – another night another – Jesus! Free in Paradise! Her head was bent down under the gothic eave of her red kerchief. Once he'd seen her gipsy hair curtaining over a desk, one arm cradling a scribbler. Ten – eleven – stark and lovely eyes – cinnamon freckles over the cheek-bones. What a heart-breaking child! And she had failed him! Utterly!

The Owl Dance had ended. The dancers had just left the centre when there came a fresh drum-roll, the sudden tinkle of bells. Matthew Bear stood in the flap. He was green; he was naked except for the salmon breech cloth with fringed ends hanging. The bells chinked at his elbows, his waist, his knees, his ankles, as he walked over to the drummers. He took a cigarette from Pete MacLeod, lit it. One hand was negligent on his hip, the inside of the wrist turned out. She was in no danger from Matthew. He jingled away from the drummers, his porcupine-hair crest fanning out from the top of his head, two pheasant feathers, their quills wrapped in tinsel, glittering down his back. Now that he was standing directly under the lamplight, he dazzled, for he was hung round the waist with horse hair and weasel tail and grizzly claws, caressed by a short cape of young eagle feathers tinted blue, alive over his painted shoulders. He displayed himself to all, still with the limp hand on his hip, the cigarette dangling from the corner of his mouth, eyes squinted against the rising smoke.

My child – my child! Oh God – you were my child – until you failed! Until he took you – now all will take you! All!

BAM BAM BAM the six drumsticks as one lambasted the opening of the Prairie Chicken Dance. Still with the smouldering cigarette in his mouth corner, Matthew dropped both arms loosely, ape-like down; with shoulders casually tilting, body lazily turning, he drifted round the tent, soft heel to hard earth, then toe behind and out and down to earth again. Current nonchalant, chip on a stream, he circled the drum. BAM BAM BAM, the impatient drummers clubbed him slowly round the ring.

My child – my child! Oh God, you were my child! How I loved you – loved you – till he took you – took you! Now all will take you – all – all – all!

BAM BAM BUHBAM, the six drummers' heads lowered together, calling upon fresh fierceness from forearm and shoulder muscles. The cigarette dropped from Matthew's mouth. Back and up his elbows came; faster his moccasins spurned the earth. Get the drum bigger – get the drum faster – get the drum wider. Steal the rope and steal the halter – steal the woman – grab the girl and steal my own! My own! My own!

BAM BAM BUHBAM! The drum was done. Victorious, Matthew walked off to the side of the tent to rest. He had barely reached it when the voices of the six singers called him back into the Prairie Chicken Dance. His back glistened green in the lamplight, was almost parallel with the ground, hips sharply angled, head back, hands clawed. It was as though the painted body hung from some great finger that idly danced him round in puppet epilepsy, shoulders working, weaving – dancing heel then dancing toe ahead, then back – across and down. Along the tent's shadowed sides small boys were infected now; with hands in pockets and elbows crooked like Matthew's, they bounded on stuttering moccasins to the bursting drum.

Carlyle stared across to Victoria.

The second episode of the Prairie Chicken Dance came to its abrupt end. Mrs. Wounded-Person passed by with a length of bone in her hand. She stopped before Tom MacLeod, who took it from her and handed it to Mary Amos. Mary crossed the tent and gave the bone to Johnny Education. With a pang, Carlyle saw that Victoria had left her place, then he found her crossing the far end of the tent, the invitation bone in her hand. He lost her as the Rabbit-dancing train obscured his view, discovered her again on his own side of the tent, stepping out to avoid the seated women and children. When he saw her next, she had stopped by Elijah Race. So, it was Elijah now! He turned his head away.

He felt an elbow nudge him, saw Peter Bush grinning. Victoria stood before him, her head turned to one side. She was holding the bone out to him. He took it. He walked with her down the side of the tent, dropped the bone into Peggy Baseball's lap, then turned to Victoria. He put his arm round her shoulders, felt her hand slide round his waist. Chastely, side by side, they slid into the reiterative beat of the drum, clasped hands ahead of themselves in pump-handle motion, swaying from the hips – forward rocking – backward tilting, their feet marking out the domino tracks of a rabbit in snow.

Victoria's head was bowed, her eyes upon the ground. Ahead of them, Sarah Bear, peeking back over one shoulder, giggled, missed a step, failed to catch up with the drum again, tore free from Lucy Wildman, ran mortified to the shelter of her mother's skirts.

When the Rabbit Dance was over, Victoria returned with Carlyle to his side of the tent.

This time Matthew was magnificent; all other things were pale and all were one under the driving drum – under the smashing drum. Who cared now – who cared for tabes and for little sabre-shinned babies in the deep trachoma dark! Who cared now if the belly sang high – if the belly rumbled low. Canvas and rags and cardboard kept you almost warm in the twenty-five below. Let the fevered baby cough and the night sweats come. To hell with warping rickets that crippled little crickets born in buckskin sin! Ottawa sends us nurses and X-ray machines for the hart that pants for cooling streams. If casual blanket marriages bring luetic babies, raise blisters for ourselves and for our sisters, in the Bull Durham sack we just let it run and run and run! The Presbytery loves us, though our sins be scarlet as the welling spit that fills the fountain full with blood. Thirty in the bucket with the agent going bail, the grabbing hold of girls and incestuous relations – they are fun – fun – fun! So we lash the hidden instinct wolf to life – we club the mirror – the Methodist glass – we break it – we smash it with disdain!

How had he arrived here in this tent flickering with lamp and firelight? He did belong with them. A wild and distant drum had pulsed for him and for Mate, when they had stood with the total thrust of prairie sun upon their defenceless heads. Together they had discovered that they were both alien from and part of a living whole. The dry husk of a dead gopher, an abandoned garter-snake skin, magpies, undertaker beetles, had taught them the terror of being human. But they knew that they were accountable to each other; the badger, the coyote, the kill-deer, the jack rabbit, the undertaker beetle, could not share their alien terror. They were not responsible for each other. Man was.

Man lifted bridges between himself and other men so that he could walk from his own heart and into other hearts. That was the great and compensating distinction: man did – the jack rabbit, the badger, the kill-deer, the weasel, the undertaker beetle, did not. How could he have forgotten that! How could he have left Victoria on that city street. Archie hadn't; Archie had not destroyed a bridge. But he had turned away from her – from all of them, lost sight of their vivid need. Victoria had not truly failed, but he had. Why? There must have grown unnoticed at first – a spent melancholy – a loosening tautness of mind – an original blinding flash of contempt for them – for all other men – for himself.

He danced again with Victoria when Wayne Lefthand had picked up the gelded thread of the Owl Dance song. Sweet rippling, frail bird of purity lifting, sinking to soar again, the others flying after him – vainly – vainly – only nearing the unattainable to drift fluttering, tilting down – helplessly – sadly down. Oh God, how important it had been to try for them – and to try again – for them – for himself – for her!

He kept his arm around her shoulder as they walked back to their place.

The singers and drummers took up the Prairie Chicken Dance again. Lower and lower Matthew danced to the wild beat of the sticks' blurred arcs.

Who cared now – who cared now! Only the now remained to them – the now so great that only death or love could greaten it. Greater than pain, stronger than hunger or their images paled with future – dimmed with past. Only the now – pulsing and placeless – now! Song and dancer and watching band were one, under the bruising drum that shattered time and self and all other things that bound them.

Her hand took his as they stood up, held it as they walked to the tent flap. The drum followed them all the way to Beulah Creek bridge, then with one lambasting sound, it was stilled.

In the luminous centre of the dance tent, as though he had been held up by the drum's solid beat, Matthew Bear fell flat to earth. Certain as birth or death or love, the faultless Prairie Chicken Dance was over and done.

THIRTY-TWO

IT WAS AS THOUGH HIS OWN PULSE HAD DRUMMED HIM AWAKE; the ruffed grouse of course. Actually it was quite distant, yet it was as though it were in the bedroom. Full daylight now. She slept. He could feel her touching warmth beside him. The drumming cut loose again outside – but inside himself as well – urgent at his throat – clubbing him with his own heart. Black was the colour of her hair, in a dark scarf laid down over her cheek. Black was the lovely curve of her lashes. Freckles still spiced beneath her closed eyes. Look at me – look at me! No – don't wake yet, my sleeping love, wearing night-gown with eyelet-embroidered bodice – overlay of lace – daisy-white. The hell she was, for his own true love was bare as Tourigny's swimming hole, and there'd be hell and heartburn all the way to Ottawa! Look what's transpired now. Sorry, Fyfe, I have disregarded your advice. It seems last night I did let myself become personally involved.

Without waking her, he got out of bed. Just as he stepped outside the agency door, he heard the distant clock of an axe echoing; somehow it gave extra clarity to the lucid morning. A dog barked, then seemed to say to hell with it, as though he hadn't really intended to bark at all. Sorry, Aunt Pearl. The poplar tree couldn't outline and shade itself, Mr. Mackey old

Kacky – but it happened all the same – sort of an accident. Oh no – oh no – it had been deliberate all right!

Why had he taken so long to know? There must have been some hidden awareness – long unadmitted. But why hadn't he admitted it sooner – given himself to it – and to her? His life just hadn't taught him how. It had given him the wrong commandments: be loved – don't love; tell – don't ask; take – don't give. The ruffed grouse down towards the river had one last try. Knock it off, ruffed grouse – let her sleep – let her sleep, my own true . . . Tell you what, Aunt Pearl and Fyfe and Old Kacky and Ottawa – I'll marry her; isn't that something to transpire: the union of two – no – two-and-a-half in the holy bonds of matrimony! Heally Richards may not have struck camp yet, and he might be as good in the marriage rites as he was in the death ritual. I'll ask her – I promise, I'll ask her. . . .

He caught the sardonic smell of willow smoke, then saw it lazing up from Old Esau's stove-pipe. Not a large and formal wedding, Aunt Pearl, mostly the bride's family. And how come the ground was so boggy under his feet? Big spring run-off year. The Powderface cabin was almost water-borne; a cottonwood log had been laid from the step to higher ground where the little four-year-old squatted with his knees up under his arm-pits. One hell of a lot of water lying around, and something had just minnowed through his mind to escape him. Well, if it was important, it would swim back again.

Buttocks bare, flawed with black-fly bites below the inadequate undershirt, but now he wore new and shining rubber boots with pencilled edges. Aunt Pearl hadn't let him wear his own lovely licorice ones that spring. He'd brought them with him purposely in his suitcase, but she had been worried they would only seduce him farther into gutter water until he went over their rims and filled them with muck.

Ezra and Old Esau had something to do with it – something Ezra had said to him. When? Just before the meeting yesterday – no – just before he'd started the school-day – early in the morning. What was it anyway – the Powderface child – rubber boots – something before that. Oh well. He and the boy must be the only humans awake in Paradise Valley. No – because somewhere there had been someone chopping, but the child must think he was the only one alive, for he was rapt over the canal system he'd dug with his tablespoon. The water did not visibly flow through his intricate pattern of tiny ditches, but as he dropped axe chips and twig bits, they were instantly and inexorably carried along. Now and again one would be drawn over to touch a side, so that a sort of earth magnetism stilled it till the child's touching finger freed it to moving life again.

It was the amount of run-off. It had something to do with that – the amount of it. He'd never seen so much in the nine springs he'd been in Paradise. But what could that have to do with Old Esau or Old Ezra or Ezra's little grandson?

Dear little bare-bum shaman, I am here – I'm standing here. Oh, let me show you to you – I want to mirror you so you may be more nearly true! Please perform your marvels for me – surprise me. Astonish me with your accidents. Trust me now. I promise you I won't destroy you with distorted image. I will not turn you into a backward person. At least will try not to. Let's you and I conjure together. You watch me and I'll watch you and I will show you how to show me how to show you how to do our marvellous human tricks together!

Hey-uh! It had been Old Ezra, taking his morning leak by the house. He'd said Beulah! That was it! Beulah!

Behind the Powderface cabin, the morning sun reflected from patches of water glittering like mirror shards scattered all the way up to the first bench. He could hear Beulah Creek now – not the usual tickling trickle of sound, but a deeper spring surf, with now and again, half-heard, the almost-human voices uncertain in stream music. Storm and Misty springs must have overcome the earth fault bumped by the seismic charges last year – farther up the canyon maybe – breaking free in a fresh place there. But the course had been dry for months, so it must have taken days – weeks – nourished by snow melt and rain as well. From first welling, pebbles – earth – desert-dry sand must have sucked and sucked, drinking to satiety. And he hadn't noticed till now! How had he failed; the others must have discovered it much earlier. No one had mentioned it to him. No – that was not true, for Old Ezra had. And others may have too.

He heard a soprano shriek overhead, then saw the high osprey coasting on stilled wings in the river direction. What a pity Old Esau had missed Beulah's renascence. The osprey worked his wings anxiously, was suddenly transformed into a feathered arrowhead that dropped from sight below the river willows, which for God's sake were in full leaf! Possibly he hadn't.

Now he heard the sound of men's voices – towards the river – urgent with exhortation. But by the height of the sun over the river willows, at the very latest, it couldn't be more than seven o'clock. Last night had been a dance night; who the hell could possibly be stirring now! He walked towards the schoolgrounds, had reached the edge when he saw the horses' heads emerge through the break in the trees made by the river trail. Very, very slowly, each foot lifting and dropping for a small gain of territory, they passed the bucking tree where Raider had left his rotting elk guts. They were in full view now, a man out at each side, importuning with shouts and cracking rope. He recognized Tom MacLeod's black team; he recognized the green truck they pulled. Archie's. The reins looped up and through the glassless windshield, and that would be Archie in the cab, holding both lines and steering wheel.

Leaning into their collars, the team moved more quickly, for they had conquered the slope lifting up from the river and the truck rolled over level ground behind them now. They veered over towards the schoolgrounds, passed through the thin line of spruce, and stopped just inside. Rod Wildman – Prince Dixon. Prince got up between the team and the truck, hooked the heels of his riding boots in the bumper, leaned back against the radiator. Archie handed the reins out to Rod Wildman, who moved off to the side. Archie called out. Rod windmilled the free ends of the lines and brought them slapping down across the horses' rumps. Prince did the same with his lasso rope. The rumps lowered and seized convulsively. The truck almost moved. Reins and lasso cracked again. The team responded mightily. The truck did move.

"Haaaagh-hawgh!" yelled Rod Wildman as he flailed the lines.

"Yaaaah-haaaaaaawh!" yelled Prince Dixon as he cracked the rope over their backs, one hand behind him for purchase on the radiator hood.

"Yaaaah-hooooeeeee!" yelled Archie Nicotine from the truck cab.

Heads moving up and down, in then out, and then in unison again, the horses achieved a faster walk, and then a trot. Rod had to jog now to keep up to them.

"Yaaaaah-high-yigh-yeeeeeeee!" screeched Archie, bouncing high on the truck seat, his hands clutching the top of the steering wheel. He looked down, freed one hand, was busy with gear shift and clutch pedal. He looked up again, gave a warning shout to the other men.

The truck bucked. The team hit an invisible stone wall. The truck let off a great, blue back-fart. The team lunged into their collars. The truck exploded and exploded and exploded again. The terrified team, pursued by the green truck, just missed the boys' and girls' toilets, avoided the teeter-totters as well, skinned the swing frame, though the truck ricocheted off one of the pipe uprights. The first buck of the truck had unhooked Prince's heels from the front bumper, but he had not fully regained balance when the right fender hit the swing frame. He was thrown backwards and up and along the motor hood, half way through the empty windshield, so that Archie stared into his crotch. It was very difficult for Carlyle to apportion speed credit either to the truck or to the team now. It was possible that the team was winning, driven only by panic, since Rod, unable to keep up with them, had thrown the reins at them and let them go on their own.

Belly to the ground, they headed for the soft-ball diamond, but before they reached it, Prince Dixon, who had foolishly released his scissor-lock on Archie's head, was squirted out through the windshield, over the radiator, and down between the team and the front bumper. His fall was successful in disengaging the team. The truck passed over him. The horses, with manes and tails wild, pounded together across the soft-ball diamond and disappeared into the bush beyond.

Rod got up and discovered his hat was missing. He brushed himself off with his hands.

Archie circled the schoolgrounds five times before he brought the truck to a halt. Carlyle walked over to him. He leaned his elbows on the open window.

"Congratulations, Archie."

Plump face glistening with sweat, Archie sat with his hands nonchalant on the top of the steering wheel. The motor was still running. "Hey-uh."

"I see you did get your rings and rebuilt carburetor."

"Hey-up."

"That's nice."

"Won't have to impose on you for a ride any more – Sinclair."

"Hey-up!" Carlyle said.

WHO HAS SEEN THE WIND *by* W.O. Mitchell *illustrated by* William Kurelek
W.O. Mitchell's best-loved book, this Canadian classic of childhood on the prairies is presented in its full, unexpurgated edition, and is "gorgeously illustrated." *Calgary Herald*

> *Fiction, 8½ × 10, 320 pages, numerous colour and black-and-white illustrations, trade paperback*

THE BLACK BONSPIEL OF WILLIE MacCRIMMON *by* W.O. Mitchell *illustrated by* Wesley W. Bates
A devil of a good tale about curling – W.O. Mitchell's most successful comic play now appears as a story, fully illustrated, for the first time, and it is "a true Canadian classic." *Western Report*

> *Fiction, 4⅝ × 7½, 144 pages with 10 wood engravings, hardcover*

FOR ART'S SAKE: A new novel *by* W.O. Mitchell
"*For Art's Sake* shows the familiar Mitchell brand of subtle humour in this tale of an aging artist who takes matters into his own hands in bringing pictures to the people." *Calgary Sun*   *Fiction, 6 × 9, 240 pages, hardcover*

LADYBUG, LADYBUG . . . by W.O. Mitchell
"Mitchell slowly and subtly threads together the elements of this richly detailed and wonderful tale . . . the outcome is spectacular . . . *Ladybug, Ladybug* is certainly among the great ones!" *Windsor Star*

> *Fiction, 4¼ × 7, 288 pages, paperback*

RAVEN'S END: A novel of the Canadian Rockies *by* Ben Gadd
This astonishing book, snapped up by publishers around the world, is like a *Watership Down* set among a flock of ravens working together to survive the harsh world of the Rockies. "A real classic." Andy Russell

> *Fiction, 6 × 9, map, 5 drawings, 336 pages, hardcover*

LIVES OF MOTHERS AND DAUGHTERS: Growing Up with Alice Munro *by* Sheila Munro
Part biography of her famous mother, part family history (with snapshots), part autobiography, this affectionate memoir will fascinate all of Alice Munro's legions of admirers.

> *Biography/Memoir, 5½ × 8½, 60 snapshots, 240 pages, hardcover*

THE GRIM PIG *by* Charles Gordon
The searing newspaper tale of getting the story, and the girl! The author of *At the Cottage* and *The Canada Trip* turns his satire on the newspaper world, and the result is very funny.   *Fiction, 6 × 9, 240 pages, hardcover*

A PASSION FOR NARRATIVE: A Guide for Writing Fiction *by* Jack Hodgins
"One excellent path from original to marketable manuscript. . . . It would take a beginning writer years to work her way through all the goodies Hodgins offers." *Globe and Mail*
Non-fiction / Writing guide, 5¼ × 8½, 216 pages, updated with a new Afterword, trade paperback

RED BLOOD: One (Mostly) White Guy's Encounter with the Native World *by* Robert Hunter
The founder of Greenpeace looks back on a wild, hell-raising career. "Hunter acts. He does things. . . . In all his adventures humour is a companion, but he can also write angry political commentary." *Globe and Mail*
Non-fiction, 6 × 9, 280 pages, trade paperback

W.O. MITCHELL COUNTRY: Portrayed *by* Courtney Milne, Text *by* W.O. Mitchell
A beautiful book for all seasons, showing prairie, foothills, and mountain landscapes. "Milne's photographs are as dramatic, as full of colour and as moving as Mitchell's best writing." *National Post*
Art / Photography, 10½ × 11½, 240 pages, 200 colour photographs, hardcover

FOR YOUR EYE ALONE: Letters 1976-1995 *by* Robertson Davies
These lively letters, selected and edited by Judith Skelton Grant, show us the private Davies at the height of his fame, writing family notes and slicing up erring reviewers. "An unmitigated delight." *London Free Press*
Belles lettres, 6 × 9, 400 pages, facsimile letters, notes, index, trade paperback

HIDEAWAY: Life on the Queen Charlotte Islands *by* James Houston
This gentle book is a song of praise to the rainforest magic of Haida Gwaii, its history, its people, and the little green cottage the author loves. "James Houston finally writes about his own backyard." *National Post*
Memoir / Travel, 6 × 9, 272 pages, 40 b&w illustrations, map, trade paperback

PADDLE TO THE AMAZON: The Ultimate 12,000-Mile Canoe Adventure *by* Don Starkell *edited by* Charles Wilkins
From Winnipeg to the mouth of the Amazon by canoe! "This real-life adventure book . . . must be ranked among the classics of the literature of survival." *Montreal Gazette* "Fantastic." Bill Mason

Adventure, 6 × 9, 320 pages, maps, photos, trade paperback

PADDLE TO THE ARCTIC *by* Don Starkell
The author of *Paddle to the Amazon* "has produced another remarkable book" *Quill & Quire*. His 5,000-kilometre trek across the Arctic by kayak or dragging a sled is a "fabulous adventure story." *Halifax Daily News*

Adventure, 6 × 9, 320 pages, maps, photos, trade paperback

THE LIFE OF A RIVER *by* Andy Russell
This story-filled history of the Oldman River area in the foothills shows "a sensitivity towards the earth . . . that is universally applicable" *Whig-Standard* (Kingston)   *History/Ecology, 6 × 9, 192 pages, trade paperback*

AT THE COTTAGE: A Fearless Look at Canada's Summer Obsession *by* Charles Gordon *illustrated by* Graham Pilsworth
This perennial best-selling book of gentle humour is "a delightful reminder of why none of us addicted to cottage life will ever give it up." *Hamilton Spectator*   *Humour, 6 × 9, 224 pages, illustrations, trade paperback*

THE CANADA TRIP *by* Charles Gordon
Charles Gordon and his wife drove from Ottawa to St. John's to Victoria and back. The result is "a very human, warm, funny book" (*Victoria Times Colonist*) that will set you planning your own trip.

Travel/Humour, 6 × 9, 364 pages, 22 maps, trade paperback

THE MACKEN CHARM: A novel *by* Jack Hodgins
When the rowdy Mackens gather for a family funeral on Vancouver Island in the 1950s, the result is "fine, funny, sad and readable, a great yarn, the kind only an expert storyteller can produce." *Ottawa Citizen*

Fiction, 5⅜ × 8⅜, 320 pages, trade paperback

BROKEN GROUND: A novel *by* Jack Hodgins
It's 1922 and the shadow of the First World War hangs over a struggling Soldier's Settlement on Vancouver Island. This powerful novel with its flashbacks to the trenches is "a richly, deeply human book – a joy to read." W.J. Keith   *Fiction, 5⅜ × 8⅜, 368 pages, trade paperback*